大学经贸英语系列教材 **21**世纪版

顾问 何泽荣　总主编 帅建林

国际结算教程

（第二版）

INTERNATIONAL SETTLEMENT

主编 傅泳

Southwestern University of Finance & Economics Press

西南财经大学出版社

大学经贸英语系列教材(21世纪版)
编 委 会

总　序

随着中国的改革开放和加入 WTO,融入到世界经济大潮中的中国和接纳了中国经济的世界对外语人才或财经人才的智力需求不是单一的。快速运行的全球经济呼唤既有娴熟的外语语言技能,又有相应专业知识的复合型人才。单纯的语言型外语专业或外语能力平平的单一专业毕业生是不能满足这种需求的,他们必将在竞争中处于劣势,而"英语＋专业"或"专业＋英语"的复合型人才必将在竞争中处于优势。这已是一个不争的事实。

目前国内许多大学外语系实行了"英语＋经贸专业"这一办学方针和复合型人才培养模式;同样,许多大学又将其财经专业教学计划细化为"经济/贸易/金融/会计/管理主干课程＋英语"的课程,实行双语教学。无论是对于"经贸英语"或"商务英语",还是对于"双语教学",本人认为他们的根本教学目标是相同的,即增强学生直接使用英语从事国际经贸的涉外能力、适应能力以及国际商务实战技能。为实现这一教学目标而采取何种切实可行的教学措施,专家学者们以及从事相关专业教学的教育工作者们一直在辛勤探索。

"经贸英语"、"双语教学"这一名称自从问世之日起,便备受人们的青睐。商务人员希望通过对"经贸英语"这一学科的学习提高其英语的实际运用能力;英语人才希望通过对该学科的学习,掌握基本的商务知识。同样,财经专业的学生渴望通过"双语教学"模式来同时提高其专业和英语水平,以及直接使用英语从事相关专业的实战能力。在飞速发展的全球经济互动的呼唤下,经贸英语已形成一门单独的学科,成为一门以国际商务为语言背景的应用性学科。它的研究对象是在这一特定语言环境下所使用的专门用途英语,以及它在使用过程中由于行业、团体、功能等因素而产生的变体及其规律。它的主要研究方向有三个:一是语体功能;二是教学法研究;三是专门用途英语的翻译理论与实践。国际商务所涉及的领域很宽泛,因此,对国际商务所涉及的主要学科的选材便显得尤其重要。显然,经贸英语的教学前提应该是首先完成对国际商务所涉的主干课程的教学,即以下所提及的**经贸专业板块**的教学。因为学生在缺乏系统的国际经贸知识的状态下,或者对国际经贸没有多少感知的前提下,要去学习一门以国际经贸为语言背景的实用英语,从而获得实战技能,是不具备可操作性的。

笔者认为"经贸英语"这一学科为学生设计的知识结构应该由三个板块组成:①**英语语言与基本技能板块**,包括英语听说、综合英语、英语写作、英汉互译、现代英语散文选读、英美文学选读、英语语言学概论、英汉同声传译、中西方文化比较等课程;②**经贸专业板块**,包括微积分、西方经济学(英语)、国际贸易实务(英语)、国际金融(英语)、经济法、管理学(英语)等主干课程;(3)**经贸英语技能板块**,包括经贸英语专业听说、经贸英语专业写作、经贸英汉互译、商务英语综合阅读、跨文化商务沟通、外事(外交)英语、商务谈判、商务实践等课程。这三个板块的教学组合秩序基本上是梯级排列的。它们之间的关系如下图所示：

因此,在确定经贸英语的专业范畴时,我们应充分考虑财经专业的骨干课程对经贸英语学科的支撑作用,即,**经贸专业板块**对**经贸英语技能板块**的支撑作用;没有经贸专业支撑,经贸英语技能也只能是空中楼阁。为此,我们针对**经贸专业板块**编写了这套**"大学经贸英语系列教材"**(21世纪版)。该系列教材旨在培养学生经贸领域的英语能力和扎实的国际经贸知识这一综合能力。具体地说,就是既使学生在国际经贸英语的语言环境中直接地、系统地学习国际贸易、国际金融、国际结算、国际投资、国际营销、国际项目管理、商务沟通等领域的专业知识,又使学生通过对国际经贸知识的学习,强化经贸英语这一专门用途英语(ESP,English for Specific Purposes)技能,掌握经贸领域的英语术语、文体和语言特点。

大学经贸英语系列教材(21世纪版)有以下特点：

(1)**系统性**:该套教材包括国际商务所涉及的主要学科,由6个分册构成：

《国际贸易实务》(*International Trade Practices*)

《国际金融教程》(*International Finance*)

《国际结算教程》(*International Settlement*)

《跨文化商务沟通》(*Business Communication：Cross Cultural Borders*)

《案释国际贸易惯例》(*Annotation by Cases to International Trade Rules*)

《经贸英语听力教程》(*Focus Listening for Business*)

(2)**案例丰富**:该套教材最大的特点是叙述上的**"案例导向"**和**"问题导向"**。教材的每一部分或每一章都从一个具体的、使人感到困惑的案例或现实问题开始,从而提高了读者的阅读兴趣,加强了读者对所学内容的记忆。

(3)**多功能**:该套教材的编委由长期从事相关学科教学的教师或研究人员以及金融界高级管理人员和中国一些知名企业的总裁组成。因此,该套教材的编写既强调实务和技能层面,又注重全方位、多功能地培养学生的综合素质。

(4)**针对性**:针对英语专业的学生、经贸专业的学生或从事国际商务活动人士阅读英语经贸专业原著颇为困难的现状,该套教材显然起了一定的改善作用。它既可作为经贸英语专业的教科书,也可作为目前诸多热衷于"双语教学"的大学经贸专业的专业教材。

(5)**适用面广**:该套教材既适用于MBA学员和英语、经济、国际贸易、国际金融、国际商务等专业的硕士研究生,或上述相关专业的本科高年级学生,也适用于成人教育和职业培训班的学生。同时,它们还对经贸界人士、银行界人士、国际商务从业人员强化其国际商务英语能力和相关专业业务能力有很大的帮助。

经济学家张维迎博士曾说过:"**读书最大的成本是时间而不是书价。要买好书,不要买便宜的书。**"谨此献给明智的读者。

何泽荣

西南财经大学国际经济研究所所长

西南财经大学教授,金融学、国际贸易学博士生导师

2003 年 9 月于成都

再版前言

在我数年于海外从事国际结算的实践活动以及回国后直接用英语从事该课程的教学活动的基础之上，经过几年的准备以及对我所编所用教案的多次修改，这本《国际结算教程》终于成书并与读者见面了。

国际结算是为了清偿国家与国家之间由于商务所引起的贸易往来以及由于政治、军事、文化活动所引起的非贸易往来而产生的债权、债务关系。从银行业务的角度来看，国际结算是银行中介业务的重要组成部分，国际上著名的大银行都把它作为其主要业务之一。从公司的角度来看，一个公司的进出口业务也离不开国际结算。一个精通该项业务的公司能够更加高效地进入国际市场并拓展其海外业务。

按照国际惯例，国际结算的整个业务运作，包括开证、制单和审单，一律使用英语而不是汉语。本书作为大学经贸英语系列教材(21世纪版)的双语类经贸课程的教材，正是为了更好地遵从这一原则，其宗旨是使读者在纯英语的语言环境下学习国际结算的专业知识，成为既懂专业又懂英语的复合型人才，并能直接用英语处理国际结算流程中的各项业务。本书不仅可以作为国际经济贸易专业本、专科学生以及研究生的教材，也可以作为银行、公司相关从业人员以及管理人员的参考资料。

国际结算是一门操作性极强的实务性课程。将结合我在海外从业的实际经验，尽量用规范、简明的英语深入浅出地介绍相关原理，并突出其实务性与操作性。本书的实务性表现在阐述各项国际结算业务时，尽可能多地提供各种单证实例，如汇票、本票、支票、各种信用证式样以及各种商业单据式样。其可操作性表现在每项业务均附有业务程序图解。而且，对于同一支付方式下的不同类型，本书都从比较的角度对单据提交规定以及制单要求进行了阐述。对于单据中的关键项目，本书不仅从理论的角度加以分析，而且还从英语语言的角度加以解读，使读者不仅能够知其然，还能知其所以然。

在编写过程中，我参阅了国内外大量有关国际结算的中、英文教材和资料。我在新加坡工作的公司 OS International Pte. Ltd. 为我提供了一个从事国际贸易的工作平台，我在新加坡的同行好友 Hongfa International(Pte.) Ltd. 的 EMY Zhang，以及 Industrial Electronics Private Limited 的 Sheila Gao 都对本书提出了许多宝贵意见并提供了一些实务单据，在此一并致谢。

我还要特别感谢西南财经大学国际经济研究所所长，西南财经大学金融学、国际贸易学博士生导师何泽荣教授以及西南财经大学出版社的各位领导及相关工作人员，他们对本书的出版与修订给予了大力的支持。

由于编者水平有限，加之国际结算业务本身的发展非常迅速，本书于2004年首次出版后，虽然根据国际结算的新规则和趋势作了一些调整和补充，但仍难免有疏漏之处，敬请读者不吝指正。

傅　泳
2012年7月于成都

内容提要

　　本书共分为三大部分计十三章。第一章至第五章为第一部分"票据理论",主要介绍金融单据——汇票、本票、支票、代理行关系以及国际结算的特点。第六章至第十章为第二部分"支付方式",主要介绍汇票、托收、信用证、国际保理以及保函和备用信用证。第十一章至第十三章为第三部分"商业单据",主要介绍不同支付方式下的汇票、发票、装箱单、保险单、提单、空运单以及其他运输单据,并介绍国际结算下的银行审单业务。这三大部分彼此依存,共同组成国际结算的实务运作系统。

　　全书用英语编写,内容丰富,讲述深入浅出,具有较强的实务操作性。本书旨在让读者于纯英语的语言环境中学习国际结算的专业知识,提高直接使用英语从事该项业务的能力。

CONTENTS

第三部分

Chapter One　Introduction

Section One　What is International Settlement

International settlement refers to the money transfer via banks to settle accounts, debts and claims among different countries. It is originated from both international trade transactions such as the sales of tangible goods and intangible service transactions and international non-trade transactions such as international lendings and investments, international aids and grants, cross-border personal remittances. For this reason, International settlement is divided into two types: international commercial settlement which is created on the basis and for the purpose of international trade, and international non-commercial settlement which is related to non-trade transactions. While international non-commercial settlement is of equal importance in international banking business, international commercial settlement will constitute the core part to this book and it will be our major focus.

International settlement centers around payment methods which in turn will cover those major items as sales amount, currency used and how to make or collect payments for each individual transaction. Thus, international settlement is also called payment terms or payment methods in a sales contract in international trade. Also, as traders are located in different countries and regions, payments in modern international settlement are not made against cash payments directly between the traders themselves. Rather, payments are made via banks against various financial instruments and/or different commercial documents in the process of settling payments. In other words, payments cannot be effected or payment methods cannot be realized without the participation of the financial instruments and/or commercial documents. So we can say that payment methods, financial instruments and commercial documents are the three important and closely related parts in international settlement. For this reason, this book will also be divided into three parts accordingly: chapter one to chapter five will be devoted to "Instrument Acts"; chapter six to chapter ten to " Methods of Payment" and chapter eleven to chapter thirteen to "Commercial Documents". The following paragraphs will talk briefly about the financial instruments, commercial documents and methods of payment respectively.

Financial instruments mainly refer to bills of exchange, cheques and promissory notes. The word "financial" implies that these instruments are made for the purpose of effecting payments. In general terms, they are the orders given to the bank by one trader who asks the bank to make/collect payments to/from the other trader. When such orders are performed by the bank, funds are successfully transferred from the buyer to the seller.

The major types of commercial documents are commercial invoice, packing list, bill of lading, insurance policy, inspection certificate and certificate of origin, etc. Various commercial documents will signify whether the responsibilities regarding the production, packing, shipment, and/ or insurance of the goods have been fulfilled by the traders. As these documents are not made directly for the purpose of effecting payment, they are referred to as commercial ones.

Methods of payment can be divided into remittance, collection, factoring, letter of credit and letter of guarantee, each with several subdivisions. Actually, different payment methods require different combinations of financial instruments and commercial documents, with the result that not only payments are effected, but also the time of making payments can be chosen to be made before, after or at the same time of the delivery of goods. As a result, modern international settlement has offered the traders with choices so that they can select different payment methods in accordance with the nature of the transaction, the market condition and the credit-granting of the seller or that of the buyer.

Another point we need to know is that the currencies used in international settlement should be convertible ones. There are three kinds of international convertible currencies: convertible currency of the export country, convertible currency of the import country and convertible currency of a third country, generally referred to as the US dollar, the British pound and the Japanese Yen. The currency is to be chosen and mutually agreed to by the traders in the sales contract before the payments are in process.

Financial instruments and commercial documents are stipulated in the relevant parts of the following major laws and uniform rules: *Uniform Rules and Practice for Documentary Credits* (1993 Revision), *ICC Publication No. 500* (UCP 500) which came into effect on 1 Jan., 1994; *Uniform Rules for Collection* (ICC Publication No. 522) which came into effect on 1 Jan., 1996; Uniform Rules for Demand Guarantee (URDG) (ICC Publication No. 458) which was published in April, 1992 and expected to be widely adopted. *Rules for Multi-modal Transport Document* (ICC Publication No. 481) which came into effect on 1 Jan., 1992. In addition to the above-mentioned laws and rules, a good knowledge of other related national and international rules and regulations is also necessary. All these constitute the legal foundation on which International Settlement practices are performed.

In summary, as international trade involves traders from different countries and goods are transferred across national boarders, it is both inconvenient and dangerous for the traders to make direct cash payments from one country to another country. This has made modern International Settlement coming into being. With the rapid development of international trade, International Settlement has evolved into a new era, totally independent from and much more complicated than domestic settlement. Its characteristics will be discussed fully in the next section.

Section Two　Characteristics of Modern International Settlement

There are five important characteristics of modern international settlement:

1. Instruments are Widely Used in International Settlement

In the early days when international trade was less developed, cash was the major medium of exchange used in international payment and the international settlement of this period was called cash-settlement. For example, if trader A in country A sold certain goods at a certain amount to trader B in country B and if, in another transaction, trader A bought some other goods at the same amount from trader C in country B, then, under the direct cash-settlement, trader B should first ship cash to trader A and the latter would again ship cash at the same amount back to country B to trader C. From the double cash shipments of the above example, the major drawbacks of cash settlement in international trade are obviously reflected. First, double shipments from and back to the same country are wasteful in terms of time, money and energy. Secondly, shipments of cash across national boundaries are risky. It is common sense that the freight costs are high and the risk of being lost, robbed or damaged is always present. In addition, the speed of transferring funds would depend largely on the speed of the transportation facilities which would often slow down the turnover of funds.

Later on, these disadvantages are largely overcome with the creation and the involvement of financial instruments. With the passage of time, financial instruments have gradually taken the place of cash to settle accounts for the traders. Financial instruments are made against the creditworthiness of the relevant parties. With its major forms such as bill of exchange, promissory note and cheque, funds can be transferred, debts can be offset and accounts will be cleared. Take the above-mentioned example again: if trader A opened an account with trader B, he could first draw an instrument on trader B and asked the latter to make payments to trader C. Trader A would then hand/give the instrument to trader C who would claim payments from trader B against the instrument. In this way, trader B cleared his debt with trader A and the latter cleared his debt with trader C. From this example, we can see clearly that the international shipment of cash is replaced by the international movement of financial instruments. When instruments are used as medium of exchange, international settlement has evolved into a new era − non-cash settlement where, compared with cash-settlement, not only the security of payment is greatly enhanced, but also the time is largely saved and the costs are significantly reduced. Wide application of instruments is the first important characteristic of modern international settlement. As a result, international settlement has evolved from cash settlement to non-cash settlement.

2. **Bank Becomes the Center of International Settlement**

Initially, credit instruments were made only on traders and the settlements were made directly among the traders themselves. Take again the above-mentioned example, we can see that the reason for trader A to draw an instrument on trader B and requires the latter to make payments to trader C is because there is a triangular sales relationship among them, with the same amount for either transaction. However, this coincidence may rarely exist in real life situations. As modern society requires large volumes of daily transactions of goods and services to satisfy its economic wants, these large volumes of daily transactions may involve a great number of traders in many different countries as well as large but varied sums of money. It may be very inconvenient and frustrating for the traders themselves to match the amounts and settle the accounts. Such problems in settlement greatly affected the development of international trade.

Later on, with the development of the worldwide banking network as well as modern banking technicality, banks have moved in as a reliable intermediary between the traders with the result that both the buyer and the seller can maintain accounts with banks. First, the buyer (the party paying the money) gives a payment order in the form of financial instrument to the bank holding the funds. Then, the bank transfers the funds to the account of the recipient (the party to receive the money) with him or another bank or financial institution. As a result, the arrangements of funds transfer via banks "smooth-out" the inconvenience of direct payment, especially when long distance and a large sum of money are involved. With its worldwide banking network and its professional services, bank has become the center of the payment system. Therefore, international payment is defined as the international money transfer via banks to settle accounts, debts and claims among different countries. In other words, the money transfer must be entrusted to banks for payments to or claims from the traders. Bank has become the center of the international payment system and this is the second major characteristic of modern international settlement. As a result, international settlement has evolved from direct payments to indirect payments.

3. Some Commercial Documents Have Become Title Documents

The word "title" signifies the right of ownership. The holder of the title document becomes the owner of the goods. With the development of shipping and insurance industries, two kinds of commercial documents, ocean bills of lading and the insurance policy, have become the title documents. For example, when the seller surrenders bills of lading, it means that he has delivered the goods and when the buyer receives the document, it means that the goods have been delivered to him. This kind of delivery is called constructive delivery in contrast to actual delivery in early international settlement where goods were delivered only when they were physically in the hands of the buyer. When goods have been documented, they have changed the landscape of the international settlement greatly because both the delivery and the payment are made against documents rather than the actual goods.

The following example will illustrate the concept of constructive delivery clearly. Now let's consider a situation when the physical goods are destroyed in transit while the shipping documents have already been handed over to the importer. Under the concept of constructive delivery, the importer has to make payments against the correct documents to the exporter, even with the knowledge that the goods can never be actually delivered to him. The loss to the importer, however, may be compensated from the insurance company if the said goods are insured. But the point here remains that the goods are constructively delivered to the importer when the title documents are in his possession. Therefore, we should always keep in mind that certain commercial documents should be treated as title documents and this is the third important characteristic of modern international settlement. As a result, both delivery and payments are made against documents and documents have become the center of modern international settlement.

4. The Seller's Rights and Responsibilities are Stipulated in the Price Terms

The fourth important characteristic in modern international settlement is that price for each transaction should be quoted in price terms. Price terms are the English initials stipulating the rights and obligations of the seller and those of the buyer. They are also called incoterms, the short form for International Rules for the Interpretation of Trade Terms. Generally speaking, price terms set out the obligations of the seller. Hence, by a process of elimination, the buyers' rights and responsibilities are implied because any obligation which does not appear in a particular price term may be the responsibility of the buyer. Price terms should be agreed upon when the sales contract is established so that the trader's rights and obligations are clearly defined at the beginning of the transaction. There are 13 different price terms and they can be classified into 4 groups:

E group

EXW Ex Works (. . . named place)

F group

FCA Free Carrier (. . . named place)

FAS Free Alongside Ship (. . . named port of shipment)

FOB Free on Board (. . . named port of shipment)

C group

CFR Cost and Freight (. . . named port of destination)

CIF Cost, Insurance and Freight (. . . named port of destination)

CPT Carriage Paid to (. . . named place of destination)

CIP Carriage and Insurance Paid to (. . . named place of destination)

D group

DAF Delivered at Frontier (. . . named place)

DES Delivered Ex Ship (. . . named port of destination)

DEQ Delivered EX Quay (Duty Paid) (. . . named port of destination)

DDU Delivered Duty Unpaid (. . . named place of destination)

DDP Delivered Duty Paid (. . . named place of destination)

It is not necessary to have a detailed understanding of all the 13 terms except the four most popular ones: FAS, FOB, CFR and CIF.

(1) FAS (Free Alongside Ship) (named port of shipment)

Obligations for the seller: Make the delivery alongside the ship at the port of loading and pay for the carriage of the goods from any inland place to the port of loading.

Obligations for the buyer: Choose the carrier to transport the goods abroad and pay for the loading costs. Arrange and pay for the export permit and export tax and the costs onward. At the same time, he may choose to arrange the insurance and pay insurance premium from the port of loading.

(2) FOB (Free on Board) (named port of shipment)

Obligations for the seller: Make the delivery on board the ship at the port of loading and pay for the carriage of the goods from any inland place to the port of loading and the loading costs. Arrange and pay for the export permit and export tax.

Obligations for the buyer: Choose the carrier and pay for the freight and the cost onward. At the same time, he may choose to arrange the insurance and pay for the insurance premium from the port of loading.

(3) CFR (Cost and Freight) (named port of destination)

Obligations for the seller: Choose the carrier to transport the goods abroad, make the delivery at the port of destination and pay the freight charges to the port of destination. Arrange and pay for the export permit and export tax as well as the loading costs if they are separated from the sea freight.

Obligations for the buyer: Pay for the unloading costs. Arrange and pay for the import permit and import tax and the costs onward. He may arrange for the insurance and pay for the insurance premium from the port of loading.

(4) CIF (Cost, Insurance and Freight)(named port of destination)

Obligations of the seller: In addition to the obligations and costs illustrated in CFR above, he must also arrange the insurance and pay for the insurance premium from the port of loading to the port of destination.

Obligations for the buyer: Pay for the unloading costs if they are not included in the sea freight already paid by the seller. Arrange and pay for the import permit and import tax and the costs onward.

From the above explanation, we will see clearly that the seller takes the least responsibilities in FAS and assumes the most obligations under CIF. This conclusion can also be applied to all the 13 price terms, that is to say, when price term moves from EXW to DDP, the responsibilities of the seller runs from the least to the most and the opposite holds true for the buyer. Hence, we should also notice the following points.

(A) Different price terms will affect the quoted price in the sales contract.

If the obligations fall heavily on the part of the exporter, the price will be quoted higher. On the contrary, if the buyer assumes the most responsibilities, the price will fall down. For example, for one sales contract, the quoted unit price (USD) may vary according to different price terms:

EXW ⟶ FOB ⟶ CFR ⟶ CIF ⟶ DES ⟶ DDP
$98 $100 $110 $115 $120 $140

Notes: The figures here are just a theoretical illustration with no practical references.

From the above we may notice that the seller charges the lowest price ($98) at EXW because it engages him the least responsibilities and he charges the highest price ($140) at DDP which implies his greatest responsibilities.

(B) Price and terms make the price terms.

"Terms" indicate the conditions under which prices are made. These conditions represent the trader's obligations and are expressed in the 13 different incoterms we have discussed above. In addition, the distance between the port of loading and that of the unloading and the currency used should also be considered as other factors affecting the quoted price. As a result, three items will make a complete and correct price term: Unit price with its currency + incoterms + place of loading /unloading. A comparison between a domestic quotation with an international price term will make the case clear. For example:

Unit price in domestic quotation: RMB100/bag.

Unit price in international quotation: USD100/bag FOB (Shanghai) or USD120/bag CIF (London).

(C) Goods can be covered by insurance under any price terms.

When dealing with price terms, we should always remember that incoterms are descriptions from the seller's point of view rather than from that of the buyer's. Therefore, goods can be protected under insurance coverage in FOB or CFR as much as under CIF. When insurance is not the seller's responsibility, such as under FOB or CFR, it can be taken by the buyer.

(D) Guiding points in choosing a proper price term.

Generally speaking, as EXW creates extreme inconvenience to the buyer while DES and

DDP brings the same trouble to the seller, these extreme price terms are seldom used in international trade. As for the four popular price terms, if the trader is not well-experienced in foreign trade, it is recommended that he may choose FAS or FOB when he is the seller and the CFR and CIF when he is the buyer. In this way, he will take fewer responsibilities and will handle the foreign trade in a more convenient way. In contrast, if the trader has gained enough experience in this field, he will do just the opposite. This is because when he chooses FAS and FOB as a buyer and CFR and CIF as a seller, the trader can do business with his familiar shipping and insurance companies. In addition to lower costs and better services he will receive, the most outstanding advantage for the trader is that he can avoid the risk of being cheated, a phenomenon that is not rare in international trade.

5. Electronic Devices are Widely Used in International Settlement

The development of the international banking network with electronic communications creates the integration of international settlement operations with electronic messages such as SWIFT, CHIPS and CHAPS to facilitate the international funds transfer.

SWIFT is the initials of the Society for Worldwide Interbank Financial Telecommunications. SWIFT also refers to a fully integrated computer transmission system where the message can be transmitted in a standard format. Established in 1977 and with its headquarter in Brussels, Belgium, the system is owned by 240 of the largest international banks. Technically, member banks will be hooked-up by computers to one the system which permits them to relay funds to another simultaneously with the computer code only known to its members. As a result, international banks are able to transfer funds at a faster speed.

CHIPS is the initials for the Clearing House Interbank Payment System. It is a computerized network established in New York in 1970 for the transfer of international payments made in US dollars. CHIPS links up more than 100 international banks and other financial institutions which have their offices or subsidiaries in the city of New York.

CHAPS is the initials for the Clearing House Automated Payment System. It is established in London in 1984 for the funds transfer made in British pounds. CHAPS is available nationwide in Britain, operated by a number of settlement banks who communicate directly through computers. Payments sent through the system are guaranteed and unconditional and cleared on the same-day basis.

Taking further steps to develop, the international settlement operations will incorporate with EDI, the initials for Electronic Data Interchange services. EDI enables all paper-based trade documentation to be sent, received and acknowledged by all parties electronically so that no documents or data need to be made on paper and sent manually. For this reason, EDI is called "trade without paper". It eliminates the repetitive and tedious paper work and thus reduces the opportunities for errors and helps to save time and resources. Although EDI has not been widely used in China today, it is developing speedily. Wide application of electronic devices is another important characteristic of modern international settlement.

After our discussion of the five major characteristics, we may have a glimpse of the process of how international settlement has evolved and moved into its present modern era where international trade has been greatly facilitated.

Chapter Two　Credit Instruments（Ⅰ）
– Bills of Exchange（Ⅰ）

Section One　Introduction

We have already known from chapter one that documents play a very important role in international settlement because payments are made against documents rather than the actual goods. There are two kinds of documents in international settlement: commercial documents and financial documents. The major function of commercial documents is to evidence that the various conditions and requirements stated in a sales contract have been fulfilled by the traders and we will discuss them in the following chapters. Financial documents refer to credit instruments made for the purpose of making/collecting payments. They have taken the place of cash and are devised as mediums of exchange to facilitate commercial transactions by eliminating the use of money in international settlement.

To define it more formally, a credit instrument is a written or printed paper issued by one person to make unconditional payment to another person up to a certain sum of money within a certain period of time either by this person himself or by another third person designated by him. By means of this instrument, funds are transferred from one person to another. The most commonly used credit instruments in international settlements are bills of exchange, promissory notes and cheques. Credit instruments can also take such forms as certificates of deposit, treasury bills, bearer securities, but the major focus of this book will be on bills of exchange, promissory notes and cheques.

All legal rules and laws with regard to credit instruments fall into two categories:

(1) British and US Legal System

This system represents the British Commonwealth of Nations and USA. It includes *Bills of Exchange Act* established in 1882 in Britain and *Uniform Negotiable Instruments Law* of 1896 in USA.

(2) Continental Legal System

This system represents the main countries in the European Continent. It refers to *Uniform Law for Credit Instruments at Geneva* which was established in 1931.

Based on the two legal systems, the United Nations have also drawn laws in this field in an effort to eliminate the major differences existing in the two systems. They are *Convention on International Bills of Exchange and International Promissory notes* and *Convention on International Cheques*. These two conventions are finalized in 1990.

Various acts and conventions provide a legal framework for the instruments so that they may be transferred from person to person to settle their debts and accounts. Instrument acts have formed the basic theoretical foundation in international settlement and we will discuss the bills of exchange act in detail in the next section.

Section Two   Bills of Exchange

1. Definition

A bill of exchange is formally defined as "an unconditional order in writing, addressed by one party (drawer) to another (drawee), signed by the party giving it, requiring the party to whom it is addressed to pay on demand, or at a fixed or determinable future time, a sum certain in money, to or to the order of a specified party (payee), or to bearer". A bill of exchange can also be called a draft or a bill.

A typical bill of exchange is drawn in this manner:

Exchange for HK $ 100,000. -   Hong Kong, June 3, 1996

At 60 days sight pay John Smith or order the sum of Hong Kong Dollars One Hundred Thousand only value received.

To: Henry Brown
      2 Hill Road
      Hong Kong   For: Mary White
                                                    (Signed)

In the sample bill shown above, the bill is drawn by Mary White on Henry Brown payable to John Smith. In other words, Mary White is the drawer who draws the bill. Henry Brown is the drawee to whom the instruction to pay the money is addressed and on whom the bill is drawn. John Smith is the payee to whom the money is to be paid. The bill is payable 60 days after the drawee's sight of it and the amount payable is HK $ 100,000. More examples of bills of exchange will be shown below:

B1-015

⊕ 中國銀行 新加坡分行

No. _____ ORIGINAL _____ 19____

Exchange for ▮▮▮▮▮▮▮▮

_____ sight of this **FIRST** of Exchange

(Second of the same tenor and date unpaid) pay to the order of

BANK OF CHINA
(INCORPORATED IN CHINA WITH LIMITED LIABILITY)

the sum of ▮▮▮▮▮▮▮▮▮▮▮▮▮▮

Value received _____

To _____

_____

B1-015

⊕ 中國銀行 新加坡分行

No. _____ DUPLICATE _____ 19____

Exchange for ▮▮▮▮▮▮▮▮

_____ sight of this **SECOND** of Exchange

(First of the same tenor and date unpaid) pay to the order of

BANK OF CHINA
(INCORPORATED IN CHINA WITH LIMITED LIABILITY)

the sum of ▮▮▮▮▮▮▮▮▮▮▮▮▮▮

Value received _____

To _____

No.   Singapore,

Exchange for

At   sight pay this **First** of Exchange

(second of the same tenure and date being unpaid) to the order of

OVERSEAS UNION BANK LIMITED   the sum of

value received

To

OUB 1445 (1)

No.   Singapore,

Exchange for

At   sight pay this **Second** of Exchange

(first of the same tenure and date being unpaid) to the order of

OVERSEAS UNION BANK LIMITED   the sum of

value received

To

OUB 1445 (2)

No.　　　　　　　　　　　Singapore,

Exchange for

At　　　　　　　sight pay this **First** of Exchange

(second of the same tenure and date being unpaid) to the order of

OVERSEAS UNION BANK LIMITED　the sum of

value received

To

OUB1445 (3) — OFFICE COPY

However, a full understanding of a bill of exchange will be achieved only after a thorough and complete study of its details in the following items and sections.

2. Essentials to a Bill of Exchange

In compliance with the *Bills of Exchange Act* 1882 of the United Kingdom, the *Uniform law on Bills of Exchange and Promissory Notes* 1930 of Geneva, and *Uniform Commercial Code of U. S. A.* of 1952, a bill of exchange must fulfill the following requisites:

(1) The Word "Exchange"

The purpose of indicating this word on a bill of exchange is to distinguish a bill from other kinds of credit instrument such as promissory notes or cheques. As the above example, we have "Exchange for HK $ 100,000". It is not definitely required in the *Bills of Exchange Act of the United Kingdom* but in practice, indicating the word can be of great convenience to the relevant parties.

(2) An Unconditional Order in Writing

(A) Unconditional.

The instrument must be made unconditional at the time of drawing. If the payment instruction is subject to any condition, it is not a bill of exchange. Please compare the following examples:

"Pay to John Smith or order the sum of one thousand US dollars." - a valid bill.

"Pay to John Smith or order the sum of one thousand US dollars when the ship 'Queen' reaches the port of Shanghai." - an invalid bill. The "when" clause makes the bill a conditional one.

"Pay to Mary White or order the sum of one thousand US dollars and debit my No. 2 account" is a valid bill, but "Debit my No. 2 account and pay to Mary White or order the sum of one thousand US dollars" is an invalid bill. The reason is that in the former bill, the order to pay comes before the order to debit. This means that the debit instruction is just an indication of a particular account to be debited. But in the latter bill, the payment undertaking will be performed only on condition that there is available balance with the No. 2 account.

However, if an instrument bears such a statement:

"Pay to ABC Co. or order the sum of one thousand US dollars drawn under XYZ bank documentary credit No. 12345" is a normal bill because "drawn under XYZ bank documentary credit No. 12345" should be treated as a statement of transaction which gives rise to the bill rather than a condition. This statement is also referred to as a "drawn clause".

(B) Order.

The bill must be an order which requires the payment instruction to be expressed in an imperative sentence. A mere request is not sufficient for this purpose. For example:

"Please pay Mary White or order the sum of one thousand US dollars" or

"I would be delighted if you would pay Mary White or order the sum of one thousand US dollars" are mere requests and are not orders on the drawee. Such expressions, as shown by the underlined parts, would make the bill invalid.

(C) "In writing".

The bill must be in writing. Oral expressions can not be admitted to vary or contradict the terms of a bill of exchange. This means when an oral expression concerning the bill is different from the bill in writing, the latter has the priority. For example, if the payable amount of a bill is at USD1,000, the payee can not say that he should be paid USD20,000 because the other day the drawee told him to pay that amount.

(3) "Addressed by One Person to Another"

A bill must be "addressed by one person to another" so that there must be one person as drawer and another person as drawee. In the case that the drawer and the drawee on the bill are the same person or the drawee is a fictitious person, the holder may treat it either as a bill of exchange or a promissory note. "The bill is drawn by us on ourselves payable to them" is an example.

It is possible to have one or joint drawees, but not drawees in alternative or in succession. For example, a bill can be drawn on "A and B" but not on "A or B" nor on "first A then B"
.

It should also be noted that the name(s) of the drawee(s) must be made in full and initials will be treated as unacceptable.

(4) "Signed by the Person Giving It"

A bill, to be a valid instrument, must be signed by the drawer or a person authorized by him. The instrument is not valid until the drawer has signed it. Forged or unauthorized signature makes the bill invalid. For a company bill, if an individual is signing for his company, these words "For", "On behalf of", "For and on behalf of" and "Per pro" should prefix the name of the company followed by the person's name and his designation. For example:

For ABC Co. , London

(Signature)

John Smith, Manager

(5) Tenor

"Tenor" means the time to effect payment and it is indicated in the definition of the bill of exchange as "on demand or at a fixed or determinable future time". Tenor often expresses the due date or maturity date. A bill must be payable on demand or at a fixed or determinable future time. Thus, according to tenor, there are two broad types of bill: demand bill and usance bill.

(A) Demand bill.

A demand bill is a bill payable on demand. It means that the drawee will be required to pay at once when he sees the bill or when the bill is presented to him for payment so the date of presentment is the due date to effect payment. A demand bill is also called a sight bill. Examples are:

"On demand pay . . . "

"On presentation pay . . . "

"At sight pay . . . "

If no time of payment is stated in a bill, it will be treated as a demand bill. For example:

"Pay . . . "

(B) Usance bill.

A usance bill is a bill which is payable at a future time. Usance bill is also called time bill or term bill. A usance bill is usually expressed in the following ways:

(a) Payable at a fixed time after sight.

The "sight" here refers to the accepting date. Accepting a bill or acceptance can be understood as a formal promise from the drawee to pay when the bill falls due and the promise is given when the drawee sees the bill. For this type of bill, acceptance is a must for the purpose of determining the actual due date. For example, "pay 30 days after sight . . . " means 30 days after the accepting date is the due date to effect payment.

(b) Payable at a fixed time after date.

The "date" here refers to the issuing date of the bill. For example, "pay 60 days after date . . . " means that the due date will be 60 days after the issuing date. Although accepting is not needed to calculate the due date for this type of bill, acceptance is recommended for the purpose of making certain of the obligations of the drawee to the bill.

(c) Payable at a fixed future date.

For example, "Pay on Sept. 30, 2008. . . "

(d) Payable at a fixed time after the occurrence of a specific event which is certain to happen

This is also called deferred payment bill. In practice, a bill is usually made at a fixed time after a B/L date. For example, "pay 3 months after the B/L date. . . " is a valid bill because the B/L date is a determinable future date. Another bill "pay 1 month after the death of B. . . " is also a normal bill because though the time of happening may be uncertain, the event is sure to happen.

On the other hand, a bill which is stated being payable on arrival of goods at a specified port, or which is payable on a person's marriage cannot be a valid bill. In these cases, at the time when the bill is drawn, no one can tell whether the event will going to take place and so the bill will be regarded as conditional instructions. "Pay 30 days after the ship 'Queen' reaches the port of Shanghai" and "pay 30 days after Susan White's marriage to John Smith" are both unacceptable as bills of exchange.

Another point to be noted with regard to tenor is how to calculate the due date.

(A) If a bill is payable at a fixed time after sight, after date or after the happening of a specific event, the time of payment is calculated by counting in the date of payment but counting out the accepting date, the issuing date or the date of happening of the specified event. After calculation, if the date of payment falls on a non-business day, the bill shall be payable on the succeeding business day. For example, if a bill is payable at 90 days after sight and the bill is presented for acceptance on April 15, 200X, this means that April 15 is the accepting date. According to the above rule, the tenor should be calculated from April 16 instead of April 15:

April 16 - 30   15 days (The accepting day, April 15, should be excluded)

May 1 - 31   31 days

June 1 - 30   30 days

July 1 - 14   <u>14 days</u> (The last date July 14 should be included)

90 days

So the maturity date of the bill is on July 14. If this due day happens to fall on a non-business day, the date of payment will be on the next business day.

(B) If a bill is payable at a fixed time from a fixed date, then this fixed date should be counted in. For example, if a bill is payable at 90 days from April 15, then the maturity date of this bill will work out to be July 13. The difference is caused by the use of the words "after" or "from". The word "after" should be understood to exclude the date mentioned and the word "from" will be understood to include the date mentioned. Compared with the bill payable at 90 days after April 15, the due date of the bill payable at 90 days from April 15 will be one day ahead. However, the word "from" is not recommended to express the tenor of a bill of exchange.

(C) If a bill is payable at x month(s) after sight/date/stated date, the word "month" here means a calendar month and the date of payment should fall on the corresponding date of the month due. For example, the maturity date of one month after Jan. 15 should be on Feb. 15. If there is no corresponding date in the month due, the maturity date should be on the last day of that month. For example, the maturity date of one month after May 31 is June 30 and the maturity date of two months after Dec. 31 is Feb. 28.

(6) A Sum Certain in Money

(A) The amount of a bill should be "a sum certain" even though the amount may be payable with interest, by stated installments or according to an indicated rate of exchange.

(a) Payable at a fixed amount.

If a bill is "payable at USD two thousand only", it is a valid bill.

If a bill is "payable at about USD two thousand", it is an invalid bill.

(b) Payable with interest.

The interest rate should be specified in order to make the amount payable a certain one. For example:

If a bill is "payable at USD one thousand with interest", it is an invalid bill.

If a bill is "payable at USD one thousand plus interest at 6% p. a. (from the date hereof to the date of payment)", it is a valid bill. In practice, interest will be calculated with the issuing date as the date of commence and the date of payment as the final date. Suppose the date of issuing is Sept. 23 and the date of payment is Oct. 22, then, the interest : $1000 \times 30/360 \times 6\% = $ USD 5.00 and

the payable amount will be: $1000 + 5 = $ USD1005.00.

(c) Payable by installments.

The installment must be clearly stated, otherwise the bill will be invalid. For example:

"Pay to the order of ABC Co. the sum of one thousand US dollars by installments" is an invalid bill.

"At one month after date pay to the order of ABC Co. the sum of one thousand US dollars by ten equal consecutive monthly installments" is a valid bill. Suppose the issuing date is July 1, a payment schedule can be worked out:

Installment Sequence	Amount	Date of Payment
1st	USD100.00	Aug. 1
2nd	USD100.00	Sept. 1
3rd	USD100.00	Oct. 1
...	...	...
10th	USD100.00	May 1

(d) Payable according to an indicated rate of exchange.

The rate of exchange must be indicated if the amount is payable in another equivalent currency.

"Pay to the order of ABC Co. the sum of one thousand US dollars converted into sterling equivalent at current rate in London" is a valid bill. The current rate of exchange is the prevailing rate in London when the bill is converted.

"Pay to the order of ABC Co. the sum of one thousand US dollars converted into sterling pound" is not a valid bill because the relevant parties do not know against which day's rate is the amount to be converted.

(B) The amount in words and in figures.

The payable amount should be expressed both in words and in figures. If they differ, the words have priority over the figures. If a bill is payable at the amount of USD1,000, the "words" should be placed after "the sum of" and expressed as "US dollars one thousand only", while the figures will be placed after the word "exchange" as "USD1,000".

(C) In money.

The bill should be made payable only in money other than in other kinds of physical goods or intangible services. For example, "pay to the order of Mary White the sum of fifty pounds and give her a suit of clothes" is not acceptable as a bill of exchange.

(7) Payable to a Specified Person or His Order or to Bearer

Finally, for a bill to be complete it must be payable to a specified person or his order or to bearer. There are three types of bill: restrictive-order bill, demonstrative order bill and bearer order bill. Different types of order will decide the negotiability of a bill and the way of negotiation. Negotiation, in simple terms, signifies the right of the payee to transfer the bill to another person. Negotiation will be discussed in the following sections. Another thing we should note here is that the word "order" in "types of order" differs from the "order" in "unconditional order". The former one actually refers to the status of the payee whereas the "order" in "unconditional order" means the payment instruction should be made as a payment command rather than a payment request.

(A) Restrictive order.

A restrictive order bill is a bill payable to a specified person only or to a specified person not negotiable/transferable. When the bill contains words such as "only", "not transferable", or "not negotiable" to prohibit transfer, it is a restrictive order bill and not transferable. Examples are:

"Pay to Mary White only"

"Pay to Mary White not transferable"

This means that Mary White can not transfer the bill to another person. This kind of bill does not have a wide application in international trade because it lacks negotiability.

(B) Demonstrative order/indicative order.

A demonstrative or indicative order bill is a bill payable to a specified person or some other person designated by him, without further words prohibiting transfer. Examples are:

"Pay to Mary White"

"Pay to the order of Mary White"

"Pay to Mary White or order"

"Pay to order" (the payee is a person designated by the drawer)

This kind of bill is negotiable. It can be transferred by Mary White, the payee, through endorsement and delivery. The negotiability is made safe by endorsement, consequently, it has found wide application in international trade.

(C) Bearer order.

A bearer order bill is a bill payable to bearer with no specified person as a payee thereon. Any person holds a bearer order bill will become the owner of the bill. Examples are:

"Pay to bearer"

"Pay to Mary White or bearer" (The word "bearer" will make the bill bearer order no matter whether or not a specified person is placed ahead of it.) A bearer order also occurs when the bill is payable to fictitious or non-existing person or the last or only endorsement is in blank.

A bearer order is also negotiable. It can be transferred by the bearer through mere delivery and no endorsement is required. It enjoys full negotiability but it is not safe for the absence of endorsement. Any forged endorsement of the payee would be disregarded since a bearer bill can be negotiated and transferred by delivery without any endorsement. For this reason, it is prohibited in China.

There are other two points to be noted when the status of the payee is discussed. First, it should be noted that the payees may be jointly stated, in alternative or in sequence. For example, "payable to A and B", "payable to A or B" or "payable first to A then to B". Second, it should also be noted that a bill may be payable to the drawer himself, such as in collection and in letter of credit. For example, "The bill is drawn by us on you payable to ourselves".

3. **Other Items in a Bill of Exchange**

(1) The Date of Issue

The date of issue refers to the date when a bill is drawn. It performs two functions: One is to make certain that the date of presentation or the date of acceptance is not before the date of issue; the other is to compute the maturity date if a time bill is payable after date.

(2) The Place of Issue

Although not a requisite, it is recommended that the place of issue is indicated in a bill because the rules or laws concerning bills of exchange may vary from country to country. When a discrepancy occurs concerning the validity of a bill, the validity is normally judged in conformity with the laws of the place of issue. Draft is normally issued in the place where the drawer resides.

(3) The Place of Payment

Payment will normally be effected in the city where the drawee resides if there is no other indication of the location. However, a bill may be payable at another city indicated by the drawee. For example, a bill drawn on Bank of England, London may be payable at Standard Charted Bank, Hong Kong.

(4) A Banker Designated as Payer

If the drawee is a company rather than a bank, the drawee may request the drawer to indicate on the draft the drawee's bank to be the banker designated as payer. For example:

A bill drawn on ABC Co. , London

Payable by Bank of England, London

If the drawee company does not indicate a banker to be the payer at the time of issue, he may indicate the name of the banker when he accepts the time bill. For example:

Accepted

(date)

payable at Bank of England, London

For ABC Co. , London

<u>Signature</u>

(5) Value Received

"For value received" indicates that the payee obtains the bill because he has given value to the drawer. Value refers to anything that is sufficient to support a simple contract and may be given in the form of goods, services or money.

(6) A Set of Bill

Bills of exchange usually are made out in duplicate which represent one liability only. When one part is paid, the other becomes void. The wordings of the 1st part of the bill will read as "pay this first bill of exchange (second of the same tenor and date being unpaid) to . . . " and the 2nd part will read as " pay this second bill of exchange (first of the same tenor and date being unpaid) to . . . ". With these wordings, double payments under one set of bills of exchange will be avoided.

(7) Referee in Case of Need (see P22, part 5)

(8) Notice of Dishonor Excused and Protest Waived (see P22, part 5)

(9) Without Recourse (see P22, part 5)

These items are not considered as essentials to a bill of exchange and Bills of Exchange Ordiance allows these parts to be optional or to be omitted.

4. **Parties to the Bills of Exchange**

Although the three major types of credit instruments are different, they share some important common characteristics. Therefore, we will use bills of exchange as an example to illustrate the parties of any credit instrument in general.

There are 3 immediate parties to a bill of exchange: the drawer, the drawee and the payee. They are the basic parties to a bill before it is transferred to another party.

（1）The Drawer

The drawer is the party who draws and signs a draft on the drawee and delivers it to the payee. He is a debtor to the draft. Before the bill is accepted by the drawee, he is primarily liable to the payee or holder of the instrument. In the event that the drawee dishonors the bill by non-acceptance or by non-payment, the drawer must redeem and pay the bill. However, when the bill is accepted, his liability becomes secondary.

（2）The Drawee

The drawee is the party on whom the bill is drawn and he is the party to honor the bill at the order of the drawer. In other words, he is the party who will effect payments to the payee. In this sense, he can also be called the payer and he is another debtor to the bill. He is called a drawee because the draft is drawn on him. However, when the bill is presented to him, the drawee can make a choice whether to honor it（agree to make acceptance and payment）or dishonor it（refuse to make acceptance and payment）because he can not prevent any party to whom he owes no debt from drawing a draft on him. This means that before the drawee agrees to honor the draft, he is not yet a debtor to the bill, and if he agrees, he acknowledges his indebtedness to the bill and in the case of a time bill, he becomes an acceptor.

An acceptor is a special drawee. When a drawee signs his name on the face of a time draft indicating his promise of payment on a due date, he becomes an acceptor. His acceptance makes the acceptor assume primary liability to the bill. As a result, the drawer holds secondary liability to the bill as mentioned above.

（3）The Payee

The payee is the party to receive payment. He is the first creditor to the bill and the first legal owner of the instrument. He can either claim payment against the bill or transfer（negotiate）the draft to another party. If the bill is transferred, he is called the original holder/transferer because the bill is taken away from him while the transferee, the person who takes the bill, becomes the new holder.

The following expression is often used to describe the three immediate parties of a bill of exchange and students must be familiar with it and have a clear mind to recognize the different parties.

The bill is drawn by A on B payable to C. Here, The drawer is A, the drawee is B and the Payee is C. If the drawer and the payee are the same person, the bill may read as: the bill is drawn by us on you payable to ourselves. If the drawer and the drawee are the same person, the bill may read as: the bill is drawn by us on ourselves payable to you.

Credit instruments can be transferred from one holder to another. In doing so, the ownership of the bill is transferred from the previous holder to the subsequent party. This process of ownership transfer is called negotiation. In the course of its negotiation, bills of exchange may have other parties as well.

(1) Endorser

An endorser is a payee or a holder who signs his name on the back of a bill for the purpose of negotiation. Because the payee is the first holder, he will be the first endorser. When the payee becomes the endorser, he transforms himself from a creditor to a debtor because he obligates himself that he will be liable to the endorsee and his subsequent parties. For example, an endorser may make a promise to his endorsee as follows: " If you, the holder of this instrument, make proper presentation for acceptance and for payment and is dishonored, I will pay the face amount of the bill upon your proper notice on me. " In the process of negotiation, we will have the first endorser, the second endorser, the third endorser and so forth and the list can go on.

(2) Endorsee

An endorsee is the party to whom the instrument is transferred. He becomes the new holder to the instrument and is the creditor to the instrument. An endorsee can also become an endorser if he wishes to transfer the instrument to another party by signing his name on its back. And by doing so, he transforms himself into a debtor. If the process of negotiation creates a sequence of endorsers, similarly, it will also bring about a series of endorsees. For example, if a bill has been transferred from A to B to C and C is the holder, from the standpoint of C, A and B will be his prior parties. If C continues to transfer the bill to D and D to E, then D and E will be called his subsequent parties.

$$A \longrightarrow B \longrightarrow \boxed{C} \longrightarrow D \longrightarrow E$$

(previous parties)   (subsequent parties)

(3) Acceptor for Honor

An acceptor for honor is the person who himself is not a liable party to a bill of exchange but with the consent of the holder may intervene and accept the bill in the event that the bill is dishonored by non-acceptance. He is the debtor to the bill and will make the payment when the bill falls due.

(4) Guarantor

A guarantor is another third party who guarantees the acceptance and the payment of a bill of exchange at the time when the bill is drawn. The guaranteed can be the drawer or drawee. The obligations of the guarantor are the same as those of the guaranteed.

(5) Holder

A holder is a party who is in possession of the instrument. A holder can be the payee/bearer or the endorsee. The payee will always be the original holder. A holder is a creditor to the bill. A person holding a forged bill or one who has stolen a bill payable to the order of another is not a holder, but a wrongful possessor. Only the legal possessor can become the holder and the perfect title to the bill will be shown as follows:

　＊ To duly present the instrument for acceptance or payments

　＊ To transfer a bill to other persons

　＊ To endorse a bill

* To give notice of dishonor to the prior party
* To exercise right of recourse against the prior party
* To sue in his own name
* To duplicate the lost bill
* To cross cheque or banker's demand draft, and to deliver it to a bank for collection

The legal possessor, the holder, can be further classified as a holder for value and a holder in due course. The perfect title to a bill will be accrued to the holder in due course.

(A) Holder for value.

As we have mentioned, value refers to anything which is sufficient to support a simple contract and may be given in the form of goods, services or money. A holder for value is the holder of a bill for which value has been given either by himself or by his prior parties. In the former case, we usually refer to the payee. In the latter case and according to *Bills of Exchange Act,* a holder for value usually refers to the holder when the value is given by his direct prior party rather than by himself. For example, If a bill is drawn by A on B payable to C and accepted by B; C endorses the instrument and gives it to D as a gift. Although D gives no value for the instrument by himself, he is qualified as a holder for value for the reason that the value has already been given by C, his direct prior party.

A holder for value is the creditor to the bill. He enjoys the same rights but is subject to the same defects in title, if any, of the transferor. That is to say, the rights of a holder for value can not be superior to his direct prior party.

(B) Holder in due course.

A holder in due course can also be called bona-fide holder. According to *Bills of Exchange Act,* a holder in due course is the person who is in possession of an instrument that is:

(a) Complete and regular on its face (A complete and regular bill is the one that contains all the essentials required) ,

(b) Taken before maturity,

(c) Taken in good faith and for value and

(d) Taken without notice of its previous dishonor and without notice of any infirmity in the instrument or defect in the title of the person negotiating it.

"Good faith" is defined as: "A thing is deemed to be done in good faith where it is in fact done honestly, whether it is done negligiently or not. " For example, if a holder is aware of some fraud or illegality in connection with the instrument or if he has actual or constructive notice of a defect in the title on the part of his transferor, consequently, he can not be a holder in due course because he has not taken the instrument in good faith.

In practice, a holder in due course usually refers to a person who has obtained the instrument through giving the value by himself. For example, if a person obtains an instrument as payment to his job done, to the goods he has delivered, to the services he has provided or as repayment for the loan he has made, he will be a holder in due course. However, it should be noted that a payee can never be a holder in due course because of the absence of negotiation. In fact, only a holder in due course has perfect title to a bill because his rights over the bill will not be affected by the title defects of his direct prior party.

Let's look at the following example and clarify a holder for value and a holder in due course.

If an instrument has been drawn by A on B payable to C, accepted by B and then delivered to C. Later on, C endorses the instrument and gives it to D as a gift but then D loses it in the street where it is found by E who transfers it for value to F who again endorses it and gives it to G as a gift. C is the payee or the original holder so he can only be the holder for value but not the holder in due course. D obtains the bill as a gift and not for value, he is not a holder in due course but he is qualified as the holder for value because the value has been given and transferred to him by his direct prior party C. E is a wrongful possessor and can not be qualified as a holder. F has taken the bill for value and he can establish himself as a holder in due course as long as he takes the instrument in good faith. This means that the defective title of the instrument on the part of E may not prevent F to become a holder in due course. G gives no value for the bill and can not be the holder in due course but he can be the holder for value because the value has been given by his prior party F. The full benefits of negotiability do not pass to a holder for value, these benefits are passed on only if the holder for value is also qualified as a holder in due course. When an instrument is dishonored, a holder in due course obtains perfect title to the bill and can claim payment from all parties liable on the instrument, and prior parties have no defense to a claim for payment by a holder in due course.

In summary, holder of a bill is the creditor to the bill and can be the payee, the bearer and the endorsee. In contrast, debtors of a bill can be the drawee, acceptor, drawer and endorser who hold the liability to make payments. Their order of liability is as follows:

Before acceptance: (a) drawer (b) the first endorser (c) the second endorser ...

After acceptance: (a) acceptor (b) drawer (c) the first endorser...

5. Acts of a Bill of Exchange

The acts of a bill of exchange refer to the legal acts carried out to bear the obligations to a draft. The main act is to issue. Other acts such as endorsement, acceptance, acceptance for honor and guarantee are based on the main act. In broad sense, the acts also include presentment, payment, payment for honor, dishonor, protest and the exercise of right recourse.

(1) Issue

To issue a draft comprises two actions to be performed by the drawer. One is to draw a draft and sign it, the other is to deliver it to the payee. Thus the liability of the bill is established and the payee becomes the creditor to the bill.

When issuing a bill, the drawer must draw it in its complete form, containing all the essentials stipulated. The drawer must sign the bill as well. A bill without a signature or with a false signature is not a valid bill. The liability on a bill of exchange is established by signature only: no person is liable upon a bill if he has not signed it. A bill can be made in the name of a person, a company or by some other person under his authority. A bill so made engages the drawer under the primary liability to the bill. A bill is not a"voucher of payment". It is "money in credit" which means that the payee's right to the bill will entirely depend on the creditworthiness of the drawer.

To deliver means to transfer the possession of the draft from the drawer to the payee. The payee is entitled to receive payments. He becomes the original holder of the bill and is the creditor to the bill.

(2) Endorsement

Endorsement is made on the back of a bill of exchange. It is an act of negotiation. A bill is negotiated when it is transferred from one person to another in such a manner as to constitute the transferee the holder of the bill. Only the holder, namely the payee and the endorsee can endorse a bill.

Endorsement comprises two actions: one is to sign on the back of a draft, the other is to deliver it to the endorsee/transferee. The transfer of a bill of exchange is effected either by delivery or by endorsement and delivery.

Endorsement is applicable only to negotiable bills of exchange and the negotiability of a bill is determined by the status of its payee, or, in other words, by the bill's type of order. In the case of a demonstrative order bill, the transfer of a bill comprises two acts to be performed by the endorser: endorsement and delivery. If a bill is of bearer order, no endorsement is required and mere delivery is sufficient to transfer the title of the bill. Endorsement is not applicable to a restrictive order bill. This kind of bill has no negotiability and transfer is prohibited.

There are five kinds of endorsement:

(A) Special endorsement (Endorsement in full).

Special endorsement bears the signature of the endorser and at the same time spells out the name of the transferee. It is also referred to as the endorsement in full. For example:

Pay to the order of B Co. , London – the endorsee

For A Co. , London – the endorser

Signature (of the endorser)

A bill so endorsed remains a demonstrative order bill. It can be further transferred by endorsement and delivery. A series consecutive special endorsements show a clear chain of endorsers

(B) Blank endorsement(General eudorsement)

Blank endorsement only bears the signature of the transferor but no transferee is specified. It is also referred to as a general endorsement. For example:

For A Co. , London – the endorser

Signature (of the endorser)

When a blank endorsement is made on a bill, it will transform the original bill from demonstrative order to bearer order. If the bill is to be further transferred, mere delivery is required. On the other hand, a blank endorsement can be changed to a special endorsement by adding above the endorser's signature such wordings as "pay to" or "pay to the order" of the transferee or some other person. However, it should be noted that if the bill is originally a bearer order bill instead of a demonstrative order bill, a special endorsement can not transform the bearer order to demonstrative order because endorsement is not required to transfer a bearer order bill.

(C) Restrictive endorsement.

A restrictive endorsement bears such indications which will prevent the further negotiation of a bill. Examples are:

"Pay to ABC Bank only . . . (the endorsee)

For A Co. , London . . . (the endorser)

Signature (of the endorser) "

Or

"Pay to ABC Bank not negotiable . . . (the endorsee)

For A Co. , London . . . (the endorser)

Signature (of the endorser) "

Or

"Pay to ABC Bank not transferable . . . (the endorsee)

For A Co. , London . . . (the endorser)

Signature (of the endorser) "

Or

"Pay to ABC Bank not to order . . . (the endorsee)

For A Co. , London . . . (the endorser)

Signature (of the endorser) "

Restrictive order will transform the demonstrative order to a restrictive order. The transferee can only claim payment against the bill and no further transfer is allowed.

(D) Conditional endorsement.

A conditional endorsement transfers ownership subject to a specified term and condition. Examples are:

"Pay to the order of B Co. on delivery of B/L to Hong Kong Bank

For A Co. , London

Signature

Two points are worth remembering in connection with conditional endorsements which should not be confused with "unconditional order" stated in the definition of a bill. Firstly, a bill of exchange should be made an unconditional order at the time of issuing. But an endorsement can be made conditional. The conditional endorsement does not affect the bill as an unconditional order to pay and it has no binding on the drawer and drawee. Secondly, when the drawee agrees to honor the draft, he can choose to honor it under the fulfillment of a certain condition or he can choose to disregard the condition. In fact, conditional endorsement is in effect a conditional delivery, which means that the bill will be delivered to the endorsee only when he fulfills the conditions.

Conditionally endorsed bill can be further transferred.

(E) Endorsement for collection.

Endorsement for collection requests that the transferee deal with the bill as he is instructed. Normally, "for collection" or other wording of instruction will be added before or after "Pay to Bank X. " Examples are:

"For collection pay to Bank A"

"Pay to Bank A for collection"

"Pay to Bank A for deposit"

"Pay to Bank A for the account of John Smith"

In the above examples, Bank A is either authorized to deal with the bill or entrusted with the bill for another person. As Bank A does not truly own the title, the bill so endorsed can not be further transferred.

(3) Presentment

Presentment/Presentation is to be made by the holder to the person designated as drawee for payment if it is a sight bill and for acceptance and payment if it is a time bill.

Bills must be presented for acceptance on the following occasions and failure to do so will make the holder lose right of recourse against his prior parties.

（A）Time bill after sight.

For this kind of bill, presentment for acceptance is a legal requirement in order to fix the maturity date of the bill.

（B）Time bill after date.

Presentment for acceptance is not legally required, the holder of this kind of bill may present the bill directly for payment at the maturity date. However, the holder is advised to make presentment for acceptance so as to secure the liability of the drawee as an acceptor.

（C）A time bill stipulates that it must be presented for acceptance.

（D）A time bill which is payable at a place other than that of the drawee must be presented for acceptance.

A sight draft should be presented for payment within a reasouable time which, according to the Uniform Law for Bills of Exchange and Promissory Notes at Geneva, is made within 1 year from the issuing date. As for a time draft, Geneva Law stipulates that the time for acceptance is made within 1 year from the issuing date. When a time draft is accepted, Bills of Exchange Act stipulates that presentment for payment should be made on due date whereas the Geneva Law stipulates that presentment for payment should be made either on due date or within two business days after the due date. If a bill is not presented within the reasonable time period, it is said to be overdue and its holder will lose right of recourse against his prior parties.

The holder should present the bill at the proper place specified on the bill. If no place is specified, the bill should be presented at the drawee or the acceptor's business office. If no business office is specified, the bill should be presented at the drawee or the acceptor's residence.

（4）Acceptance

Acceptance of a bill is the signification by the drawee of a time bill of his assent to the order of the drawer. The drawee has no liability on the bill until he signs the bill in such a way as to signify acceptance of liability to pay the money stated in the bill.

A valid acceptance requires two actions: one is for the drawee to write the word "Accepted" on the face of a bill and sign below. The mere signature of the drawee, without additional words, is sufficient. The other is for the drawee to return the accepted bill to the payee. In practice, the return of the accepted bill can be replaced by the drawee's issuing of an acceptance notice to the payee. In the case that the bill is a time bill after sight, the accepting date is deemed to be the sight date from which the maturity date can be worked out. After acceptance, the drawee will then credit the amount payable to the payee's account at maturity.

The drawee is allowed to have reasonable time to deliberate whether or not to accept the bill. According to *Bills of Exchange Act 1882*, acceptance is generally to be made at a reasonable hour on a business day subsequent to the presentment of the bill. According to *Uniform Law for Bills of Exchange* and *Promissory Notes at Geneva of 1930*, acceptance should be made between the 1st presentment and the 2nd presentment made on the next day. In order to be convenient, the accepting date and the due date will be stated when the acceptance is made:

ACCEPTED

(date)

to mature

(date)

For name of the drawee

Signature

When the drawee has made his acceptance, he is known as the acceptor instead of the drawee and he becomes primary liable on the bill. When this happens, the drawer will be secondarily liable to the bill. In practice, an accepted bill can be transferred more easily than an unaccepted one because it has the definite undertaking of the drawee to make payment on the due date.

Acceptance can be classified into two types: general acceptance and qualified acceptance.

(A) General acceptance.

A general acceptance assents without qualification to the order of the drawer. For example:

ACCEPTED

1 Feb. , 200X

For Bank of China, Shanghai

Signature

(B) Qualified acceptance

A qualified acceptance in express terms varies the effect of the bill as drawn. Examples are as follows.

(a) Conditional acceptance.

A conditional acceptance indicates that payment by the acceptor will depend on the fulfillment of conditions stated therein.

ACCEPTED

1 Feb. , 200X

Payable on goods are up to Board of Trade standards

For ABC Bank, London

Signature

(b) Partial acceptance.

A partial acceptance means that only part of the amount of the bill will be accepted. For example, suppose the face amount of the bill is GBP1,000. 00

ACCEPTED

1 FEB. , 200X

Payable for amount of GBP800. 00 only.

For ABC Bank, London

Signature

(c) Local acceptance.

A local acceptance means that payment will be effected only at a particular place. Acceptance to pay at a particular place is a general acceptance unless it expressly states that the bill is to be paid there only and not elsewhere. For example:

ACCEPTED

1 Feb. , 200X

Payable at the Bank of China, Singapore only

For Hong Kong & Shanghai Banking Corp. , H. K.

<u>Signature</u>

（d）Time qualified acceptance.

A time qualified acceptance is an acceptance to alter the time to effect payment. For example, suppose the tenor of the bill is 3 months after date.

ACCEPTED

1 Feb. , 200X

Payable at 6 months after date

For ABC Bank, London

<u>Signature</u>

Qualified acceptance by the drawee is allowed because the drawee can choose whether or not to assent the order to pay given by the drawer. This means he can choose to agree, to disagree or to insist on having proof that certain conditions has been fulfilled before he accepts the bill. Qualified acceptance will not make a bill invalid if the bill itself is made unconditional at the time of issue. However, the holder may refuse to take a qualified acceptance, and, if he does not accept a qualified acceptance, he may treat the bill as dishonored by non-acceptance.

（5）Payment

The ultimate purpose for a bill of exchange is to get paid. Payment is carried out when the bill is paid. Payment of a sight bill is made when the bill is presented to the drawee and payment of a time bill is made at maturity. A bill will be discharged only when payment is made in due course. The so-called payment in due course includes the following:

（A）Payment should be made by or on behalf of the drawee or the acceptor and not by the drawer or any endorser. The payment made by the drawer or any endorser is not a final payment because he may claim payment from the drawee or the acceptor.

（B）Payment should be made on or after the maturity date of the bill and can not be made in advance.

（C）Payment should be made to the holder and if the bill has been transferred, the bank will check the endorsements or at least the sequence of the endorsements before making payment.

（D）Payment should be made in good faith, without knowing that the holder's title thereto is defective.

In short, payment in due course means payment made by the drawee or acceptor at or after the maturity of the bill to the holder thereof in good faith and without notice that his title to the bill is defective. When the payment is made in due course, it is the final payment and the bill is discharged. That is to say that the drawee's or the acceptor's liability to the bill ends and so does the liabilities of other debtors to the bill such as the drawer and the endorsers, if any.

Payment may be made in the national currency of the drawee's country or in the currency stated on the draft, depending upon the foreign exchange regulations enforced in the drawee's country.

(6) Dishonor

Dishonor is a failure or refusal to make acceptance on or payment of a bill of exchange when presented to the drawee. A bill of exchange may be dishonored either by non-acceptance or by non-payment. When a bill is only offered a qualified acceptance, the holder may take it or treat it as dishonored by non-acceptance. Other instances of dishonor may arise when the drawee's deliberate avoidance, his bankruptcy or even his death has made the acceptance or the payment impossible.

When a bill is dishonored either by non-acceptance or by non-payment, the right of recourse will be accrued to the holder at once. That is to say, the holder may exercise his right of recourse against his prior endorsers and drawer for payment.

(7) Notice of Dishonor

When a bill is dishonored by non-acceptance or by non-payment, the holder must give notice of dishonor to the drawer and all the endorsers for whom the holder may wish to make liable. The purpose of giving such notice is to inform the drawer and prior endorsers the default of acceptance or payment so that they may get ready to honor the payment. According to the *Bills of Exchange Act 1882*, if the notice of dishonor is not given, the holder shall lose right of recourse against the drawer and all the endorsers. For a holder in due course, however, his recourse claim shall not be prejudiced by such an omission. According to the *Geneva's Uniform Law 1930*, the right of recourse of the holder shall remain unless the drawer and/or the endorsers do suffer loss due to his omission of giving the notice, in which case the holder must compensate for the loss. Notice of dishonor should be given on the next business day after the dishonor of the draft. There are two methods in which the notice of dishonor may reach the prior parties and the drawer.

For the first method, the notice of dishonor is given by the holder to his direct prior party who shall do so in quick succession till the notice is given to the drawer. Any party failing to do so shall remain liable to the holder and lose his own right of recourse against all his prior endorsers and the drawer. For a holder in due course, however, his recourse claim shall not be prejudiced by such an omission. The first method will be shown below:

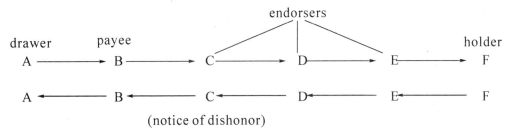

(notice of dishonor)

For the second method, the holder gives the notice of dishonor to each endorser and the drawer separately in order to retain their liability thereon. In this case, there is no need for each subsequent party to inform his direct prior party. Take the above-mentioned example, F, the holder will give notice to E, D, C, B till A. In practice, the 1st method is preferred as the holder may have no knowledge of every prior party and he can be fairly certain that each prior party will pass on the notice. The second method will be shown below:

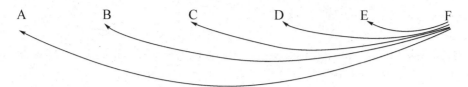

If the drawer or the endorser states besides his name on the bill such wordings as "notice of dishonor excused", it means that in the event the bill is dishonored, the holder can claim compensation from him without giving him a notice of dishonor.

(8) Protest

Protest is a formal certificate given by a notary party or another authorized person to evidence that a bill of exchange has been dishonored. The protest should be done on the very day or no later than the next business day from the day of dishonor.

After a bill is dishonored and a notice of dishonor is given, the holder may hand the bill again to a notary party who will present it again to the drawee so as to obtain a legal proof of the act of dishonor. If it is dishonored again, the notary party then will draw a protest and return it to the holder together with the bill, against which the holder may exercise his right of recourse against the prior parties.

According to the *British Bills of Exchange Act*, foreign bills should be protested whereas inland bill need not. If a foreign bill is not so protested, the holder will lose his right of recourse against his prior parties.

The protest fee is to be borne by the drawer and will be charged to him at the time when the compensation is made. However, the drawer may indicate besides his name on the bill such wordings as "protest waived" or "please do not protest if dishonored" so that he will not be responsible for the protest fee. In this case, the holder may claim payment from him without protest and if the holder still wants the notary party to draw up a protest, he himself will pay the protest fee.

(9) Right of Recourse

Right of recourse means that the holder of bills of exchange has the right to claim compensation from the drawer and the endorsers in the event that the bill has been dishonored. The compensation should include the amount payable on the bill with interest, the fees for giving the notice of dishonor and protest and other incurred expenses.

The holder may exercise his right of recourse only when he has completed the following procedures:

(A) Present the bill to the drawee for acceptance or payment and it is dishonored by non-acceptance or non-payment.

(B) Give notice of dishonor to his prior party in one business day following the day of dishonor.

(C) Make a protest for non-acceptance or non-payment in one business day following the day of dishonor.

The recourse claim should be enforced within the legal limit of time which is 6 years according the *British Bills of Exchange Act* or 6 months according to the *Geneva's Uniform Law*.

It should be noted that the endorser can only file his recourse claim against his prior parties but not his subsequent parties. For example:

A ——————→B ——————→C ——————→D ——————→E ——————→C

The holder C is actually the prior party to D and E. Therefore, if the bill is dishonored, C can only sue B and A but not E and D.

Let's take again the example of item 5, part IV, section two in this chapter to discuss the different rights of recourse accrued to the various possessors of a bill:

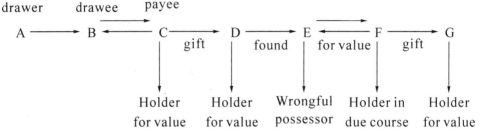

In the event that the drawee B has dishonored the draft, the rights of recourse accrued to each individual party will be shown as follows:

Party	Status	Right of recourse against			
G	Holder for value	E	D	C	A
F	Holder in due course	E	D	C	A
E	Wrongful possessor	Not applicable			
D	Holder for value	A			
C	Holder for value	A			

If the drawer or any endorser writes on the bill such words as "without recourse" or "sans recourse", he will be discharged of his liability on the bill. However, such wordings will affect the negotiability of the bill.

(10) Acceptance for Honor

When a bill has been dishonored by non-acceptance, any person who is not a liable party thereon may intervene and accept the dishonored bill supra protest after he gains the consent of the holder. This act is known to be acceptance for honor and the purpose is to vindicate the honor of the drawer or a particular endorser. If the acceptance for honor does not expressly state for whose honor it is made, it is deemed to be an acceptance for the honor of the drawer. It should be noted that if the bill so accepted is payable after sight, its maturity date is calculated from the date of protest, not from the date of acceptance for honor. The form of an acceptance for honor is as below:

Accepted for honor

Of (the person for whose honor the bill is accepted)

On (the date of acceptance for honor)

Signed by (the acceptor for honor)

The acceptor for honor is liable to the holder and all the parties subsequent to the one for whose honor he accepts the bill. And when the payment is effected, on the one hand, all the parties subsequent to the one for whose honor the bill is accepted are discharged of their liability to the holder. On the other hand, the acceptor for honor becomes the holder in due course and he can exercise his right of recourse against the party for his honor the bill is accepted, all his prior parties and the drawer. For example:

$$C +$$
$$A \longrightarrow B \longrightarrow C \longrightarrow D \longrightarrow E \longrightarrow F$$

Notes: In the above chart, A is the drawer; B is the prior party of C; D and F are the subsequent parties of C and F is the holder.

If C + accepts the bill for the honor of C, then he will be liable to C's subsequent parties D, E and F. After the payment is effected by C +, D and E will be discharged their liability to the holder F, and C + becomes the new holder and he can claim compensation from C, B or A.

In practice, however, when the bill is dishonored by non-acceptance, it will be difficult to have a third party to accept the bill for honor. As a result, acceptance for honor is seldom used in international settlement.

(11) Payment for Honor

When a bill has been dishonored by non-payment, any person who is not a party liable thereon may intervene to pay the bill. The act is known as payment for honor and the purpose is to vindicate the honor of a drawer or a particular endorser. Unlike acceptance for honor, payment for honor can be made without the consent of the holder and the holder must agree to such an act, otherwise he loses his right of recourse against the person for whose honor the payment is to be made.

When a bill has been paid for honor, all parties subsequent to the one for whose honor the bill is paid are discharged of their liability thereon, and the payer for honor becomes the holder and has the right of recourse against the person for whose honor he has made the payment as well as against all prior parties thereon.

In practice, however, when the bill is dishonored by non-payment, it will be difficult to have a third party to pay the bill for honor. As a result, payment for honor is seldom used in international settlement.

(12) Guarantee

Guarantee is performed by a person called guarantor, who is not a liable party on the bill and who engages at the time when the bill is drawn that the bill will be paid on presentation if it is a sight bill or accepted and paid if it is a time bill. The guarantor assumes the same liability to the bill as that of the drawer, and drawee.

Guarantee is normally made on the face of the instrument. The common forms are as follows:

GUARANTEED	PER AVAL	PAYMENT GUARANTEE
For a/c of _____	Given for _____	Signed by _____
Guarantor _____	Signed by _____	Dated on _____
Signature _____	Dated on _____	

If the guaranteed bill is dishonored by non-acceptance or by non-payment, the guarantor shall pay it. And after the payment is effected by the guarantor, he will become the new holder and exercise the right of recourse against the drawer or the drawee.

In practice, the creditworthiness of an instrument will be enhanced by guarantee. Its negotiability will also be improved. As a result, guarantee has found wide application in the field of financing.

6. Peration of a Bill of Exchange

A bill of exchange can go different routes from its issue to its discharge. The operation can be affected by the following three factors: (a) Whether or not the bill is negotiated/transferred, (b) Whether or not it is dishonored; and (c) Whether or not its acceptance or payment is intervened by a third party. When the route is different, the parties involved will vary accordingly. The following is a summary of some typical routes:

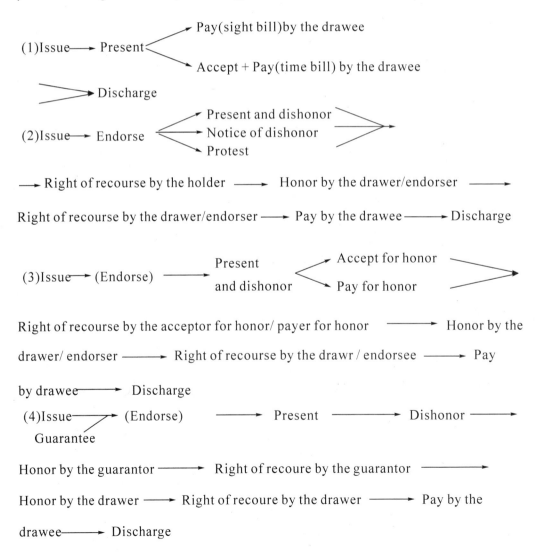

Chapter Three　Credit Instruments(I)
− Bills of Exchange (II)

Section One　Classification of Bills of Exchange

Bills of exchange can be classified according to the tenor, currency and the different status of the relevant parties. The followings are the major types:

1. According to Different Places of the Three Immediate Parties

(1) Domestic Bill or Inland Bill

When the three immediate parties, namely the drawer, drawee and payee reside in the same country, the bill is a domestic bill. Normally a domestic bill is drawn and payable in the same country.

(2) Foreign Bill

When two of the three immediate parties reside in different countries, the bill is a foreign bill. Normally a foreign bill is drawn in one country and payable in another country.

2. According to the Tenor

Tenor refers to when the bill will reach its maturity.

(1) Sight Bill

As its name implies, a sight bill is supposed to be paid when it is first seen by the drawee. It can be expressed as payable at sight / on demand / on presentation. When a bill specifies no time of payment, it is also considered as a sight bill.

(2) Time Bill

It is a bill payable at a fixed or determinable future time. It will be further classified into payable at a fixed future time / at a fixed future time after date / after sight / after the happening of a certain event.

3. According to Types of Order

(1) Restrictive Order Bill

It is a bill payable to a specified person only. No negotiation is allowed.

(2) Demonstrative Order Bill

It is a bill payable to a specified person or to the order of a specified person. Negotiation is allowed and the bill will be transferred by endorsement and delivery.

(3) Bearer Order

It is a bill payable to bearer. Negotiation is allowed and the bill will be transferred by mere delivery, no endorsement is required.

4. According to the Drawer and the Drawee

(1) Banker's Draft or Bank Draft

It is a draft drawn by a bank on another bank or on its head/branch office. When a banker's draft is accepted by the drawee bank, it is called a banker's acceptance bill. This kind of bill is most preferable in international settlement because it has a bank's undertaking to the bill.

(2) Commercial Bill / Trader's Bill

It is a draft drawn by a trader on another trader or a banker. When the bill is drawn on another trader and accepted by him, it is called a trader's acceptance bill. If the bill is drawn on a bank and accepted by the bank, it can be called a banker's acceptance bill.

5. According to Whether or not Shipping Documents are Attached

(1) Clean Bill

A clean bill is one that has no relevant shipping documents attached and is normally used alone in international settlement. Such a draft may be drawn for many purposes, among which are the collection of open accounts, payments for services, personal remittances and other transactions that arise in international trade but for which no shipping documents exist.

(2) Documentary Bill

A documentary bill is one that should be accompanied by the relevant documents to complete an export transaction. It will not be used alone and will always be used together with the shipping documents.

Clean bill and documentary bill may look the same in form. The way to distinguish one from the other is to see whether it is used alone or with shipping documents attached in a given payment method.

It should be noted that the classification of a bill of exchange is not clear-cut. In fact, a bill can be one type or a combination of several types to serve different purposes. For example, a bill can be a foreign time banker's acceptance bill payable to a specified person only.

Section Two   Finance under Bills of Exchange

A trader can get financed by making use of a bill of exchange. These different ways of finance are achieved by discounting, forfeiting and accommodating.

1. Discounting

(1) Definition of Discounting

Discounting a bill of exchange means that a holder of an accepted bill sells the bill to a financial institution at a price less than its face value before it reaches its maturity. The financial institution can be a bank and when this financial institution specializes in discounting bills of exchange, it is also referred to as a discount house. The present value the holder receives is called the net proceeds. And the balance between the face value and the net proceeds is called the discount interest which represents the profits of the financial institution.

The purpose for the holder to discount the bill is to obtain funds before the due date. In this way his turnover can be speeded up and he is thus financed. On the other hand, the financial institution will also make a profit by discounting a bill of exchange and his profit is represented by the discount interest.

(2) The Procedure

The procedure of discounting a bill of exchange is illustrated as follows. Let's see how the holder is financed and how the financial institution makes a profit through this process.

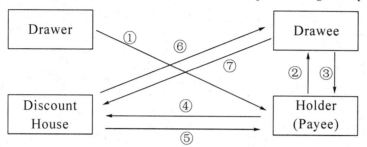

① The drawer draws a time bill on the drawee and delivers it to the payee/holder.

② The payee presents the bill to the drawee for acceptance.

③ The drawee accepts the bill and returns it to the payee.

④ Before due, the payee as the original holder discounts (sells) the accepted time bill to a discount house.

⑤ The discount house discounts (buys) this bill and pays the net proceeds to the payee. The discount house becomes the new holder.

⑥ At maturity, the discount house presents the bill for payment to the drawee.

⑦ The drawee pays the face value to the discount house.

(3) Calculation

The discount interest and the net proceeds will be calculated according to the following formulas:

Discount interest = (Face value × Discounting days × Discounting rate) / 360 (365) days

Net proceeds = Face value − Discount interest, or

Net proceeds = Face value × [1 − Discounting days /360 (365) days × Discounting rates]

Suppose a bill for USD10,000 is payable at 90 days sight. The bill is accepted on June 20, 200X and the holder decides to discount it on June 30, 200X. If the discount rate is 10% and a year is based on 360 days, then,

When the holder discounts it on June 30, the days left to maturity date is 90 − 10 = 80 days. So discounting days would be 80 days.

Discounting interest = (10,000 × 80 × 10%) / 360 = USD222.22

Net proceeds = 10,000 − 222.22 = USD9777.78

The example shows that the holder will get USD9777.78 when he discounts the bill on June 30, 200X. The discount house will receive USD10,000 when he presents the bill to the drawee for payment on its due date. Therefore, the discount house has made a profit at USD222.22.

(4) The Discount House

The discount house acts as an endorsee who receives the bill from the endorser (the payee/holder) to provide finance to the holder. By discounting, the payee (the original holder) becomes the endorser and the discount house becomes the endorsee. However, the discount house is a special endorsee because the purpose of the endorsement is for the purpose of financing the endorser. Normally, if no further negotiation occurs, the discount house becomes the new holder of the bill. As any holder, the discount house bears the risk of non-payment at maturity. For this reason, the creditworthiness of the acceptor is of great concern to him. Generally speaking, the creditworthiness of a banker is more reliable than that of a trader and a big, first-class bank is better than a small one. As a result, a first-class banker's accepted bill is more preferable and acceptable than a trader's acceptance bill in the discounting market. As any holder, in the event that the drawee defaults the bill by non-payment, the discount house will obtain the right of recourse against his prior endorsers, the payee and the drawer.

There exists a well-known discount market in London, which is composed of twelve discount houses, operating business independently of any other financial institutions. These discount houses are also members of the London Discount Market Association.

(5) Rediscounting

Rediscounting is an operation by which the discount house sells the discounted bill to another bank. Rediscount may occur when money is tight for the discount house or when the discount house is short of funds. In England, the Bank of England usually acts as the "lender of the last resort" and the rediscounting bill must bear the names of two first-class British banks. Normally, the drawee should be one British bank who later accepts the bill and the discount house should be another British bank who previously discounted the bill.

2. Forfeiting

(1) Definition

Forfeiting is a special kind of discounting. It is the discounting without recourse the medium-term large amount promissory note or draft by the forfeiter to the payee/holder and for the purpose of financing the latter in international trade transactions.

Forfeiting is used as a means of financing when the goods involved are capital goods for which the payment may be made within five to seven years. The financial institute who discounts the bill without recourse is called the forfeiter. "Without recourse" means that the forfeiting is made with the understanding that the forfeiter can not exercise his right of recourse against his prior endorser in the event that the instrument is dishonored by the drawee. Thus, the payment to the payee is secured and the forfeiter will charge a higher fee than the ordinary discounting for the higher risk he takes. In the case of promissory note, The payee of the note will be the exporter and the maker of the note is the importer. Whereas in the case of a draft, the drawer and the payee is the exporter and the drawee is the importer. By forfeiting, the payee, namely the exporter will only look to the forfeiter for payment and he is free from the worry whether the importer will dishonor the instrument or not.

(2) Procedure

For the higher risk involved in forfeiting, the instrument should be guaranteed by an importer's bank before the forfeiting is carried out. If the importer (the drawee) dishonors the instrument, the guarantor bank will intervene and make the payment. For a promissory note, the procedure is as follows:

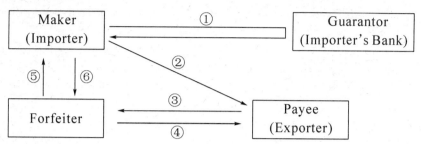

① The importer issues a promissory note and gets it guaranteed by his bank. The importer becomes the maker of the note.

② The maker delivers the promissory note to the payee (the exporter) .

③ Before maturity, the payee forfeits (discounts) the note to the forfeiter.

④ The forfeiter forfeits (buys) the note and makes payment without recourse to the payee at an amount less than the face value to the payee. In other words, the payee receives net proceeds from the forfeiter.

⑤ The forfeiter, as the new holder of the note, presents the note to the maker (importer) for payment at maturity.

⑥ The maker makes payment to the forfeiter at the face value of the note.

For a draft, the procedure of forfeiting is shown as follows:

① The exporter draws a time daft on the importer payable to himself and presents the bill to the drawee for acceptance.

② The drawee accepts the bill and has it guaranteed by his bank.

③ The drawee returns the accepted and guaranteed bill to the payee.

④ Before maturity, the payee discounts (sells) the bill to the forfeiter.

⑤ The forfeiter discounts (buys) the bill without recourse and makes the payment to the payee at an amount less than the face value to the payee.

⑥ At maturity, the forfeiter, as a new holder, presents the bill for payment to the drawee.

⑦ The drawee makes payment to the forfeiter at its full face value.

(3) Differences between forfeiting and discounting

Forfeiting is a special discounting. And a comparison between the forfeiting and an ordinary discounting will highlight the major differences.

Discounting	Forfeiting
Amount will not be large with the maturity less than one year.	The amount is usually large with maturity ranging between 5 – 7 years.
The discount house has the right of recourse against the prior endorser.	The forfeiter has no right of recourse against the prior endorser.
The risk is lower.	The risk is higher.
No guarantee of the accepted bill is required.	The accepted bill must be guaranteed by the importer's bank.
The discount rate is lower and no other fees need to be paid.	The discount rate is higher and other fees such as financing commission, commitment fee should be paid to its forfeiter.

3. Accommodating

(1) Definition

Accommodation is a finance to a company by a financial institution's consent to be the drawee of the accommodating bill drawn by the company. The drawer and payee of the bill are the company who wants to get finance this way. Such a bill is established when the company succeeds in "inviting" a financial institution to be the drawee when he gives no value to the bank. In other words, the company "borrows" the credit standing of the bank to draw such a bill. Therefore, the company is the party accommodated and the financial institution is the accommodating party who lends its credit standing for a fee to the company. When the bill is later accepted by the financial'al institution, the company can discount the bill to get finance.

The financial institution (the accommodating party) which specializes in accepting a time bill drawn on himself for the pure purpose of financing is called an accepting house. In London there are 17 accepting houses and they are members of the London Accepting Committee. The difference between a discount house and an accepting house is that the former acts as an endorsee and the latter acts as a drawee, though the purpose of both is to provide finance to traders. Another difference to be noted is that only the discount house will get involved in discounting whereas in accommodating, both the accepting house and the discount house will be included for the trader to receive funds.

(2) Procedure

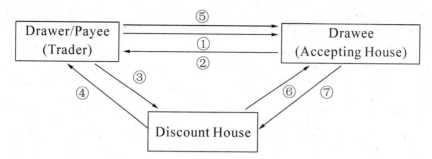

① The trader draws a time bill on an accepting house payable to himself and presents the bill to the drawee for acceptance.

② The accepting house accepts the bill and returns it to the payee.

③ Before maturity, the payee discounts (sells) the bill to the discount house.

④ The discount house discounts (buys) the bill and makes the payment to the payee at an amount less than the face value of the bill.

⑤ The trader provides funds to the accepting house just before maturity so that the drawee can honor the bill at maturity.

⑥ At maturity, the discount house, as the new holder of the bill, presents the bill to the accepting house for payment.

⑦ The drawee makes payment to the discount house at the face value.

(3) Calculation of the Face Value of an Accommodating Bill

When a trader draws an accommodating bill to raise funds, the face value of the bill must be larger than the target amount so that the discount interest can be covered. The face value of the bill is calculated as follows and the net proceeds represent the target amount the trade wants to raise:

Face value = Net proceeds / [1 – (Tenor × Discount rate) / 365 (360)]

For example, suppose that a trader wants to raise funds at the amount of USD30,000 by drawing an accommodating bill. If the tenor is 90 days and the discount rate is 9% based on 365 days a year, the face amount for the accommodating bill will be:

Face value = 30,000 / [1 – (90 × 9%) /365] = USD30,680. 86

So, in order to raise funds at USD30,000, the trader should draw a bill at the amount of USD30,680. 86.

(4) The Liabilities of the Trader and the Accepting House

The accommodating bill is a special bill in the sense that the bill is drawn on the accepting house when the trader gives no value to the accepting house before such a bill is established. For this reason, it is necessary to further consider the liabilities of these parties.

For the trader – the party accommodated:

(A) As a drawer to an accommodating bill, he is always primarily liable to the bill though the drawee and the acceptor is the accepting house.

(B) The drawer has to provide funds to the drawee (the accepting house) just before the due date so that the latter can honor the bill by making payment at maturity.

(C) Closely related to point (A), an accommodating bill is discharged only when the drawer (the accommodated party) makes the payment, not the drawee.

For the accepting house — the accommodating party:

(A) As a drawee and acceptor to the bill, the accepting house is liable to the endorsee (the discount house) to make payments. For this reason, the accepting house may require some forms of security before he agrees to be the drawee and acceptor of such a bill.

(B) As a special drawee, he is not liable to the drawer because he receives no value from the former.

4. Comparison of Lending, Discounting and Negotiating

As ways of financing, lending, discounting and negotiating share some similarities with distinct differences. In the first place, all of them can provide funds to the traders for a period of time in return for interest payments and the funds are to be returned at the time of maturity. However, while lending is a bank loan to the trader, discounting and negotiating are methods of finance by making use of the financial instruments. Furthermore, negotiation is used together with payment methods. Their differences will be outlined in the following table:

	Lending	Discounting	Negotiating
a	Neither financial instruments nor shipping documents are required.	Discounting is not used with payment methods. The bank will only purchase the financial instruments.	Negotiating is used together with payment methods. In most cases, bank will purchase both the financial instruments and the shipping documents.
b	Acceptance is not applicable.	The time instruments should be accepted before discounting.	The time instruments need not to be accepted, but the documents attached, if any, should be made in compliance with the stipulations of the payment methods before the negotiation.
c	Once the loan is granted, the lending bank will collect the lending interest at the maturity.	When discounting the time drafts or time notes, the discounting bank will collect the discounting interest immediately.	When discounting the time drafts or time notes, the negotiating bank will collect the discounting interest immediately.

	Lending	Discounting	Negotiating
d	Only the right to use the funds is transferred from the bank to the borrower.	Both the ownership and the right to use the financial instruments are transferred from the borrower (the payee) to the bank.	Both the ownership and the right to use the financial instruments as well as the title to the shipping documents are transferred from the borrower to the bank.
e	The bank can not recall the loan before maturity.	When the bank is in short of money, he may arrange to rediscount the instrument to get the fund bank.	The instruments should first be accepted before any rediscounting can be carried out.
f	The loan will be refunded only when the borrower makes repayment at the time of maturity.	The funds in the form of net proceeds will be refunded when the acceptor makes payment at maturity. In the event of non-payment, the bank can exercise the right of recourse against the payee to get refunded.	The bank will forward the instruments and the shipping documents to the issuing bank to claim reimbursement after the negotiation is done under L/C. In the event of non-payment, the bank can sell the goods to recover the funds, or the bank can exercise the right of recourse against the payee to call back the funds.
g		There is a discounting market to discount clean drafts.	There is no separate negotiating marketing to negotiating drafts.

Chapter Four　Credit Instruments (Ⅱ)
－ Promissory Note and Cheque

Section One　Promissory Note

1. Definition

Bills of Exchange Act defines a promissory note as: "A promissory note is an unconditional promise in writing made by one person (the maker) to another (the payee) signed by the maker engaging to pay on demand or at a fixed or determinable future time a sum certain in money to or to the order of a specified person or bearer." For example:

Promissory Note for USD40,000　　　　　　　　　Singapore, June 1, 200X

At 60 days after date we promise to pay to the order of ABC Co. the sum of US dollars forty thousand only.

　　　　　　　　　　　　　　　　For XYZ International Pte. Ltd., Singapore

　　　　　　　　　　　　　　　　　　　　　Signature

---

2. Essentials to a Promissory Note

With the knowledge of the essentials to a bill of exchange, we may easily understand the essentials to a promissory note. As some items in this part will be similar to those under the essentials to a bill of exchange, readers may need to turn back to the corresponding parts under bills of exchange for reference.

(1) The Word "Promissory Note"

The word "promissory note" should be clearly indicated in order to distinguish the note from other types of instruments like bills of exchange or cheques.

(2) An Unconditional Promise to Pay

This promise is given by the maker of the note. The promise should be made unconditional at the time of making.

(3) Status of the Payee

The payee can be a specified person, to his order or to the bearer.

(4) Signed by the Maker

Only the signature of the maker will make the note a valid one. A note will be made invalid if the signature is absent or forged.

(5) The Time and Place of Issue

The time of issue is the date the note is issued.

If there is no place indicated, the place besides the name of the maker will be deemed as the place of issue.

(6) Tenor

Promissory note can be either a sight one or a time one. In the event that no tenor is indicated on the note, the note is deemed to be a sight one. Banker's notes are usually made on demand.

(7) A Certain Sum in Money

(8) Place of Payment

If no place of payment is indicated, the place of issue is deemed as the place of payment.

3. A Comparison between a Promissory Note and a Bill of Exchange

As another major type of credit instruments, promissory notes are equally subject to the provisions of *Bills of Exchange Act* except for the following differences:

(1) Immediate Parties

There are only two immediate parties to a promissory note, namely the maker and the payee; whereas there are three basic parties to a bill of exchange, namely the drawer, the drawee and the payee. The maker of a note corresponds to the drawer and the drawee of a bill.

(2) Payment Undertaking

The maker of a note is the person who draws an instrument on himself. That means that the payment will be made by himself. So the maker of a note will make a promise to the payee that he will make payment at maturity, rather than an "order" to himself to make such a payment. The maker is primarily liable on a promissory note.

However, a bill of exchange is an order to pay. The order is given by the drawer to another person, the drawee. The drawer is primarily liable to a sight bill or a time bill before acceptance and the acceptor assumes the primary liability only after the bill is accepted by him.

(3) Acceptance Requirement

Acceptance is not applicable to a promissory note, neither is the presentment for acceptance nor the accepting for honor. For this reason, time note is seldom made after sight.

However, acceptance is generally required for a time bill.

(4) Protest

Protest is not applicable to a foreign note in the event of dishonor; whereas a dishonored foreign bill must be protested.

(5) The Issuer and the Payee

The maker and the payee can not be the same person for a note; whereas a bill of exchange allows the drawer and the payee to be the same person.

(6) Full Set

A promissory note is a solo note when issued; whereas a bill of exchange is usually in a duplicate set when issued. When one part of a bill is accepted or paid, the other part becomes void.

4. Major Forms of Promissory Notes

(1) Trader's Note

Trader's note is a promissory note whose maker is a firm or a trader. By issuing a trader's note, the firm can raise funds from the public. However, because of its low creditworthiness, trader's note is acceptable only when it is guaranteed by the firm's or trader's bank. For this reason, a trader's bill is generally replaced by a letter of guarantee.

(2) Banker's Note

The promissory note has found its wide application in banks. A banker's note made by a bank payable to a specified person can be deemed as cash. A sight banker's note payable to bearer is a "legal tender" which is part of the currency realm and an uncontrolled issue of banker's sight bearer order notes by commercial banks will certainly disturb a country's monetary system. Therefore, commercial banks can only issue notes payable to a specified person. Banker's sight bearer order notes are put under special statutory basis and can be issued by the central bank or the authorized banks only.

(3) International Money Order

International money order is usually denominated in US dollars with the maximum amount not exceeding USD2,500. It is issued by clearing banks in New York for the payee's convenience when he is travelling outside the U. S. It can also be used to settle payments in international trade when the amount is small. International money order is favorable to the maker because the clearing bank can take hold of the capital from the time of the purchase of the note by the payee to the time that the note is exchanged in for collection.

(4) Treasury Bill

It is also referred to the government bond with the maker to be the Ministry of Finance. In Britain, it is a short-dated government security. Treasury bills bear no formal interest, but are promises to pay in 91 days time. It is issued at a discount on their redemption price. The amount of purchase is to be calculated as follows:

The amount of purchase = net proceeds = principal − (principal × tenor × redemption rate/365 days

For example, suppose a GB treasury bill at GBP100,000 payable 91 days after date with the redemption rate at 7. 5%, the purchase amount would be:

$$\text{The purchase amount} = 100,000 - (100,000 \times 91 \times 7.5\%) / 365$$
$$= GBP98,130.14$$

(5) Traveler's Cheque

A traveler's cheque can be either considered as a promissory note or a cheque. It is a promissory note because it is drawn by the issuing bank upon itself payable to a traveler. However, a customer who wishes to obtain a traveler's cheque should first make payment equivalent to the face value to the issuer of the cheque. Then as a payee, the customer can cash the cheque or make use of the cheque to pay for the commodities he bought and services he enjoyed in a foreign country. To the customer, to purchase a traveler's cheque is similar to deposit money into the issuing bank while to cash it is like to withdraw the money from the issuing bank or his agents. So it can also be called a cheque. Similar to the international money order, the major advantages for the traveler's cheque are that it is easy to carry and safe to use because they are replaceable. It has gained a large popularity.

The denominations of a traveler's cheque can be \$10, \$20, \$50, \$100, \$500 and \$1000. To prevent fraud, the customer is required to sign his/her name on the cheque in the presence of the issuer or his selling agent at the time of purchase. The customer will also be required to countersign the cheque in the presence of the cashier at the time when the cheque is cashed or used to pay for the commodities he bought or the services he enjoyed. The amount he receives will be less than the face value because a small commission will be deducted which will be earned by the banks. An additional benefit to the issuing bank is that he can hold the capital from the time the cheque is purchased by the customer to the time the cheque is exchanged in by the cashier to claim compensation.

Section Two   Cheque

1. Definition

A cheque is defined as: "An unconditional order in writing addressed by the customer to a bank signed by that customer authorizing the bank to pay on demand a sum certain in money to or to the order of a specified person or bearer. " In simple words, a cheque can also be defined as a bill of exchange drawn on a banker on demand. For example:

Cheque for USD3,000	Shanghai, May 20, 200X

Pay to the order of John Smith the sum of US dollars three thousand only.

To: Bank of China
    Shanghai, China

William Smith
Signature

Usually, cheques will be pre-printed by the banker for its customers. Blank cheque books will be held by the customer who will fill in (draw) a cheque when needed and deliver it to the payee. Pre-printed blank cheque will be shown as follows:

It is worth remembering that the drawer of a cheque should first obtain/open an account with a banker. To "draw" actually means writing out a cheque for a certain amount of money in the account with the banker. Hence, the drawer can draw a cheque on a banker. There are three immediate parties to cheque:

(1) The Drawer

The drawer is the person who writes the cheque. He should first be the banker's customer in the sense that he maintains an account with the banker. Secondly, when he draws a cheque, it is his responsibility to make sure that there is enough balance in his account to cover the cheque amount. Otherwise, the cheque will be bounced.

(2) The Drawee

The drawee is the banker on whom the cheque is drawn and to whom the order to pay is given. He is the banker with which the drawer maintains an account.

(3) The Payee

The payee is the person to whom a cheque is expressed to be payable.

2. Essentials to a Cheque

(1) The Word "Cheque"

The word "cheque" should be clearly indicated in order to distinguish it from other types of instruments like the bills of exchange and the promissory notes.

(2) Unconditional

Payment can not be made on certain conditions to be met by the payee.

(3) Writing

It must be in writing.

(4) Signed

A cheque must be signed by the drawer, from whose account the money is paid out.

3. Clearing Cheques

The payee should deposit the cheque into his bank before he can obtaining payments expressed in the cheque. When a payee deposits a cheque into his bank and asks the latter to obtain funds for him, the process is refrred to as cheque clearing. Normally, two banks will be involved in the clearing process with one bank acting as the collecting bank and the other as the paying bank. The payee's bank may or may not be the drawee bank. In the case that the payee's bank happens to be the drawee bank, this bank should also play two roles, one as the collecting bank and the other as the paying bank. Therefore, the clearing system identifies two roles to be played by the banks, one is the role of the collecting bank and the other is the role of paying bank.

(1) The Collecting Bank

The collecting bank is the payee's bank. When a customer (the payee) deposits a cheque drawn on another bank into his bank, he is asking his bank to obtain payment on his behalf.

There are three major functions for the collecting bank. First, the bank is to receive a cheque and to scrutinize the cheque carefully to ensure it is a complete and valid instrument. Second, the bank is to collect the money from the bank on which the cheque is drawn. Third, the bank must ensure that the amount is paid to the payee or the amount has been credited to the account for which it is intended.

(2) The Paying Bank

The paying bank is the drawee's bank. The paying bank is to debit the cheque amount from his customer's (the drawer's) account when the cheque is passed in to him through the clearing system and to transfer the amount to the collecting bank. Before an account is debited, it is the paying bank's responsibility to ensure that the cheque is correctly completed and it is not overdue, i. e. six months from the date of issue. When the payment is made, the cheque is said to be cleared.

However, when both the drawer and the payee maintain their accounts with a common bank, this bank can assume the role of the collecting bank as well as that of the paying bank.

4. Classification of a Cheque

According to different criteria, cheques can be classified into the following types:

(1) According to Order

(A) Demonstrative order.

When a cheque is payable to a named person or his order, it is a demonstrative order cheque and can be transferred by endorsement and delivery.

(B) Restrictive order.

A restrictive order cheque is one that is payable to a named person only. It is non-negotiable.

(C) Bearer order.

A bearer order cheque is one that is payable to the bearer. It is transferable by mere delivery.

However, it should be noted that cheques are not designed to be negotiated, the rules on negotiation have little significance on cheques.

(2) According to the Drawer

(A) Banker's cheque.

A banker's cheque means that the drawer is a bank. It is a cheque drawn by one bank on another bank. And the drawer banker becomes the customer of the drawee banker.

(B) Personal cheque / Trader's cheque.

When the drawer is an individual or a company, it is a personal cheque / trader's cheque.

（3）According to Whether or not the Cheque is Crossed

This is the most important classification of cheque, which demands our full attention.

（A）Uncrossed cheque/Open cheque.

An uncrossed or open cheque refers to the one which is written on "plain" bank form, implying that the cheque can be exchanged for cash over the counter when the payee/holder presents the cheque for payment to the drawee bank.

（B）Crossed cheque.

A crossed cheque refers to two parallel lines drawn on the face of the cheque, and usually this is done on the top left corner of the cheque. It implies that the cheque amount should be paid into a bank account of the payee and can not be exchanged for cash over the counter. The purpose of crossing a cheque is to ensure the right holder to obtain the payment.

The procedure to clear a crossed cheque is shown as follows:

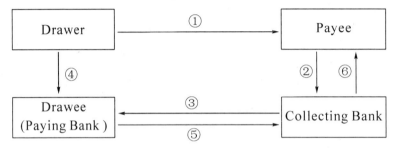

① The drawer draws a cheque and delivers it to the payee.

② The payee deposits the cheque to the collecting bank and asks the latter to collect payments for him.

③ After scrutiny, the collecting bank forwards the cheque to the drawee bank on behalf of the payee.

④ After scrutiny, the drawee debits the amount from the drawer's account with him.

⑤ The paying bank transfers the funds to the collecting bank.

⑥ The collecting bank credits the amount to the payee's account.

Crossed cheque can be further divided into two types:

（1）General Crossing

A cheque is generally crossed when the cheque bears two parallel lines across its face, either with or without the words "and company", "& Co.", "not negotiable", "A/C payee" between the lines. For example:

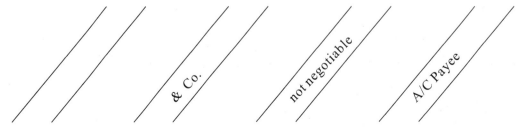

The effect of a general crossing is to make the cheque payable through a bank only and not to make cash payment over the counter. In this case, no bank is specified as the collecting bank. That is to say, the paying bank should honor the cheque presented by any bank provided it is a correctly complete valid cheque.

(2) Special Crossing

When a cheque bears across its face an addition of the name of a banker, either with or without the words "and company", "& Co. ", "not negotiable", "A/C payee" and the two parallel lines, that addition constitutes a special crossing. For example:

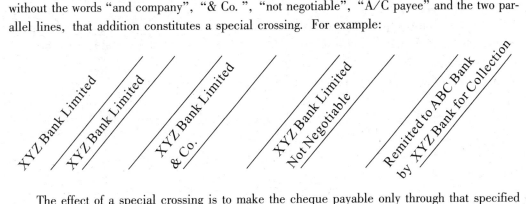

The effect of a special crossing is to make the cheque payable only through that specified bank (XYZ Bank) which is to act as a collecting bank. Only this bank(XYZ Bank) can present the cheque to the paying bank (ABC Bank) for payment. In other words, the paying bank will honor the cheque presented only by the specified collecting bank.

It should be noted that both the drawer and the payee can do the following:

(A) Cross an uncrossed cheque.

(B) Change a general crossing to a special one.

(C) Add the words "not negotiable" to the cheque.

5. Countermand of a Cheque

It is commonly known as "stop payment". It is an order of payment cancellation in writing given by the banker's customer (the drawer) to his banker (the drawee) to stop payment to a particular payee. The drawer is the only party who can instruct the bank to do so. In the event that the holder has the cheque stolen or lost, he can only inform the bank of the condition and seek instructions of the drawer. When the drawee receives such an order from the drawer, he must obey and stop payment.

On the other hand, the banker is obliged to honor a customer's cheque up to the amount of his credit balance or agreed overdraft. In this case, the banker can neither pay a "stopped" cheque nor wrongly dishonor a customer's cheque. For both cases, the banker is to bear the full responsibility and will make the necessary compensation.

6. Differences between a Cheque and a Bill of Exchange

As another major type of credit instruments, cheques are equally subject to the provisions of *Bills of Exchange Act* except the following differences:

(A) A bill of exchange may be drawn by any person upon another, whereas a cheque can only be drawn by a customer on his banker where he maintains an account with sufficient credit balance in it.

(B) The tenor of a bill may be either sight or time whereas a cheque can only be made payable on demand.

(C) After a bill is accepted, the acceptor is primarily liable for payment. Acceptance is not applicable to a cheque and the drawer should always hold primary liability to a cheque.

(D) Acceptance made by the acceptor of a bill is irrevocable. Whereas the duty and authority of the drawee bank to pay a cheque may be terminated by the countermand of payment by the drawer.

(E) A bill must be presented to payment upon due, or else the drawer will be discharged. Whereas delay in presentment of a cheque does not discharge the drawer unless he suffers an actual loss from the delay.

(F) The rules concerning crossing are applicable to cheques only.

Section Three　Functions of Credit Instruments

The major functions of credit instruments are that they can be used as means of negotiation, means of payment and means of credit.

1. Means of Negotiation

(A) A Credit instrument is negotiable, it can be transferred to another person by mere delivery if it is a bearer order or by endorsement and delivery if it is a demonstrative order instrument. Similar to money, an instrument can be negotiated without informing the drawer or the drawee. That is to say, no notice of transfer needs to be given to the person liable on the instrument.

(B) Perfect title of the holder in due course is protected under the *Bills of Exchange Act*. The title to the instrument passes fully and legally from the transferor to the transferee provided that the latter obtains the instrument for value and in good faith. This transferee is called the holder in due course whose title to the instrument will not be affected by the defects of his prior parties. Thus, the negotiability of the instrument is greatly enhanced.

2. Means of Payment

(A) As a medium of exchange, credit instruments take the place of money to settle debts and accounts. That is to say, payment order is made in the form of instruments rather than money in the era of non-cash settlements.

(B) As a medium of exchange, credit instruments have some advantages over money in international settlement. They are more safe and convenient when the amount is large and when the payment is to be transferred across national borders.

(C) As a negotiable instrument, the debtor can transfer the instrument to his debtor to clear his debt if the former obtains consent from the latter.

3. Means of Credit

(A) Time instruments to defer payment.

International trade is seldom carried out on cash-on-delivery basis. Rather, payment will be made either before or after the delivery of goods or the provision of services for a particular transaction. Thus, the party who fulfils his obligations first would be the creditor and the other party becomes the debtor. For example, when payment is deferred, it is the party who delivers the goods who extends credit to his trader partner, and the credit is extended by making use of time instruments.

(B) Finance through bills of exchange.

If the holder of an accepted time bill finds himself in short of funds, he may discount the bill to obtain the payment in advance. The credit standing of both the acceptor and the trader is taken into consideration in the discounting business. Another alternative to get financed through a bill of exchange is through an accommodating bill where a trader draws a time bill on a financial institution upon the latter's consent. The trader then discounts the accepted accommodating bill in the discount market to raise funds and get financed.

From the above discussion, we may see clearly the advantages of financial instruments over cash and we may also understand why financial instruments have found much wider application in modern international settlement.

Chapter Five   Correspondent Banking Relationship

Section One   Introduction

1. The Importance of Correspondent Relationship

In order to be an "intermediary" of its international customers/traders and to "smooth-out" the funds transfer for them, bank should go internationally either through establishing its own foreign presence or through cooperating with other foreign banks. The result is a worldwide banking network which has undoubtedly facilitated international banking operations.

A bank can expand its business abroad in various ways. The first method is to achieve its own foreign presence by setting up its own representative offices, agencies, subsidiaries or branches in foreign countries, and the second alternative is to establish a correspondent banking relationship with a foreign local bank. The major difference between these two methods is that in the first method, the home bank maintains ownership over its foreign offices, subsidiaries or branches while in the second method, the correspondent bank is a separate local bank, independent from the home bank.

(1) The First Method – to create a bank's own foreign presence

(A) Representative office.

A representative office is established in the host country to do business on behalf of the home bank. However, the office can not conduct normal banking operations such as accepting deposits, issuing loans, dealing with drafts and letters of credit. The basic function of a representative office is to collect and provide information for the home bank. It is the lowest form of a presence in a foreign country.

(B) Subsidiary and affiliate.

A subsidiary is a separately incorporated bank, owned entirely or in large by a parent home bank. It is controlled by the parent bank though part of the equity may belong to local banks or other foreign banks. Affiliate is also a locally incorporated bank which is partly owned by but not necessarily controlled by the parent bank. Similar to a branch, both the subsidiary and the affiliate can perform normal banking business.

(C) Branch.

A foreign branch is a legal and operational part as well as a subordinate institution of its parent bank, conducting banking business in the host country, with its full resources, including both the capital and staff provided by the head office at home. The loss and profits of a branch will also be reflected in the balance sheet of its head office. It is an expensive form of foreign presence. But it remains an important form when a bank wants to be competitive in international banking business.

(D) Agency.

An agency resembles a branch except that it is not allowed to accept deposit from the local public. It is to perform a number of non-depositary banking services related to international trade.

(2) The Second Method — to find a correspondent bank

A correspondent banking relationship is established between two independent banks, one being the bank at home and the other being the local bank in the host country. When two such banks exchange their control documents, sign a cooperate agreement and open accounts with each other, they will become correspondent banks. For example, if Bank of China and United Overseas Bank, Singapore have established correspondent banking relationship, then Bank of China is the correspondent bank of United Overseas Bank, Singapore and the latter will also be called the correspondent bank of the former. A detailed information concerning the steps to establish a correspondent banking relationship will be provided in the next section.

2. A Comparison of the Two Different Methods will Highlight the Importance of Establishing a Correspondent Banking Relationship in a Foreign Country

(A) The representative office, agency, subsidiary or branch will be treated by the host country as a foreign entity. Therefore, not all banking businesses in the host country are allowed to be performed by it. A foreign correspondent bank is a local bank, and it will not be subject to this restriction.

(B) It would be very difficult to do business in a foreign country without the cooperation of a local bank. In this sense, a foreign correspondent bank can better help the home bank to explore the market in the host country.

(C) Setting its own entities abroad requires substantial amount of capital to be invested in and a number of home staff to be sent to the host country. Not every bank can afford such an investment.

(D) The foreign correspondent bank can do well the international business entrusted with in the same way as the home bank's own branches or subsidiaries.

(E) Correspondent relationship enables one bank to utilize the staff, services, management skill and customer resources of another bank so that its international banking business can be smoothly conducted in the host country.

(F) The home bank can learn valuable experiences from the cooperation with its foreign correspondent bank.

For these reasons, a bank, no matter how large it is and no matter how many subsidiaries and branches it has been established abroad, still lays great emphasis on the establishment of correspondent banking relationships with foreign local banks. For example, large international banks such as Lloyds Bank International Limited and Barclays Bank International Limited have made great efforts to establish correspondent relationships despite the fact that they have already had thousands of branches and subsidiaries worldwide. In China, the four major commercial banks have already set up extensive correspondent relationships with a great number of foreign banks all over the world. Bank of China has had over 5,000 correspondent banks up to 1992 and the Chinese Agricultural Bank has had over 400 correspondent banks worldwide.

Section Two　Establishment of Correspondent Banking Relationship

The establishment of correspondent banking relationship will undergo three stages: exchange the control documents; sign a cooperate agreement or an agency agreement and open accounts with each other.

1. Exchange the Control Documents

Booklet of authorized signatures, test key and schedule of terms and conditions constitute the control documents. When establishing a correspondent relationship, the two banks concerned will first exchange their control documents. This becomes the first step because once correspondent relationship is established, the correspondent banks will provide services to each other. Such services will include remittance, collection and letter of credit, etc., which will be dealt with through mail or telegraphic messages. These messages should be authenticated before they are sent out and followed up. A mail message needs to be authenticated by an authorized signature and a telegraphic one needs to be authenticated by a test key. And the service fees provided by the correspondent bank will be charged according to the schedule of terms and conditions.

(1) Booklet of Authorized Signatures

The authorized signatures are used for the authentication of the mail message addressed by one bank to its correspondent bank. The booklet contains the specimen of signatures of the authorized officers with their corresponding authorities. The mail messages, certificates and instruments issued by one bank will be valid with an authorized signature and the correspondent bank should check the signatures on the documents against the specimen before the mail instructions are carried out. For example, a banker's demand draft will not be paid if it bears no authorized signature. If a bank does not send the specimen signatures to the advising bank abroad, its issuance of credit by airmail could not be advised by the advising bank to the beneficiary.

(2) Test Key

The test key is code arrangements agreed upon by the two correspondent banks in advance in order to authenticate telegraphic messages. The test key will be sent together with the cable, telex or SWIFT message so that the bank receiving the message can verify whether the message is the right one from the right bank. For example, if a bank does not send the test key arrangements to the advising bank abroad, its issuance of credit by cable could not be advised by the advising bank to the beneficiary.

The code of the test key consists of a series of tabulated numbers, each representing a particular month, date, amount, currency and other related items. The indicated numbers are totaled and make the test key. In the case that both the correspondent banks are members of SWIFT, a SAK (SWIFT authentic key) will be used. These codes are strict confidential and the arrangement will be renewed every few years.

(3) Schedule of Terms and Conditions

It is a list of service fees which a bank will charge its foreign correspondent bank. It should be made clear to its counterpart before the services are provided. The actual rate set for a particular service will also take into consideration of their relationship.

2. **Sign a Cooperate Agreement or an Agency Agreement**

The second step to establish a correspondent banking relationship is to sign a cooperative or an agency agreement. The agreement will provide a guideline by which international banking business will be carried out.

Major items in the cooperative or agency agreement should include the following:

(1) Office Concerned

The cooperate agreement should be established between the head offices of the two banks. It should state clearly whether the agreement is applicable to branches (if any) and the names of the branches should also be indicated.

(2) Control Documents

Booklets of authorized signature: The exchanging of the booklets should be stated in the agreement.

Test key: The agreement should specify whether the test key of one bank is for mutual use or each bank uses its own test key.

Schedule of terms and conditions: The agreement should specify whether the fee is charged according to the schedule or charged at a favorable rate.

(3) Currency for Transactions

The agreement should specify the convertible currency to be used, be it US dollars, Japanese Yen or Swiss Franc, etc.

(4) The Methods to Remit Covers and Claim Reimbursement

The agreement should specify how to remit covers under remittance and collection and how to claim reimbursement under letter of credit.

(5) Other Items

Other items such as credit facilities should also be specified.

The sample agency agreement and cooperate agreement will be shown as follows:

Agency Agreement

Bank A and Bank B through friendly negotiation and on the basis of equality and mutual benefits agree to establish correspondent relationship for the cooperation of banking business as follows:

(A) office Concerned:

1. Bank A including its xx branches.

2. Bank B including its xx branches.

Additional branches will be included through negotiation whenever business requires.

(B) Control Documents:

1. Each party will send its Booklet of Authorized Signatures and Schedule of Terms and Conditions to the other party.

2. Bank A's telegraphic test key is supplied to Bank B's office for mutual use.

(C) Currency for Transactions:

US dollars, Hongkong dollars, Pound sterling.

Other currencies will be included through negotiation whenever it is necessary.

(D) Business Transactions:

1. Remittance

Each party mentioned in (A) may directly draw on the other party mentioned in (A) by drafts, mail transfer or telegraphic transfer. At the time of drawing, covers is to be remitted as follows:

For Party A:

For US dollars: .... The Chase Manhattan Bank, New York, A/C No. 123

For Hongkong dollars: ...... The Standard Chartered Bank, Hong Kong A/C No. 456

For Party B:

For US dollars: .... The Chase Manhattan Bank, New York, A/C No. 678

For Hongkong dollars: ...... The Standard Chartered Bank, Hong Kong A/C No. 910

2. Collections

Each party may send collections directly to the other party with specific instruction in each individual case regarding disposal of proceeds.

3. Letter of Credit

Each party may issue by mail or by cable the letter of credit to the other party nominated as advising bank. Appropriate instructions are to be embodied in each credit advice with regard to reimbursement.

4. Each party may request the other party to provide the credit standing of their clients.

5. Credit facilities

Credit facilities of both party shall be subject to separate arrangement.

This arrangement becomes effective immediately on the date of signing of both parties and will terminate after receipt of either party's advice three months prior to the date of termination.

Signed on _____ Signed on _____
Bank A   Bank B
Senior Managing Director   Senior Managing Director
Signature   Signature

Cooperation Agreement

This agreement is concluded on to strengthen the cooperation of banking business and promote the development of business transactions between Bank A and Bank B, both parties agree on the basis of equality and mutual benefits as follows:

1. Both parties will establish correspondent banking relationship in 200X.
2. Bank A and Bank B will exchange information on the situation of laws, regulations, policies and provide banking and financial advisory services to each other.
3. Bank A will provide Bank B with loans and / or credit facilities at favorable condition and provide its know-how in this field.
4. Bank A undertakes to prepare and carry out, at its own expense, trainee programs for senior officers from Bank B.

This agreement shall take effect on the day of signing.

Signed on _____   Signed on _____

Bank A	Bank B
Chairman and President	General Manager
Signed	Signed

After the signing of the cooperate or agency agreement, the control documents should be sent to the correspondent banks. The head offices shall be responsible for the posting and they may be required to send the documents directly to the relevant branches, if any.

3. Maintain Current Accounts with Each Other

Current accounts should be maintained with each other so that the international funds transfer can be achieved and the purpose of establishing correspondent banking relationship will be realized. This current or deposit accounts can be called your account (vostro account) or our account (nostro account) depending on the standpoint of the correspondent banks. Before opening a current account in its correspondent bank, the bank must be aware of such detail conditions as the amount of initial deposit, minimum credit balance, interest rate of the account, and how often the statement of balance will be sent, monthly or weekly.

(1) Your Account (Vostro Account)

From the point of a domestic bank, a current account opened by a foreign bank with this domestic bank is referred to as your account (vostro account). For example, when a US bank opens an account with a Chinese bank, then the latter (the Chinese bank) will call this vostro account, meaning your account. Usually, the vostro account may be opened in local currency (RMB), or in the currency of the foreign country (US dollars), or even in another convertible currency, such as the Pound sterling. Having opened a vostro account, the foreign bank can directly receive payment from and make payment to the local customers in the local currency through that account.

(2) Our Account (Nostro Account)

From the point of view of a domestic bank, a current account opened by a domestic bank with a foreign bank abroad is called our account (nostro account). For example, When a Chinese bank opens an account with a US bank, then the former (the Chinese bank) will call this nostro account, meaning our account. Usually, nostro account may be opened in foreign currency (US dollars), or in the currency of the domestic country (RMB), or even in the currency of another convertible currency. Having opened a nostro account, the domestic bank can directly receive payment from and make payment to its foreign customers in the currency of that account.

In fact, an our account (nostro account) from the viewpoint of a domestic bank is a your account (vostro account) from the viewpoint of a foreign bank and vice versa.

Section Three　International Funds Transfer

As we already know, international funds transfer is carried out via banks among different countries and is greatly facilitated by the establishment of the correspondent banking relationship and the worldwide banking network. Banks involved will perform at least two roles in the process. One role is that of a remitting bank and the other is that of a paying/receiving bank. When funds are transferred from the former to the latter, international funds transfer is realized.

The remitting bank is the one which transfers the funds to a bank located in a foreign country. The paying/receiving bank is the one which receives funds from the remitting bank located in a foreign country. Instructions to transfer funds are always given by the remitting bank to the paying bank. These instructions can also be called reimbursement clauses because it is possible that the paying bank will make the payment to the customers before it receives funds from the remitting bank. Or, the payment made to the paying bank is to cover the payment he has made or he is about to make to the customer. In practice, the phrase "in cover" is used to indicate that the payment to the paying bank is made for reimbursement.

However, not all banks are correspondent banks or head/branch offices with each other. So, according to whether or not a direct current account is maintained with the remitting bank and the paying bank, funds transfer will undergo three different routes.

1. Direct Accounts are Available

When direct accounts are available with the remitting bank and the paying bank, then these two banks will be correspondent banks. or head/branch offices

(A) If the remitting bank maintains a current account with the paying bank, the current account will be referred to as a nostro account (our account) by the remitting bank. The remitting bank will give instructions to the paying bank as follows to transfer the funds to him:

"Please debit the sum to our account with you. "

"You are authorized to debit the sum to our account with you. "

The process can be illustrated as follows:

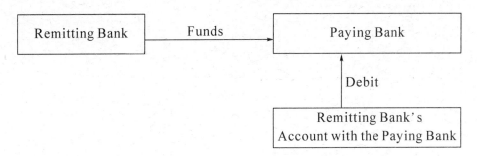

After the paying bank debits the sum to the nostro account of the remitting bank, the funds are transferred from the remitting bank to the paying bank.

(B) If the paying bank maintains a current account with the remitting bank, this account will be called vostro account (your account) from the viewpoint of the remitting bank. And the instructions to transfer funds will be as follows:

"(In cover), we have credited the sum to your account with us".

The process can be illustrated as follows:

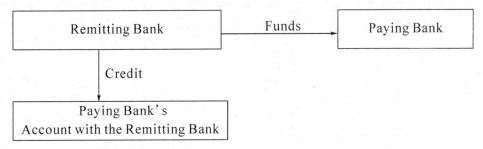

After the remitting bank credits the sum to the vostro account of the paying bank, the funds are transferred from the remitting bank to the paying bank.

2. Accounts are Maintained with a Third Mutual Correspondent Bank

When the remitting bank and the paying bank are not directly related, a third bank will be involved in the process of funds transfer. And this third bank is usually the mutual bank of the remitting bank and the paying bank and it is most likely to be a clearing bank in the clearing centers like London and New York. This is made possible because banks, if they want to engage in international banking business, will normally open accounts with clearing banks. For example, they will open a US dollar account with a bank in New York or a sterling account with a bank in London or a Japanese yen account with a bank in Tokyo. As a result, chances are that both the remitting bank and the paying bank will maintain their accounts with the same clearing bank. This clearing bank becomes the third mutual bank and through which funds are transferred from the remitting bank to the paying bank. The instruction to transfer the funds will read as follows:

"(In cover), we have authorized the xx bank to debit our account and credit your account with them. "

Please note that "we" here refers to the remitting bank. "xx bank" is the mutual third bank with which the remitting bank maintains "our account" and the paying bank maintains "your account". The process can also be illustrated as follows:

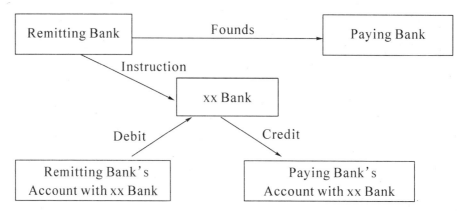

After xx bank debits the sum to the account of the remitting bank and credits the account of the paying bank, funds have been transferred from the remitting bank to the paying bank.

3. No Mutual Bank is Available

Although banks doing international banking business will normally maintain accounts with clearing banks, chances are that the remitting bank and the paying bank may open accounts with different clearing banks, though in the same clearing center. As a result, no mutual bank is available.

(A) When the clearing banks are correspondent banks.

When the clearing banks maintain correspondent relationship with each other, funds will be transferred from the remitting bank to the paying bank through the accounts of the clearing banks. For example, if the remitting bank maintains accounts with Bank A and the paying bank maintains account with Bank B, the instruction to transfer funds will read:

"(In cover), we have authorized Bank A to pay the proceeds to your account with Bank B. "

"(In cover), please reimburse yourselves to the debiting of our account with Bank A. "

Because Bank A and Bank B are correspondent banks, the funds transfer from the former to the latter please refer to item 1 of this section.

The process will be illustrated as follows:

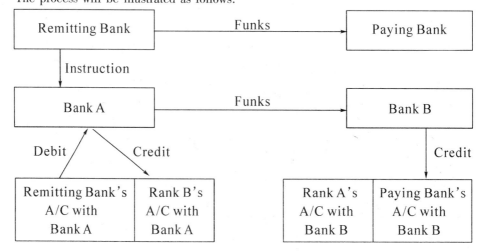

(B) When the clearing banks are not correspondent banks.

If there is no correspondent banking relationship between the clearing banks, then it is necessary to look for still another bank which is the mutual bank of the clearing banks. The process will be more complicated since it is the combination of all the above mentioned ones. It will be observed that enlarged worldwide banking network will get more and more banks to be connected more and more directly with each other and international settlement will be made easier, more convenient and more effective.

Chapter Six　Payment Methods（Ⅰ）
－ Remittance

Section One　General Introduction to Payment Methods

1. Introduction to Payment Methods

In the last chapter, we have discussed how funds are transferred via banks from one country to another. But what are the reasons for the funds transfer? Funds transfer is mainly for the purpose of:

* Settlement of debts as a result of international trade;
* Personal remittance from friends to relatives or friends abroad;
* Government aids to foreign countries.

Traditionally, the largest funds transfer is the settlement of debts resulting from international trade, which is generally known as commercial settlement. As payments can not be directly settled by the traders, to a great extent, banks transfer funds across national borders at the request of their customers (traders) , or, that the traders will require the banks to transfer funds for them to their foreign counterparts to whom the payments are due. We usually say that customers (traders) are "principals" who give instructions to banks to transfer money to their foreign counterparts, known as the "beneficiary". Banks become the "intermediaries" or the "agents" of their customers ("principals"). The "principal"-"agent" relationship is significant in international settlement. The instructions from the "principal" to the "agent" to make/collect payments are reflected in the payment methods and they are varied to serve different purposes of the principals.

Before we move to payment methods, two points need to be clarified. Firstly, it is important to distinguish payment methods from payment tools. Payment tools can be either cash or credit instruments. Although credit instruments are more popular in the non-cash settlement era, cash is needed to calculate the amount of payments. Payment methods will combine payment tools (cash and credit instruments) with various trade terms (incoterms) and/or different commercial documents. Major payment methods are remittance, collection, letter of credit, factoring and letter of guarantee. Different payment methods represent different risks and/or credit to the traders because they can make the time of payment either before, after or at the same time as the time of delivery. Secondly, it should also be noted the distinction between payment methods and reimbursement clauses. The former reflects the customer-bank relationship while the latter refers to the clearing methods among banks after they have transferred funds for their customers.

2. Classification of Payment Methods

Payment methods are various and they can be classified according to the following criteria:

(A) According to payment tools.

(a) Cash settlement.

Cash is used as the medium of exchange when international settlement has not been fully developed.

(b) Non-cash settlement.

Credit instruments such as bills of exchange, promissory notes and cheques are used as mediums of exchange. Non-cash settlement is an indicator that international settlement has moved into its modern era.

(B) According to the credit standing.

(a) Trader's credit.

In trader's credit, the payment undertaking is given by a trader. Remittance and collection are payment methods based on trader's credit.

(b) Banker's credit.

In banker's credit, the payment undertaking is given by a bank instead of a trader. Letter of credit, factoring and letter of guarantee are payment methods based on banker's credit.

(C) According to the direction of the movement of the instruments in relation to that of the funds flow.

(a) Remittance.

In remittance, the debtor gives proceeds (payments) to the bank and asks the bank to transfer the funds via certain credit instrument or certain payment iustruction to the creditor. In international trade, the creditor is the exporter while the debtor is the importer. Remittance indicates that the funds flow in the same direction as the credit instrument or certain payment instruction transmitted therefrom. The movements of both the funds and instrument will be shown as follows:

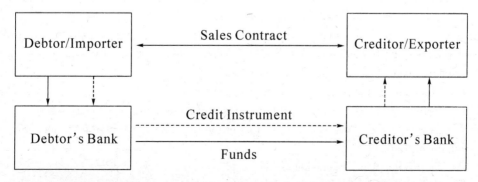

Notes: The straight lines represent the movement of the funds and the dotted lines represent the directions of the instruments.

(b) Reverse remittance.

In reverse remittance, the creditor (exporter) draws an instrument on the debtor (the importer) or his banker requiring the bank to collect payment for him based on the instrument. Reverse remittance indicates that the funds flow in an opposite direction of the credit instrument transmitted therefrom. Collection, letter of credit and factoring fall into this category. The movements of both the funds flown and the instrument will be shown as follows:

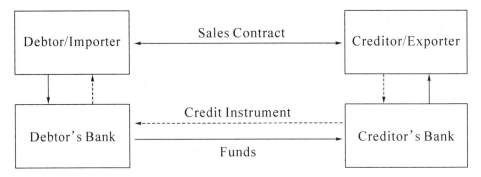

Notes: The straight lines represent the movement of the funds and the dotted lines represented the direction of the instruments.

Section Two　Remittance

1. Definition and Parties

Remittance refers to a bank (the remitting bank), at the request of its customer (the remitter), transfers a certain sum of money to its overseas branch or correspondent bank (the paying bank) instructing it to pay to a named person (the payee/beneficiary) domiciled in that country. Remittance is used for the settlement of both commercial and non-commercial settlements. Therefore, it is an important payment method in international banking business.

There are four immediate parties in remittance:

(1) Remitter

A remitter is the party who will make the payment. He is the person who requires his bank to remit funds to the beneficiary in a foreign country. In international trade, he is often the buyer and the importer.

(2) The Remitting Bank

We have talked about the remitting bank in reimbursement methods where the focus is on how banks transfer funds and make reimbursement among themselves. In this part, we will talk about the remitting bank in connection with payment methods where the focus is on the customer-bank relationship. A different point of view is adopted here and the distinction between the reimbursement methods and payment methods should always be kept clear in mind.

Remitting bank is the bank who remits the funds at the request of a remitter to the paying bank and instructs the latter to pay a certain amount of money to a beneficiary. The remitting bank will usually locate in the same city as that of the remitter and is often the importer's bank in international trade.

(3) The Paying Bank/Receiving Bank

A paying bank is the bank entrusted to by the remitting bank to pay a certain sum of money to a beneficiary. From the point of view of payment methods, it is called the paying bank because it is the bank to make payment to his customer. From the angle of reimbursement methods, it can also be called the receiving bank because this bank will receive proceeds from the remitting bank. The paying bank usually locates in the same city as that of the exporter and is often the exporter's bank in international trade.

(4) Beneficiary or Payee

The beneficiary or payee is the person who is addressed to receive the funds by remittance. He is the exporter in international trade.

2. Outward and Inward Remittance

An outward remittance or an inward remittance is the description of a given remittance from the point of view of the handling bank.

(1) Outward Remittance

When the home bank is acting as the remitting bank, the remittance handled by him is called an outward remittance.

(2) Inward Remittance

When the home bank is acting as the paying bank, the remittance handled by him is called an inward remittance.

3. Types of Remittance and the Procedure

According to different ways to give payment instruction, remittance can be classified as remittance by airmail (M/T), remittance by telegraphic transfer (T/T) and remittance by banker's demand draft (D/D).

(1) Remittance by Airmail (M/T)

The remitting bank, at the request of the remitter, transfers the funds by means of sending/posting a payment instruction to the paying bank, asking the latter to pay a certain sum of money to the payee. M/T makes use of post service to transfer the payment instructions. A payment instruction is an authenticated order in writing addressed by the remitting bank to the paying bank. In M/T, the payment instruction can take the form of Mail Transfer Advice or Mail Transfer Payment Order or Debit Advice.

M/T payment order is made based on the M/T application form. An application form is pre-printed by the Remitting Bank and should be filled in by the remitter before he requires his banker to transfer the proceeds for him. When filled in and signed by the customer and stamped by the banker, M/T application becomes a contract between the banker and the customer (the remitter). The bank will transfer the funds accordingly. Both the remitter and the beneficiary's full names and addresses will be clearly indicated in the application form. The form will be made in sets with the first part being the banker's copy, the second being the Mail Transfer Payment Order and the third being the customer's copy. Thus such items as the beneficiary's name, address and the name of the remitter will be exactly the same in these three parts except that the Mail Transfer Payment Order must contain reimbursement instructions and be authenticated by the authorized signature of the remitting bank. Remitter may choose the collecting bank or he may leave it to be decided by the remitting bank.

A sample M/T application form is shown below:

中国银行 新加坡分行
BANK OF CHINA SINGAPORE BRANCH

信汇申请书 APPLICATION FOR
MAIL TRANSFER

请以正楷书写
PLEASE COMPLETE IN BLOCK LETTERS

金额 AMOUNT

收款人姓名 PAYEE	申请人 REMITTER
住址 ADDRESS	住址与电话 ADDRESS & TEL
附言 MESSAGE	

上列申请，如遇邮误，申请人自负责任。
Remitter shall bear all consequences resulting from any postal discrepancy.

所需费用，请
In reimbursement please

☐ 收入现金 receive cash
☐ 付我帐，帐号 debit my/our A/C No. _____ with you
☐ 收入支票号码 receive Cheque No. _____ 付款银行 on _____
　　(收妥作实 Subject to final payment)

银行专用 FOR BANK USE ONLY
汇率　RATE
新币　SGD
手续费 COMM
邮费　POSTAGE
合计　TOTAL

REM 32

申请人签章 Signature of Applicant
Signature Verified

Notes: The Remittance Application Form (1st part − Banker's copy).

中国银行 新加坡分行
BANK OF CHINA SINGAPORE BRANCH

信汇委托书
MAIL TRANSFER PAYMENT ORDER

请解付下列汇款，如有费用，由收款人支付
Please effect the following payment, charges if any to be borne by beneficiary.

金额 AMOUNT

收款人姓名 PAYEE	申请人 REMITTER
住址 ADDRESS	住址与电话 ADDRESS & TEL
附言 MESSAGE	

For **BANK OF CHINA**
· SINGAPORE

AUTHORIZED SIGNATURES

Notes: The Remittance Application Form (2nd part – M/T Payment Order).

BANK OF CHINA   SINGAPORE BRANCH

客户存根 CUSTOMER'S COPY		金额 AMOUNT
收款人姓名 PAYEE		申请人 REMITTER
住址 ADDRESS		住址与电话 ADDRESS & TEL
附言 MESSAGE		

我行已于今日办理你的申请，如遇邮误、责任由你/你司自负
We confirm that the above transfer has been effected today at your own risk should there be any postal discrepancy.

所需费用，我行已
In reimbursement we have

收入现金
☐ received your cash
付我账，账号
☐ debited your A/C No. _____ with us
收入支票号码   付款银行
☐ received your Cheque No. _____ on _____
（ 收妥作实 Subject to final payment）

中国银行新加坡分行
BANK OF CHINA, SINGAPORE

银行专用 FOR BANK USE ONLY	
汇率 RATE	
新币 SGD	
手续费 COMM	
邮费 POSTAGE	
合计 TOTAL	

_____
申请人签章 Signature of Applicant

Notes: The Remittance Application Form (3rd part – Customer copy).

As for T/T or D/D application form, readers may turn to the next page for reference. Although the lay out may appear to be different, the remitting bank generally follow the same principle to devise the form.

M/T procedure is shown as follows:

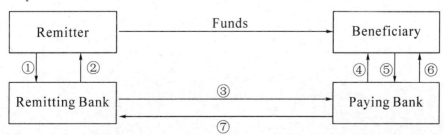

① The remitter gives his signed written application to his bank, instructing it to transfer the funds through M/T.

② The remitting bank will check the remitter's account. If it is positive, the remitting bank will stamp on the application form and return the customer's copy to the remitter for record

(In the case of a personal remittance, the customer will give proceeds to the remitting bank together with the application form).

③ The remitting bank will debit the remitter's a/c with the amount to be remitted together with its commission and airmail expenses (if any) and then issue and post a Mail Transfer Payment Order to the paying bank.

④Upon receipt the Mail Transfer Payment Order, the paying bank verifies the authorized signature before it notifies the beneficiary with a copy of the payment order.

⑤The beneficiary presents the copy of the payment order to the paying bank for payment.

⑥The paying bank checks the identity of the beneficiary before releasing the funds to him.

⑦The paying bank will claim reimbursement according to the reimbursement clause stated in the Mail Transfer Payment Order.

(2) Telegraphic Transfer (T/T)

Remittance by cable/telex/SWIFT is called telegraphic transfer (T/T). That is, the remitting bank, at the request of the remitter, transfers funds by means of cable/telex/SWIFT message to the paying bank, asking the latter to pay a certain sum of money to the beneficiary.

T/T shares many similarities with M/T in both the application form and procedures, the fundamental difference lies in the way the payment instruction is sent. Like M/T, the cable message should also bear such items as the beneficiary's full name, address and the name of the remitter in the same way as they appear in the M/T application form. The payment order must contain reimburse instructions, and the T/T application form should also be made in full sets. Unlike M/T, the payment instruction under a T/T is sent by cable instead of by airmail and the cable message must be authenticated by test key or SWIFT key instead of the authorized signature.

OVERSEAS UNION BANK LIMITED	APPLICATION FOR DEMAND DRAFT/TELEGRAPHIC TRANSFER
	DD/TT No.

Name of Applicant Address Contact Tel. No.	Agent/Correspondent

I/We wish to apply for a	FOR BANK USE	
☐ Demand Draft Drawn on _____ (Location) ☐ Telegraphic Transfer to _____ (Location)	FX Contract No. (If applicable)	

For Demand Draft only	Currency/Amount	Exchange Rate	SGD Equivalent
Beneficiary's Name			
		Commission	
For Telegraphic Transfer only		Cable Charges	
Beneficiary's Bank			
		Total	

Beneficiary's
Account No :
Name   :

This application and the issue of the above item is subject to the Bank's Terms and Conditions (printed overleaf) receipt of which I/we hereby acknowledge, and which I/we have read and agree to abide by.

In Settlement:

☐ Debit my/our Account No. _____

☐ Bank _____ Cheque No. _____

☐ Cash

Details of Payment

Charges Imposed by Agent/Correspondent

☐ To be borne by me/us   ☐ To be borne by beneficiary

_____   _____
Signature(s) of Applicant(s)   Date

Instruction for Beneficiary's Bank (if any)

TELLER   OFFICER

OUB 1924 (1) Bank Copy

ACCOUNTING VOUCHER

APPLICATION FOR DEMAND DRAFT/TELEGRAPHIC TRANSFER

DD/TT No.

Name of Applicant
Address

Contact Tel. No.

Agent/Correspondent

I/We wish to apply for a

☐ Demand Draft Drawn on _____ (Location)

☐ Telegraphic Transfer to _____ (Location)

FOR BANK USE

FX Contract No.
(If applicable)

For Demand Draft only	Currency/Amount	Exchange Rate	SGD Equivalent
Beneficiary's Name		Commission	
For Telegraphic Transfer only		Cable Charges	
Beneficiary's Bank		Total	

Beneficiary's
Account No :
Name :

This application and the issue of the above item is subject to the Bank's Terms and Conditions (printed overleaf) receipt of which I/we hereby acknowledge, and which I/we have read and agree to abide by.

In Settlement:

☐ Debit my/our Account No. _____

☐ Bank _____ Cheque No. _____

☐ Cash

Details of Payment

Charges Imposed by Agent/Correspondent

☐ To be borne by me/us ☐ To be borne by beneficiary

Signature(s) of Applicant(s)　　　　　Date

Instruction for Beneficiary's Bank (if any)

Validations

Cr : Remittances Suspense Account No 9 9 - 0 0 2 8 7 - 5

Description : ☐☐☐☐☐☐☐☐☐☐☐☐☐☐☐☐☐☐ Ref ☐☐☐☐☐

Cr : Commission Foreign Account No 9 9 - 0 0 6 5 7 - 3

Description : ☐☐☐☐☐☐☐☐☐☐☐☐☐☐☐☐☐☐ Ref ☐☐☐☐☐

Teller	Checked	Authorised

OUB 1924 (2) Accounting Voucher

OVERSEAS UNION BANK LIMITED

APPLICATION FOR DEMAND DRAFT/TELEGRAPHIC TRANSFER

DD/TT No.

Name of Applicant
Address

Contact Tel. No.

Agent/Correspondent

I/We wish to apply for a

[ ] Demand Draft Drawn on _____ (Location)

[ ] Telegraphic Transfer to _____ (Location)

FOR BANK USE

FX Contract No.
(If applicable)

For Demand Draft only   Currency/Amount

Beneficiary's Name

Exchange Rate   SGD Equivalent

Commission

For Telegraphic Transfer only

Beneficiary's Bank

Cable Charges

Total

Beneficiary's
Account No :
Name   :

This application and the issue of the above item is subject to the Bank's Terms and Conditions (printed below) receipt of which I/we hereby acknowledge, and which I/we have read and agree to abide by.

In Settlement:

[ ] Debit my/our Account No. _____

[ ] Bank _____ Cheque No. _____

[ ] Cash

Details of Payment

Charges Imposed by Agent/Correspondent

[ ] To be borne by me/us   [ ] To be borne by beneficiary

Signature(s) of Applicant(s)   Date

Instruction for Beneficiary's Bank (if any)

TELLER   OFFICER

TERMS AND CONDITIONS

1   The encashment or payment of outward remittance (which in these Terms and Conditions shall mean drafts or any other form of transfer of funds) is subject to rules and regulations of the country where the outward remittance is to be encashed or payment is to be made. In view of exchange restrictions prevailing in some countries, the liability of the Bank with respect to the encashment or payment of the outward remittance shall not exceed in any case the extent to which payment is allowed in the currency in which the outward remittance is to be made.

2   For the issue of outward remittance, the Bank shall be free on behalf of the Applicant to remit funds in any manner determined by the Bank (whether by mail, telex, cable, SWIFT or otherwise) and to appoint or use any correspondent, agent or sub-agent whether at the specific request of the Applicant or as determined by the Bank as indicated on the form. For the avoidance of doubt, the relationship between the Applicant and the Bank herein is that of Principal and Agent, and the said correspondent, agent, or sub-agent appointed or used whether at the specific request of the Applicant or as determined by the Bank shall be deemed to have been appointed by the Applicant as Principal, without responsibility on the Bank's part as Agent. The Applicant agrees to assume all risks and shall not hold the Bank liable for any loss or damage arising out of:

(i)   interruptions, omissions, distortions, errors or delays occurring in the wire, cable or mail or on the part of any postal authority, telegraphic, cable or wiring company, or made by any employee thereof beyond the control of the Bank or the correspondents, agents or sub-agents;

(ii) the failure of any correspondent, agent or sub-agent to locate, or error in identifying the named payee, or from failure to effect payment or from the refusal or inability of such correspondent, agent or sub-agent to pay the outward remittance by reason of any law, decree moratorium, regulation, compulsion or control of public authority or of domestic or foreign government, de jure or de facto, or an agency thereof, or resulting from declared or undeclared war, censorship, blockade, revolution, insurrection, civil commotion or resulting from any other cause whatsoever beyond the control of the Bank, the correspondent, agent or sub-agent;

(iii) any correspondent, agent, or sub-agent becoming insolvent, unable to pay its debts as they fall due, stopping, suspending or threatening to stop or suspend payment of all or a material part of its debt, beginning negotiations or taking any proceedings or other steps with a view to readjustment, rescheduling or deferral of all or part of its indebtedness, proposing or making a general assignment, arrangement or composition with or for the benefit of its creditors or on a moratorium being agreed or declared in respect of or affecting all or a material part of its indebtedness, or on any step being taken by any person for the dissolution or winding up of the correspondent, agent or sub-agent.

3   A refund or repurchase by the Bank of the amount of the outward remittance shall be made at the Bank's discretion only to or from the Applicant. In the case of drafts, upon receipt by the Bank of the drafts duly endorsed by the Applicant, the currency in question shall be converted at the current "on demand" buying rate less all costs, charges and expenses incurred by the Bank provided the Bank is in possession of the funds, for which payment instructions were issued, free from any restrictions.

4   In the event of the draft being lost, stolen or destroyed, the Bank must be informed at the earliest possible time and the issuance of a replacement or a refund of the amount of the draft may be requested by the Applicant on the condition that the Applicant provides the Bank with an acceptable letter of indemnity protecting the Bank against liability with respect to the lost, stolen or destroyed draft.

5   Instructions to stop payment are accepted in the Bank's sole discretion and subject to the practices rules regulations laws and acts of the country where the order is made payable, all international rules and regulations applicable to the transaction and the practices rules and regulations of the Bank's correspondent and shall be executed by the Bank in such manner as the Bank may in its sole and absolute discretion deem fit. It is hereby irrevocably and unconditionally agreed that while the Bank may execute the Applicant's instructions to stop payment, the Bank shall not be liable for any failure to do so howsoever arising and the Applicant shall indemnify the Bank against any expense, loss, damage or liability whatsoever which may be incurred or suffered by the Bank as a result of its endeavours.

OUB 1924 (3) Customer Copy

The T/T procedure is shown as follows:

APPLICATION FOR TELEGRAPHIC/ELECTRONIC TRANSFER

CUSTOMER'S COPY

To:

_____ LIMITED

A MEMBER OF THE UNITED OVERSEAS BANK GROUP

Please tick [✓] the relevant box.
Collection Instruction - Advice Slip ☐ Collect Personally ☐ Mail To Me

Date :

Applicant's Name	
Address	
Telephone No	
Currency & Amount	
Beneficiary's Name	
Address	
Beneficiary's A/c No	
Beneficiary's Bank	
Address (Branch/Street/City/Country)	
Payment Details (Max 70 Characters)	
Special Instructions	

BANK USE ONLY		
Reference No.		

Remittance System		
Input By	Verified By	Approved By

Rate _____
S$ Equivalent _____
Commission _____
Cable _____
Agent Charges _____
Total _____

Signature Verified By	Earmarked By	Confirmed With Applicant By

FOR BRANCHES ONLY		
Checked By	Approved By	Branch Stamp

Settlement
☐ Cash
☐ Debiting Account No _____
☐ Others _____

FX Contract (If Applicable)
☐ FX Contract   Contract No/Rate _____
                 Value Date _____
                 Dealer's Name _____

Remitting Bank's TT Charges
☐ To My Account   ☐ To Beneficiary's Account

FRN-9.97 (5.94) (1.98)

I/We agree that you may at your discretion confirm this application with me/us before acting on it. I/We have read and agree to the conditions shown overleaf.

_____
Signature(s) & Company Stamp (If Applicable)

① The remitter gives his signed written application to his bank, instructing it to transfer the funds through T/T.

② The remitting bank will check the remitter's account. If it is positive, the remitting bank will stamp on the application form and return the customer's copy to the remitter for record (In the case of a personal remittance, the customer will give proceeds to the remitting bank together with the application form).

③ The remitting bank will debit the remitter's a/c with the amount to be remitted together with its commission and cable charges (if any) and then issue and send the payment instruction by cable/telex/SWIFT to the paying bank.

④Upon receipt the cable message, the paying bank verifies it against the test key or SWIFT authenticate key (SAK) before it notifies the beneficiary with a copy of the cable message.

⑤The beneficiary presents the copy to the paying bank for payment.

⑥The paying bank checks the identity of the beneficiary before releasing the funds to him.

⑦The paying bank will claim reimbursement according to the reimbursement clause stated in the cable message.

Telegraphic transfer is faster and safer than mail transfer but the cost is much higher. It is often chosen by traders, especially when the remitted amount is large and the transfer of funds is subject to a time limit.

(3) Remittance by Banker's Demand Draft (D/D)

The remitting bank, at the request of the remitter, draws a bill of exchange on the paying bank ordering the latter to pay on demand a certain sum of money to the beneficiary who will also be the payee of the draft.

The bill of exchange drawn in such a way is a banker's draft because it is drawn by the remitting bank on its overseas branch or correspondent bank acting as the paying bank. The draft is drawn after the remitted amount has been provided by the customer (the remitter). For example:

Mr. Lee, the importer, requests the Hong Kong Royal Bank to transfer the proceeds to the exporter, Mr. CHAN H. M. A. in Canada at the amount of US dollars ten thousands. The Draft of the D/D will be made as follows:

REF. No.	**THE ROYAL BANK LIMITED** Hong Kong	
No. R 12345		Date: June 8, 200X
Pay to the order of: <u>Mr. CHAN H. M. A.</u> * * * * * * * * * * *		
The Sum of: <u>US DOLLAR TEN THOUSAND ONLY</u> * * * *		USD 10,000 * * *
To:		
The Royal Bank of Canada International Center 22 XYST. Toronto, Canada		The Royal Bank Mongkok Br. HK _____

Please note that the remitter Mr. Lee will not be a party in the banker's draft.

D/D application form should first be filled in and signed by the customer before he requires the bank to transfer funds for him. The full set of D/D application form should also be filled in by the remitter but the payment instruction for a D/D is represented by a banker's draft shown above which must be authenticated by the authorized signature. For the D/D application form, please turn back to T/T application form for reference.

The Procedure of D/D is different from that of M/T and T/T and will be shown as follows:

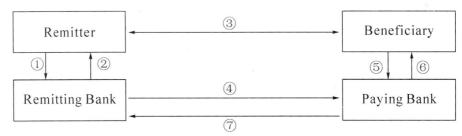

① The remitter gives his signed written application to his bank instructing the bank to transfer the funds by D/D.

② The remitting bank will check the remitter's account with him. If it is positive, the remitting bank will debit the account and draw a draft on the paying bank payable to the beneficiary. The draft will be made in a set and one part will be handed back to the remitter (In the case of personal remittance, the customer will provide the remitted amount to the bank before the latter draws a banker's draft).

③ The remitter will send the draft to the beneficiary.

④ The remitting bank will keep the paying bank aware of the remittance via inter-bank system.

⑤ Upon receipt of the draft, the beneficiary will present the draft for payment to the paying bank.

⑥ After authentication of the draft against authorized signature, the paying bank will release the funds to the beneficiary.

⑦ The paying bank will claim reimbursement against the remitting bank.

4. Comparison of the M/T, T/T and D/D

A customer can request his banker to transmit the funds by any method. However, in addition to the differences mentioned above, the remitter should also understand that the costs, the speed and the reliability of the different methods of remittance could be significantly varied.

D/D: A bank draft sent by the customer himself is the least expensive, but is the slowest form of transmission and the customer should also bear the risk of theft, destruction or loss of the draft in transit by airmail.

M/T: A mail transfer by the banker instead of the customer is a little safer and is not very expensive, but the speed of the transfer is low and the mailed M/T payment order could be delayed, destroyed or even stolen. Such delay involves additional interest payment to be made by the remitter to the beneficiary.

T/T: A telegraphic transfer, on the other hand, is the most expensive, but its speed could save substantial interest payment if the transferred funds are large. It is one of the most reliable forms of money transfer because it will depend on the inter-bank transfer system rather than the mailing system of the post office. As a result, traders always use this form of transmission if they are to settle the payments by remittance.

5. Characteristics of Remittance

Compared with other payment methods such as collection and letter of credit, remittance is the most simple and the least expensive method. It has found a wide application in international commercial settlement in the form of open account, consignment and payment in advance, which will be discussed in detail in the next section.

Remittance is based on the trader's credit. That is, banks only transfer the funds at the request of the remitter and they assume no payment undertaking to the beneficiary. Even in D/D, the remitting bank will not draw a banker's draft before he receives the proceeds from the remitter or before he debits the remitter's account. In this sense, a banker's demand draft under D/D will not vary the fact that remittance is based on trader's credit.

Section Three   Application of Remittance in International
Commercial Settlement

Remittance has found its applications in open account, payment in advance and consignment. It should be remembered that although these applications make significant difference to the traders, that is, the importer and the exporter, they remain a business of remittance for the banks.

1. Payment in Advance

By its very name, payment in advance signifies that the time of payment comes before the time of the delivery of goods or the provision of services. That is, the importer makes payment to the exporter before the latter makes the delivery. Obviously, this method is favorable to the exporter while putting the importer at a great risk of non-delivery. The benefit to the exporter lies in that he can make use of the funds before he makes the delivery of the physical goods or the provision of services.

Payment in advance is unfavourable to the importer on the following grounds:

(A) He pays in advance, tying up his capital prior to the receipt of the goods or services.

(B) He bears the risk of non-delivery.

(C) He has no assurance that what he contracted for will be supplied, received or received within the agreed time period or received in quality or quantity ordered.

As a result, payment in advance will be used under the following conditions:

(A) When the market is in the seller's market with conditions favoring the exporter, in order to secure the goods, the importer has to offer favorable terms to the exporter.

(B) When the manufacturing process or services delivered are to be specialized or capital intensive, the importer may agree to finance the exporter by partial payment in advance and partial progress payment.

(C) The exporter may insist to settle the payment in advance when the buyer's credit standing is doubtful or when there is an unstable political and economic environment in the buyer's country which is beyond the seller's control and will result in the delay in receipt of funds.

On the whole, in order to protect himself, the importer should make sure that the credit standing of the exporter must be exceedingly good or that he will agree to pay in advance only a certain percentage of the amount with the balance to be paid through other payment methods.

2. Open Account

Open account is just the opposite of payment in advance. Open account means that the exporter will make the delivery of goods or the provision of services before the importer makes payment. Although the time of payment is agreed to be made on a predetermined future date, the exporter is in fact selling on credit without any safeguards about the performance of the importer. The method is in the importer's favor and he can make payment only when the goods or services are received or inspected.

Open account is unfavourable to the exporter on the following grounds:

(A) He bears the risk of non-payment.

(B) He releases the title to the goods without having assurance of payment.

(C) His own capital is tied up until he receives the payment.

(D) There is possibility that political events will impose regulations which defer or block the movements of funds to him.

Open account is used when:

(A) The market is in the buyer's market with conditions favoring the importer. In order to be competitive, the exporter has to offer this favorable term to the exporter, though O/A is not the only way to make the exporter competitive.

(B) There is a long-standing or regular business relationship between the importer and the exporter.

(C) When a multi-national company ships the goods to its foreign branches or subsidiaries.

On the whole, in order to protect himself, the exporter should make sure that the credit standing of the importer must be exceedingly good or that he will require the open account be taken under a bank guarantee.

3. Consignment

Under a consignment, the exporter ships the goods to the importer and retains the title to the goods until the importer makes payment. The exporter is called the consignor and the importer is called the consignee. Similar to open account, the method is in favor of the importer who will make payment only when the goods are sold to a third party.

The method is disadvantageous to the exporter on the following grounds:

(A) He bears the risk of non-payment though he retains the title to himself.

(B) There is the possibility that political events will impose regulations which will defer or block the movement of funds to him.

(C) His capital is tied up until the goods are sold to a third party.

Similar to open account, the exporter may require the consignment be used under a bank guarantee. Consignment is used when:

(A) The exporter wants to make a trial sale for a new product in order to get to know the market conditions for its subsequent sales.

(B) The exporter wants to maintain large inventories in a local market in order to compete with local competitors.

(C) The goods are unsalable ones.

(D) The exporter wants to dispose of exhibits after a sales promotion.

Whether it be a payment in advance, open account or consignment, it is a business of remittance in the eyes of the handling banks. As we have already pointed out, remittance is made on trader's credit, the trader will suffer a loss by the other party's non-performance, either in the form of non-payment or in the form of non-delivery.

Chapter Seven　Payment Methods（Ⅱ）
－ Collection

Section one　Introduction

In payment in advance, consignment and open account, banks play little role because the documents are sent directly from the exporter to the importer. Whereas in collection, these documents can be sent through banks and payment is collected through banks who are acting as the intermediaries.

1. Definition

Collection means the handling of documents by banks in accordance with instructions received to:

(A) Obtain payment and/or acceptance; and

(B) Deliver documents against payments and/or against acceptance.

The word "documents" here include both financial documents and commercial documents. Financial documents are bills of exchange, promissory notes and cheques; commercial documents are invoices, transport documents, title documents and other similar documents.

In simple terms, collection means an arrangement whereby the goods are shipped and the relevant bills of exchange are drawn by the seller on the buyer, and / or document(s) is sent to the seller's bank with clear instruction for collection through one of its correspondent banks (branches) located in the domicile of the buyer.

2. Parties to a Collection

(1) The Principal

He is the person who entrusts the collection items to his bank. The term is based on his principal-agent relationship with his banker. He is the exporter and the drawer of the draft. He can also be called a shipper because he will consign the goods to shipment.

(2) The Drawee

He is the drawee because the draft is drawn on him. He should honor the draft by payment and/or acceptance. He is the importer.

(3) The Remitting Bank

The remitting bank is the exporter's bank. It will receive the collection items from the principal and forward the draft and/or other document(s) to its overseas branch or correspondent bank, asking the latter to collect proceeds from the importer. It should be noted that collection is a reverse remittance. Therefore, the exporter's bank will be called the paying bank in remittance while it is called the remitting bank in collection.

(4) Collecting Bank

The collecting bank is to receive the collection items from the remitting bank and present the draft to the drawee. It is the correspondent bank or a branch/head office of the remitting bank. The importer's bank plays different roles under remittance and collection. In remittance, it remits the proceeds to the exporter's bank while in collection, it collects the proceeds from the importer.

When the principal specifies a collecting bank, the remitting bank will forward documents to that bank. When no collecting bank is specified, the remitting bank will choose a collecting bank. In practice, it is better for the choice to be left to the remitting bank. Not all overseas banks can be relied upon, and it is much safer for the remitting bank to select one which it knows to carry out instructions properly.

(5) Presenting Bank

The presenting bank is to notify the drawee of the arrival of the collection items, to present the draft to the drawee on behalf of the collecting bank and to request payment or acceptance from the drawee. The collecting bank and the presenting bank will normally be the same bank, but they could be different banks. This may happen in the case that the drawee's residence or place of business is not in the same city as that of the collecting bank, or that the drawee does not maintain an account with the collecting bank. Then the collecting bank can only present the draft through another bank which meets the two conditions above and this bank becomes the presenting bank.

3. Outward and Inward Collection

(1) Outward Collection

When a bank acts as a remitting bank, the collection is referred to as an outward one on his part because he will send the collection items abroad to the collecting bank.

(2) Inward Collection

When a bank acts as a collecting bank, the collection business will be referred to as an inward one on his part because he is to receive the collection items forwarded to him from an overseas bank.

4. Uniform Rules for Collection (URC)

The Uniform Rules for Collection (URC) was published by International Chamber of Commerce. It is an internationally accepted code of practice covering documentary collections. It has a legal binding on all parties because all bank authorities will state that the collection is subject to URC. URC will apply unless the collection order states otherwise or the laws in one of the countries concerned specially contradict the rules in URC.

Section Two   Types of Collection

1. Types of Collection

According to whether commercial documents are attached to financial documents when submitted to the remitting bank, collection can be divided into clean collection and documentary collection.

(1) Clean Collection

Clean collection is the collection on financial instruments alone without being accompanied by commercial documents. Shipping documents will be forwarded by the exporter directly to the importer. When a credit instrument is accompanied by a non-shipping document such as invoice, the collection will also be considered as clean one.

Clean collection is mainly used to collect incidental expenses occurred in a transaction such as freight, insurance premium, commission or any other supplementary charges. On other occasions, clean collection is also used in the collection of down-payment or in the case of service transactions where there are no shipping documents available.

(2) Documentary Collection

Documentary collection is the collection on financial instruments being accompanied by commercial documents or the collection on shipping documents without financial documents. When financial instruments are not included, the stamp duty can be avoided and the invoice can do the job of financial documents by indicating clearly the amount to be collected. Compared with clean collection, documentary collection means that banks will assume higher liability because they have the shipping documents in their hands.

Documentary collection can be further divided into documents against payment and documents against acceptance. The division is based on different conditions against which the documents are released to the importer.

(A) Documents against payment at sight (D/P at sight).

D/P at sight means that the collecting bank may release the documents against payment of the sight drafts or simply against sight payment of the importer. The draft used under D/P at sight is a sight draft. When payments are made at sight by the importer/drawee, the shipping documents are released to him immediately. However, draft may not be a must under this method since the collecting bank can release the documents against the invoice, a commercial document clearly indicating the amount to be paid.

(B) Documents against payment after sight (D/P after sight).

D/P after sight means that the collecting bank may release the documents against payment of a time bill. The draft used under this method is a time draft. Because of this, when the importer/drawee accepts the bill upon presentation, the bill must be returned to the collecting bank. As a result, both the accepted draft and the shipping documents are held in the hands of the collecting bank. The documents are to be released to the importer only when he makes the payment on due date.

The process of D/P after sight will create a problem because the tenor of the draft may take much longer time than the transit of goods. That is to say, while the goods covered by the collection documents may have arrived or waited at the destination, the drawee will not be able to take the delivery because the documents are in the possession of the collecting bank awaiting payments till due date which may be months away. And in the mean time, the goods are landed at the quay and are exposed to risks. Therefore, according to *Uniform Rules for Collection* under *ICC* publication No. 522, D/P after sight is not encouraged. In practice, however, D/P after sight is widely used when it has been modified by the involvement of another document, trust receipt.

（C）D/P after sight against Trust Receipt（D/P, T/R）.

D/P after sight against T/R is a modification to D/P after sight. The T/R is issued in exchange of shipping documents. In fact, it is a kind of credit extension by the collecting bank to the importer so that the latter can obtain shipping documents in advance before he makes payment.

Trust Receipt（T/R）is a contract between the collecting bank and the importer. It is an acknowledgement of the pledge of the goods to the bank and an undertaking of the importer to deal with the goods as a trustee for the bank. T/R signifies the ownership of the bank over the goods and is thus a security for the importer to obtain finance from the bank. After T/R is established between the bank and the importer, documents will be released immediately to the importer under the importer's promise to make payment to the collecting bank on due date.

The obligations of the trustee（the importer）are:

* To arrange for the goods under D/P after sight against T/R to be warehoused in the name of the bank and to be separated from other goods;

* The proceeds from selling the goods should be handed over to the bank or he holds the proceeds on behalf of and in trust for the bank. A separated account should be opened for the said proceeds;

* Not to put the goods under D/P after sight against T/R in pledge to other persons.

The rights of the collecting bank are:

* Trust Receipt can be cancelled at any time to recover the said goods;

* To collect the proceeds at any time after the goods have been sold;

* To have priority in settling claims of the bank before liquidation in the case of the trustee's bankruptcy.

When D/P after sight against T/R is arranged between the collecting banks and the importer, the collecting bank will bear the risk of non-payment in the event that the importer defaults his responsibilities on due date. However, an exporter may also ask the collecting bank to arrange T/R with the importer. In this case, it is the exporter rather than the collecting bank who is to finance the importer. As a result, the exporter will bear the risk of non-payment on due date and it does not concern the collecting bank.

A typical T/R will take the following forms:

TRUST RECEIPT

To: **Malayan Banking Berhad**

Date:

Dear Sirs,

1. In consideration of your delivering to us shipping documents for goods/shipping guarantees to take delivery of the goods as follows:

MARKS AND NUMBERS	NO. OF PACKAGES/DESCRIPTION	STEAMER

which have been hypothecated/pledged to the Bank as security for the due acceptance and payment of the under-mentioned draft drawn upon us and accepted by us, we hereby undertake to land store hold and deliver to purchasers the said goods and receive their proceeds as Trustees for you and as Agents on your behalf and not otherwise and in the event of the said goods or any portion thereof being sold and cleared before full complete payment of the said draft, we pledge ourselves that the proceeds of such sales shall be received and retained by us as Trustees for you and that they shall be kept separate and apart from our other moneys, and to pay to you the proceeds of such sales as soon as the goods are realised as and when received by us, in order that the same may be applied in or towards payment of the draft we at the same time furnishing to you all necessary particulars to enable you to apply the same to the relative draft in each case.

2. We expressly agree that you shall remain the Owners of the goods and that we are to be and we hereby undertake to act as your Agents for the sale of the said goods and to receive and account to you for the proceeds thereof and that they shall be open to inspection at all times by you or your duly accredited representative and you are at liberty (at our expense) if you think fit so to do to retake possession of them without any reference to or consent obtained from us and to remove the same or any part of them from the place where they have been stored to any other place you may choose and place the same under the care of any one you may select and to dispose of them by sale or otherwise if so required, we also undertake to keep the goods referred to fully insured against fire and also (if required) against marine risks and to hand over to you the amount of any claims on the underwriters; the policies of insurance being in the meantime held by us as Trustees for and on behalf of the Bank.

3. We undertake not to sell the goods or any part thereof on credit unless with your prior consent in writing.

4. You shall be entitled without prior notice to us to debit on the maturity date of the Trust Receipt, or at any time thereafter, any of our account(s), current or otherwise with you (regardless of whether such account(s) be in credit or debit) for payment of the Trust Receipt sum together with interest and all other moneys due and payable in connection with the Trust Receipt. Provided always that no such debiting shall operate as payment or satisfaction of any sum due (except to the extent of any amount in credit in the account concerned) or a waiver by you of any breach or default on our part, and you shall not in any way be held liable for any cheque(s) dishonoured as a result of such debiting. If any such debiting causes our account(s) to be overdrawn, interest on the overdrawn amount shall be payable accordingly. Where the currency of the amount due is different from the currency of the account(s), your then prevailing rate of exchange for conversion of the currency of the amount due to the currency of the account(s) shall be used to convert the same. For the avoidance of doubt, your rights over the goods described herein shall remain and continue for so long as any amount remains unpaid under or in connection with the Trust Receipt.

5. Prior to any exercise of your rights under paragraph 4 above, we hereby agree and undertake to pay Default Interest in respect of any moneys payable in connection with the Trust Receipt ("TR") not paid on due date as follows:

    1. if interest on the TR is payable at or at a margin above (i) Prime Lending Rate (ii) Foreign Centre Rate or (iii) Overseas Centre Rate (each of these rates as may be applicable shall hereinafter be referred to as the "Prescribed Rate"), at the rate of 2% above the applicable Prescribed Rate;

    2. if interest on the Singapore dollar TR is payable at or at a margin above Costs of Funds, at the rate of 5% above the Bank's Prime Lending Rate;

    3. if interest on the foreign currency TR is payable at or at a margin above (i) Singapore Interbank Offered Rate or (ii) Costs of Funds, at the rate of 5% above the Overseas Centre Rate;

    such Default Interest to commence from the due date of payment of the TR up to and including the actual date when payment is made (both before and after judgment).

    A certificate by the Bank as to the Prime Lending Rate, Costs of Funds, Foreign Centre Rate, Overseas Centre Rate or Singapore Interbank Offered Rate, as the case may be, shall be conclusive for all purposes against us.

    In the event of any conflict or inconsistency between the terms relating to Default Interest herein and in any other agreement, document or letter between the parties hereto, the terms herein shall apply.

Yours faithfully,

....
Authorised Signatories

PARTICULARS OF DRAFT		
DRAFT NO.	AMOUNT OF DRAFT	DUE DATE

Malayan Banking Berhad
Form No 98-0298(1/3)

押1(2)

TO: 🏦 中 国 银 行
BANK OF CHINA

From:

Date:

TRUST RECEIPT

Under L/C No............................　Ref:IC/AB................................

covering goods specified hereunder for amount ....

Maturity :..

** Subject to fluctuation and based on the Ruling Rate at the time of Reimbursement to the Negotiating Bank.

B/L No.	Vessel's Name	Quantity and description of goods
AWB No.		

In consideration of your delivering to us the shipping documents relating to the goods specified above, (receipt of which is hereby acknowledged) and which documents are now pledged to your Bank as security for banking facilities.

WE UNDERTAKE AND AGREE as follows:—

1. To hold the shipping documents and the goods to which they relate on Trust for your Bank and to deal with them as the property of your Bank.

2. To return to you immediately on demand at any time the Documents and/or any other documents received by us in exchange or substitution for them and to comply promptly and fully with any instruction which you may give as to the manner of dealing with goods or any of them or the removal of them to, or storage of them at, any place.

3. Not to charge or purport to charge the goods or proceeds of sale thereof with the payment of any money to any person or to use or purport to use the same as security for the performance of any obligation whatsoever.

4. Not to dispose of the said goods otherwise than by sale at such price or prices and upon such terms as the Bank may previously approve and upon such sale to hold the proceeds thereof in trust for your Bank. Pending such sale we further undertake to keep the goods insured at our cost against all risks in their full value and to hold the proceeds of insurance effected hereunder on trust for your Bank as aforesaid.

5. That all sales shall be for cash and not on credit without your previous consent in writing.

6. To keep the said goods, manufactured product or proceeds thereof, whether in the form of money or bills receivable or accounts, and all insurance money, separate and capable of identification as the property of your Bank.

7. That notwithstanding anything herein contained we will on demand by your Bank at any time before sale deliver possession of the said goods to your Bank and we authorise your Bank its servants or agents for the purpose of taking possession or making inspection thereof to enter our godown or other places where the goods may be and we agree that your Bank may at any time after receiving possession thereof and without notice to or further authority from us sell the said goods in such manner and for such price as you shall think fit and apply the net proceeds of sale on or towards satisfaction of the amount then owing by us to your Bank.

8. That the goods shall be a security to the Bank for the payment on demand of all other monies now or at any time hereafter to become due to the Bank from us alone or jointly with any other or others, whether on current account or for money advanced or paid in respect of bills, notes or drafts accepted paid or discounted interest commission or any other or lawful charge or on any other account whatsoever together with all costs, charges and expenses.

9. This Trust Receipt is of continuing effect notwithstanding the death, bankruptcy, liquidation, incapacity or any change in the constitution of us or any settlement of account or other matter whatsoever and is in addition to and shall not merge with or otherwise prejudice or affect your general bankers lien or any contractual or other right or remedy or any guarantee, lien, pledge, bill, note, mortgage or other security (whether created by the deposit of documents or otherwise) now or hereafter held by or available to you and shall not be in any way prejudiced or affected thereby or by the invalidity thereof or by you now or hereafter dealing with exchanging, releasing, varying or abstaining from perfecting or enforcing any of the same or any rights which you may now or hereafter have or giving time for payment or indulgence or compounding with any other person liable.

10. If signed by a firm, this Trust Receipt shall be binding on all persons from time to time carrying on business in the name of such firm or under the name in which the business of such firm may from time to time be continued notwithstanding the retirement or death of any partner or the introduction of any further partner.

AND WE DECLARE that we are not indebted to any other person in respect of the goods specified above and confirm that we will not sell the goods to buyers to whom we are indebted or under any liability.

Dated at Singapore this　　　　　　　day of　　　　　　　19

S/G No...............................　dated ....

In case the goods have been released under Shipping Guarantee the effective date of this Trust Receipt commences from the date of the issuance of the relative Shipping Guarantee.

_____
Authorised Signature (s)
& Company Stamp

TRUST RECEIPT

ORIGINAL   1

To:

_____ LIMITED
(BANK'S NAME)

A MEMBER OF THE UNITED OVERSEAS BANK GROUP

SHIPPING DOCUMENTS DELIVERED TO	T/R NO.	CN NO.	UNDER LC/IBC NO.
	MATURITY	SHIPMENT FROM	PER SS
A/C NO.: _____	COVERING GOODS SPECIFIED HEREUNDER FOR $ _____		

MARKS & PACKAGES	QUANTITY	DESCRIPTION OF GOODS

Sirs

The Bill(s) of Lading and/or other documents of title and/or other documents (collectively "the Documents") representing or purporting to represent the goods specified above have been delivered to you as security for payment by us at Singapore of the Trust Receipt amount stated above together with interest thereon at such rate(s) as you may decide from the date of advance/the date of collection note, until full repayment is received by you, including all costs, charges and expenses.

In consideration of your releasing to us the Documents (receipt of which is hereby acknowledged) WE UNDERTAKE AND AGREE as stated overleaf.

Dated at Singapore this   day of   19

Yours faithfully

_____
AUTHORISED SIGNATURE(S) & COMPANY STAMP

FRN-5.1 (R8.94) (8.96)

TRUST RECEIPT

TERMS & CONDITIONS

1. To receive the said documents and the said goods to which they relate in trust for you and to land store and hold the goods for your account and under trust and lien to you and as your agent and bailee and to deal with them as your property.

2. Not to charge or purport to charge the goods or the proceeds of sale thereof with the payment of any money to any person or to use or purport to use the same as security for the performance of any obligation whatsoever. We hereby declare that we are not indebted to the buyers of the goods or to any other person(s) having possession of the said goods.

3. To hold the said goods when received in trust for you and on your behalf, with authority to sell the said goods for your account but not to make any other disposition whatsoever of them. We undertake not to sell the goods or any part thereof on credit or for non-monetary consideration or at a loss without your previous consent in writing.

4. To remit the proceeds of sale of the goods to you as soon as received or within such time as you may allow in reduction or extinguishment of our indebtedness to you and to notify you at once should the goods not be sold or the proceeds of sale not be received within 28 days from this date in order that you may, if you wish, make other arrangements for the sale of the goods or the recovery of the proceeds of sale, as the case may be.

5. To keep the said goods fully insured for an amount not less than the invoiced value of the said goods in your name, against all risks usually insured against (including fire and theft) and against any other risks you may deem desirable and to hand you the evidence of such insurance; the sum insured to be payable, in the event of loss, to you. In case such insurance is not arranged to your satisfaction you are hereby authorised to effect insurance, the cost of which we engage to pay and failing payment you are authorised to debit the cost to our account with you.

6. To keep the said goods when received by us stored to your satisfaction, to advise you of the whereabouts of the goods at all times and if requested by you to remove them at our expense to any other place of storage indicated by you. It is understood that all charges and expenses in connection with the removal or storage of the said goods are for our account and failing payment of such charges and expenses by us you are authorised to make payment and debit our account with you accordingly.

7. To keep the said goods and the proceeds thereof (whether in the form of money or bills recoverable or accounts receivable) identifiable and separate from any other transaction. You are irrevocably authorised, if you shall think fit so to do, to notify and to receive direct from the buyers the proceeds of any sale.

8. It is also understood that you may without notice to us at any time cancel the transaction evidenced by this trust receipt and resume possession of the shipping documents or the goods specified therein. We authorise you, your servants or agents for the purpose of taking possession or making inspection of the said goods to enter our premises or other places where the said goods may be.

9. That the goods shall be a security to you for the payment on demand of all other monies now or at any time hereafter to become due to you from us alone or jointly with any other or others, whether on current account or for money advanced or paid or in respect of bills, notes or drafts accepted paid or discounted interest commission or any bank charges or on any other account whatsoever together with all costs charges and expenses including but not limited to expenses incurred in retaking possession of the goods and the (re) storage of the same.

10. That no failure or omission on your part to enforce or to require that we carry out fully any of the provisions of this or any similar receipt or agreement, or of the agreement under which you issued the Letter of Credit under which the said goods were purchased, shall be deemed to be a waiver by you of any of your rights or remedies hereunder or thereunder.

11. That it is hereby understood and agreed that the handing to us of any of the Documents as above mentioned is entirely at your option and does not in any way alter or affect our personal liability or your rights under any other security or document(s) you may hold.

12. That notwithstanding that the maturity date of this trust receipt or of any negotiable instrument given hereunder shall not have expired, the aforesaid sum together with all accrued interest cost, charges and expenses shall be due and payable immediately without demand upon the happening of any of the following events:-

    a) If we default under any agreement relating to any loan or credit facility whatsoever given by any other party to us or if any of our indebtness is declared due prior to its stated maturity.

    b) If we fail to pay any debt in the ordinary course of our business or any legal proceedings or suits of any kind is instituted against us which in your opinion adversely affects our financial position.

    c) If we are in breach of any of our undertakings or obligations under any agreement binding on us, including this trust receipt.

13. Without prejudice to any other term herein, you shall be entitled without prior notice to us to debit on the maturity date of this trust receipt, or any time thereafter, any of our account(s), current or otherwise, with you (regardless of whether such account(s) be in debit or credit) for payment of the trust receipt sum together with interest and all other moneys due and payable in connection with this trust receipt. Provided always that no such debiting shall operate or have any effect as payment or satisfaction of the sums due (except to the extent of any amount in credit in the account concerned) or a waiver by you of any breach or default on our part. If any such debiting causes our account(s) to be overdrawn, interest on the overdrawn amount shall be payable accordingly. Where the currency of the account(s) is different from the currency of the amounts due, your then prevailing rate of exchange for conversion of the currency of the account(s) to the currency of the amounts due shall be used to convert the same.

14. (i) If we should make (a) new object(s) from the goods, mix the goods with (an) other object(s) or if the goods in any way whatsoever becomes a constituent of (an) other object(s) you will be given the ownership of this (these) new object(s) as surety for the full payment of what we owe you. We agree that the ownership of the object(s) in question whether finished or not, are to be transferred to you and that this transfer of ownership will be considered to have taken place through and at the moment of the single operation or event by which the goods are converted into (a) new object(s), or is mixed with or becomes a constituent of (an) other object(s).

    (ii) Until the moment of full payment, we shall keep the object(s) in question for you in our capacity of fiduciary owner and, if required, shall store this (these) object(s) in such a way that it (they) can be recognized as such.

    (iii) We will be entitled to sell these objects to bona fide purchasers for value within the framework of the normal carrying on of our business and to deliver them on condition that — if you so require — we, as long as we have not fully discharged our debt to you shall assign to you the claims we have against our buyer emanating from this transaction.

15. If this trust receipt is signed by or for and on behalf of two or more of us our liabilities shall be joint and several. In the construction of this trust receipt the singular number shall be deemed to include the plural and vice versa.

16. The term hereof shall be construed and shall take effect according to the laws of the Republic of Singapore and shall be subject to the non-exclusive jurisdiction of the Court of the Republic of Singapore.

(D) Documents against acceptance (D/A).

Documents against acceptance means that the collecting bank may release the documents against the buyer's acceptance to the draft. The draft required under D/A is a time draft.

Compared with D/P at sight, D/A enables the importer to obtain shipping documents against mere acceptance instead of payment. Compared with D/P after sight, no T/R is required after acceptance if the importer wants to obtain shipping documents without the delivery being delayed till the due date. Generally speaking, D/A is more favorable to the importer while D/P is more favorable to the exporter.

2. Collection Order

Collection order is a standard form of authority which enables the exporter to include specific instructions to his bank regarding documentary collection. When signed between the exporter and the remitting bank, it is called application form for collection. When signed and forwarded by the remitting bank to the collecting bank, it is called collection order. Collection order can serve as a covering letter to the collection items and the collection will be carried out only when collection order is received by the banks. An Application for Documentary Collection/A Collection Order will be shown as follows:

<u>APPLICATION FOR DOCUMENTARY COLLECTION</u>

TO: BANK OF CHINA   DATE:
    SINGAPORE

Dear Sirs

I/We enclose herewith the following draft(s) and document(s) for collection subject to the terms and conditions set out overleaf:

Bill No	Amount	Due Date/Tenor	Drawee

Documents	Drafts	B/L	Invoice	P/W List	Ins Cert	Cert Origin	Cert of Qly/Qty	AWB	D.O.	

Kindly act in accordance with my/our instructions marked "X" as indicated hereinbelow:
(   ) Deliver document (s) against payment. (   ) Deliver document(s) against acceptance.
(   ) All banking charges are for account of drawee.
(   ) All Collecting Bank's charges are for account of drawee and your charges are for my/our account.
(   ) Protest for non-payment.   (   ) Protest for non-acceptance.
(   ) Overdue interest to be collected from the drawee at   % per annum from due date to the approximate date of return remittance in Singapore.
(   ) Interest to be collected from the drawee at   % per annum from first presentation to the approximate date of return remittance in Singapore.

In case of need or difficulties, please communicate with (SELLER'S representative):

Address:

Tel:

who will endeavour to obtain the honouring of the aforesaid draft(s), without any alteration of my/our instructions.

In case of dishonour, the goods may, in the option of your correspondent or agent, be landed, cleared through the customs, warehoused and insured at my/our costs and expenses.

It is understood and agreed that, having exercised due care in the selection of any correspondent to whom the abovementioned items may be sent for collection, you shall not be responsible for any act, omission, default, suspension, insolvency or bankruptcy of any such correspondent or sub-agent thereof, or for any delay in remittance, loss in exchange or loss of items or their proceeds during transmission or in the course of collection; but your responsibility shall be only for your own acts.

<u>PAYMENT INSTRUCTIONS:</u>
(   ) Please advance/discount the bill
(   ) Please pay us only upon receipt of funds
(   ) Please credit proceeds to our account no.:
(   ) Please offset Import Bill(s) ref.:
(   ) Please utilise Forward Contract no.:
(   ) Hold proceeds and contact: at Tel. No.
(   )

<u>SPECIAL INSTRUCTIONS:</u>
Please deliver the documents through: Yours faithfully
(Drawee's Banker)

(X) Whichever is applicable.

(Subject to Uniform Rules for Collections ICC Publication No. 322)

TERMS AND CONDITIONS FOR ADVANCE

In consideration of your accepting the Bill and relative documents detailed overleaf as security and advancing to me/us thereon the sum of S$_____ being _____% of the Invoice Value of the merchandise covered by the documents (the remaining _____percent of such sum to be retained by you as margin for payment to me/us only after collection by you and/or after receipt by you of remittance from your Agents at destination of the total proceeds of the bill):-

(A) We guarantee and assume full responsibility for the genuineness, regularity and validity of the bill of lading and other documents attached to the bill of exchange drawn by us on the said drawees_____ and also the character, quantity, quality and condition of the merchandise mentioned in the bill of lading and/or other documents.

(B) We agree to be responsible for and to bear the consequences of the loss or late or non-arrival of part or all of the aforesaid bill and documents, or for any loss or damage which may happen to the said merchandise whether during its transit by sea, air or land or after its arrival or by reason of the non-insurance or insufficient insurance thereof or by whatever cause, or for the stoppage, or detention thereof by the shipper or any party whosoever, engaging ourselves duly to reimburse you with whatsoever sum that may be due to you with respect to the discount and purchase of the said bill.

(C) We also agree that the title to property in the said bill and the documents relative thereto and the merchandise represented thereby and the whole of the proceeds thereof shall be and remain in you until payment of the said bill and of all sums that may be due on the said bill or otherwise and the payment of any and all other indebtedness and liability, now existing or now or hereafter created or incurred by us to you due or not due, it being understood that the said documents and the merchandise represented thereby and all our other property, including securities and deposit balances which may now or hereafter be in your and/or your branches' possession or otherwise subject to your control shall be deemed to be collateral security for the payment of the said bill. And, we hereby authorise you to dispose of the aforementioned property by public or private sale at your discretion without notice to us whenever the said bill from any cause or for any reason whatsoever be dishonoured by non-acceptance or non-payment on the due date or whenever in your discretion it is deemed necessary for the protection of yourselves and after deducting all your expenses to reimburse yourselves out of the proceeds.

(D) We further agree that the bill and accompanying documents, after receipt from us by you on the terms and conditions stated above will be on our responsibility, received and held by you, and forwarded by you for realisation by your collecting Agents at destination subject to all Governmental regulations, restrictions and taxes and other dues both at Singapore as well as the place of destination of the shipment and the bill; and we hold ourselves fully responsible to you and to your Agents for the due compliance with each requirement, regulation, order or restriction, of any Government Department or of any competent naval or military authority made given or imposed in connection with the shipment of the merchandise or with the Bill of Exchange or its negotiation and collection. All charges, costs and expenses relative to all matters herein are chargeable to and payable by us, if not paid or not fully paid by the drawee.

(E) Any advance to us at our request and upon your approval will be applied at your bank's current T/T buying rate. We further agree that interest for the first 10 days will be at the rate determined by you, and will be deducted from the amount advanced. Subsequently, interest shall be payable upon the expiry of such interest period as you may conclusively determine and if not paid, shall itself bear interest at your prescribed rate.

PLEASE COLLECT THE UNDERMENTIONED FOREIGN BILL AND/OR DOCUMENTS   A

Full Name and Address of Drawer/Exporter	For Bank Use Only	Date	I.S.B. Collection No.
	Drawers reference (to be quoted in all correspondence)		
	For Bank Use Only	Due Date	Correspondents Reference

Consignee - Full Name and Address	Drawee (if not Consignee) - Full Name and Address
	For Bank Use Only	Fate Dates

TO Barclays Bank PLC	Drawers Bankers Barclays Bank	Sorting Code No. 20-	Ref. No.
S.W.I.F.T. ADDRESS BARC GB22	Account No.		

Subject to uniform rules for collections (1978 Revision) International Chamber of Commerce Publication No. 322.

PLEASE FORWARD DOCUMENTS ENUMERATED BELOW BY AIRMAIL. FOLLOW SPECIAL INSTRUCTIONS AND THOSE MARKED X

Bill of Exchange	Comm'l. Invoice	Cert'd./Cons. Inv.	Cert. of Origin	Ins'ce Pol./Cert.	Bill of Lading	Parcel Post Recpt	Air Waybill

Combined Transport Doc.	Other Documents and whereabouts of any missing Original Bill of Lading

RELEASE DOCUMENTS ON	ACCEPTANCE	PAYMENT	If unaccepted	Protest	Do Not Protest
If documents are not taken up on arrival of goods	Warehouse Goods	Do Not Warehouse	and advise reason by	Cable	Airmail
	Insure Against Fire	Do Not Insure	If unpaid	Protest	Do Not Protest
Collect ALL Charges	Yes	No	and advise reason by	Cable	Airmail
Collect Correspondent's Charges ONLY	Yes	No	Acceptance/Payment may be deferred until arrival of goods	Yes	No
Goods and carrying vessel.			After final-payment remit proceeds by	Cable	Airmail

For Bank Use Only

In case of need refer to	For Guidance	Accept their Instructions

SPECIAL INSTRUCTIONS 1. Represent on arrival of goods if not honoured on first presentation

Date of Bill of Exchange	Tenor	Amount of Collection

Bill of Exchange claused		
	Please apply proceeds of this collection as indicated with an 'X'	Credit us in Sterling	
		Credit our Foreign Currency Account No.	
		Apply to Forward Contract No.	
	I/We agree that you shall not be liable for any loss, damage, or delay however caused which is not directly due to the negligence of your own officers and servants. Any charges and expenses not recovered from the drawees, including any costs of protecting the merchandise, may be charged to us.	
For Bank use Only	Date & Signature	

371 (OC206) 1/85

Specimen Collection Order

We will illustrate the major items of the two documents from the point of view of an application for documentary collection:

(A) Name and address of the drawer/exporter.

(B) Name and address of the remitting bank (the drawer's bank).

(C) Particulars of the draft where the information of the drawee/importer will be shown. This item will be further discussed in item 3.

(D) Documents covered/submitted. The exporter is expected to indicate clearly the name and the numbers of original and/or duplicate documents he will submit.

(E) Documents release conditions.

Documents will be released to the importer against D/P or against D/A. Normally D/P will require either a sight draft or a time draft and D/A a time draft. Failing to give such instructions, documents will be released against payment.

(F) Store and insurance clause.

If documents are not taken up on arrival of goods, instructions are required on whether or not to warehouse and insure the goods. In the event that the importer does not pay or accept the draft, the collecting bank will be instructed by such a clause to warehouse and insure the goods. The cost of this operation will be borne by the exporter and it will be claimed from the exporter's bank, who will in turn debit their customer, the principal. When the goods are protected, the exporter will have time to find an alternative buyer or to ship the goods back. If a waybill or a B/L shows the importer as consignee, this clause will be superfluous because the collecting bank has no control over the goods.

(G) Bank charges.

The application will state whether or not bank and other charges such as interest and collection charges are for the account of the drawer or that of the drawee. The exporter should complete the clause in accordance with the details agreed in the sales contract.

(H) Protest clause.

Specific instructions are required whether or not to protest in the event of dishonor by either non-payment and/or non-acceptance.

In some countries, the law requires a dishonored bill to be protested within one-working day, otherwise the drawer can not sue on the bill. If a bill is to be protested, the collecting bank may instruct a lawyer in his country to undertake formal procedures whereby he asks the drawee to reason for his dishonor and makes appropriate notes. The protest fee will be borne by the collecting bank who will be reimbursed by the exporter's bank who will in turn debit his customer.

(I) Overdue interest.

Overdue interest to be collected at such and such rate from the drawee.

(J) The case of need.

The case of need is an agent of the exporter who resides in the importer's country. In the event of default, the collecting bank will refer to him in the settlement process.

(K) Payment instructions.

After the payment is effected by the importer, funds can be transferred by either debiting the vostro account of the collecting bank with the remitting bank or crediting the remitting bank's nostro account with the collecting bank. T/T is obviously the best way to remit the funds from the exporter's point of view, but this is the more expensive method than mail transfer.

(L) The signature of the drawer/exporter.

(M) Special instructions.

This is a space where the information of the collecting bank (the drawee's bank) is entered. The collecting bank may be indicated by the exporter or he may leave it up to the remitting bank to decide.

(N) Subject to URC.

It is a must that the collection order should bear clearly the following wordings: Subject to *Uniform Rules for Collections* (1978 Revision) International Chamber of Commerce publication No. 322.

3. Collection Draft

Draft used under collection is called the collection draft. The tenor can be either sight or time. The drawer of a collection bill is always the exporter or the seller and the drawee of the bill is the importer or the buyer. The payee can be made as follows:

(A) To be the beneficiary.

The beneficiary, namely the exporter is the payee. When he forwards the draft with other collection items to the collecting bank, he should endorse the bill in collection endorsement.

(B) To be the remitting bank.

The remitting bank can also be the payee. Usually, a drawn clause will be added to the draft to indicate that it is for the purpose of collecting that the remitting bank has been made the payee. A collection endorsement is required when the bill is forwarded to the collecting bank.

(C) To be the collecting bank.

The collecting bank can be the payee as well. And again, a drawn clause will be added to the draft. No endorsement is required for this type of bill.

4. Procedures under Documentary Collection

(1) Procedure under D/P at Sight

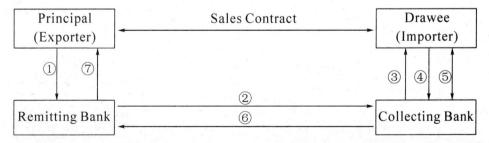

① After shipment is made and shipping documents are obtained, the exporter draws a sight draft on the importer for the value of the goods, fills in the application form for collection indicating clearly that documents will be released under D/P sight. The exporter then submits it together with draft and shipping documents to his banker for collection.

② The remitting bank completes its own collection order based on the application form and forwards it together with the other two collection items it receives to the collecting bank.

③ Acting as an agent for the remitting bank, the collecting bank notifies the importer upon receipt of collection items and presents draft to him for payment.

④ The importer makes payment to the collecting bank.

⑤ The collecting bank releases shipping documents to the importer against his payment.

⑥ The collecting bank will remit the proceeds to the remitting bank according to the instructions on the collection order.

⑦ The remitting bank credits the payment to the exporter's account.

(2) Procedure under D/P after Sight

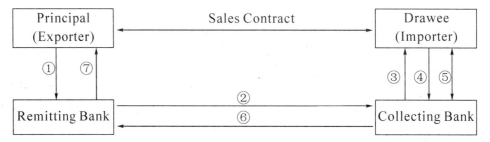

① After shipment is made and shipping documents are obtained, the exporter draws a time draft on the importer for the value of the goods, fills in the application form for collection, indicating clearly that documents will be released under D/P after sight. The exporter then submits it together with draft and shipping documents to his banker for collection.

② The remitting bank completes its own collection order based on the application form and forwards it together with the other two collection items it receives to the collecting bank.

③ Acting as an agent for the remitting bank, the collecting bank notifies the importer upon receipt of collection items and presents draft to him for acceptance.

④ The importer accepts the draft upon presentment and returns the accepted draft to the collecting bank.

⑤ At maturity, the collecting bank presents the accepted draft again for payment. Once payment is made by the importer, the collecting bank will release shipping documents to him.

⑥ The collecting bank will remit the proceeds to the remitting bank according to the instructions on the collection order.

⑦ The remitting bank credits the payment to the exporter's account.

(3) Procedure under D/P, T/R

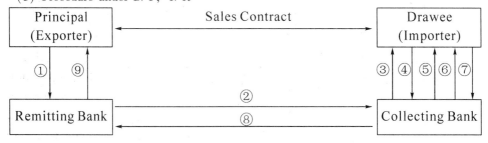

① After shipment is made and shipping documents are obtained, the exporter draws a time draft on the importer for the value of the goods, fills in the application form for collection, indicating clearly that documents will be released under D/P after sight. The exporter then submits it together with draft and shipping documents to his banker for collection.

② The remitting bank completes its own collection order based on the application form and forwards it together with the other two collection items it receives to the collecting bank.

③ Acting as an agent for the remitting bank, the collecting bank notifies the importer and upon receipt of collection items and presents the draft to him for acceptance.

④ The importer accepts the draft upon presentment and fills in and signs a T/R. The importer returns the accepted draft together with the signed T/R to the collecting bank.

⑤ The collecting bank releases shipping documents to the importer against T/R.

⑥ Upon due date, the collecting bank will present the accepted bill again for payment.

⑦ The importer makes payment to the collecting bank on due date.

⑧ The collecting bank will remit the proceeds to the remitting bank according to the instructions on the collection order.

⑨ The remitting bank credits the payment to the exporter's account.

（4）Procedure under D/A

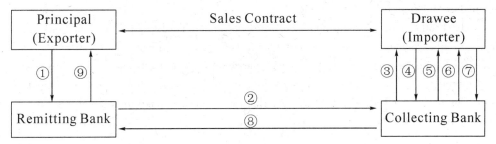

① After shipment is made and shipping documents are obtained, the exporter draws a time draft on the importer for the value of the goods, fills in the application form for collection, indicating clearly that documents will be released under D/A. The exporter then submits it together with draft and shipping documents to his banker for collection.

② The remitting bank completes its own collection order based on the application form and forwards it together with the other two collection items it receives to the collecting bank.

③ Acting as an agent for the remitting bank, the collecting bank notifies the importer upon receipt of the collection items and presents the draft to him for acceptance.

④ The importer accepts the draft and returns it to the collecting bank.

⑤ The collecting bank releases the shipping documents to the importer against his acceptance.

⑥ Upon due date, the collecting bank will present the accepted bill for payment.

⑦ The importer will make payment on due date.

⑧ The collecting bank will remit the proceeds to the remitting bank according to the instructions on the collection order.

⑨ The remitting bank credits the payment to the exporter's account.

Section Three　Characteristics, Risks and Bank's Liabilities under Collection

1. Characteristics of Documentary Collection

（A）In comparison with payment in advance and open account, we should say that collection, particularly the documentary collection, is a compromise to payment in advance and open account. This is because documentary collection provides both the importer and the exporter a better protection on the following two grounds:

(a) Once the documents are passed to the bank by the exporter rather than being sent directly to the importer under either open account or consignment, the bank has an absolute right over the goods through the title documents. The right includes the arrangements concerning the release of documents, protection, warehousing and shipment of the goods on behalf of the exporter. Normally, title to the goods does not pass to the buyer (unless the buyer is the named consignee on the transport document) until the draft is paid and/or accepted. Therefore, the exporter is better protected than under open account when there is no assurance of the coming payment after the delivery.

(b) On the other hand, when the importer makes acceptance or payment, he is sure that goods are shipped and documents are available to him. In this case, the importer is better protected than under payment in advance.

(B) Another characteristic about collection is that it is also a payment method based on trader's credit. In the event that the importer fails to make payment, the exporter will suffer a loss. If the exporter is dishonest, the importer may get inferior goods after making payment (D/P), or acceptance (D/A). Generally speaking, collection is more favorable to the importer because whether under D/P or D/A, the exporter should always make the delivery first and place the documents in the hands of the banks.

2. **Risks under Collection**

(1) To the Exporter

(A) Under D/P

Although D/P gives the exporter better protections than D/A in the sense that when the title documents are used, the buyer can not obtain the goods without paying the bill of exchange.

However, when a buyer intentionally refuses to take delivery, the exporter will not get paid. Furthermore, the physical goods are at the overseas port, in chance of being damaged, stolen or possibly incurring demurrage (Demurrage means charges levied by port authorities for goods which are not collected on time). When this happens, on the one hand, the exporter must arrange proper protection and insurance for the goods and pay for the charges that might occur. On the other hand, he has to find an alternative buyer in the importing country or pay to ship the goods back to the home country.

On other occasions when the market for the imported goods shrinks or the market price falls, some dishonest importer will purposely reject the goods on some excuses after their arrival, in hope of driving the exporter into a price reduction. All these would expose the exporter to risks. Therefore, when a payment method is on trader's credit, the credit standing of the trader is very important.

(B) Under D/A

The additional risk with a D/A is that the documents, and therefore the goods are released on acceptance, with no guarantee that payment will be forthcoming at maturity. Once the bill of exchange is accepted, the exporter is in no better position than under an open account terms, except that he has a trader's accepted bill with him on which he can sue the importer if it is dishonored at maturity.

Despite these risks under collection, the exporter will have to choose this favorable term to the importer in a highly competitive market, or when goods are unsalable ones or are of inferior quality, etc. However, as a measure of self-protection, the exporter may incorporate a store and insurance clause in the collection order and specify a case of need as well. Under a store and insure clause, the exporter knows that the goods will then be protected until an alternative buyer is found. The case of need will be given full authority in the event of default and he will arrange the selling and the settlement on behalf of the exporter.

(2) To the Importer

Although collection is generally in his favor, the importer is exposed to risks as well.

(A) Under D/P

Under D/P, the importer has to make payment prior to the possession of the goods. That is to say, no opportunity is then available to inspect goods before making payment. Whether goods are of the contract description or not will entirely depend on the exporter's credit standing.

(B) Under D/A

Under D/A, even the importer has a chance to check the goods before making payment, according to *Bills of Exchange Act,* however, the importer's credit-worthiness will be harmed if he refuses to make payment against the accepted bill in the event that the imported goods are inferior to the conditions described in the sales contract.

3. **Banks Liabilities under Collection**

According to URC, banks doing collection business will act in good faith and exercise reasonable care. Banks must check that they appear to have received the documents which are specified in the collection order, but they have no obligations to exam the documents any further. However, in practice banks do check the documents for common errors. For example, the remitting bank will make the following checks before it sends the items abroad:

(a) Correct endorsements are made on the draft, on the bill of lading and on the insurance policy.

(b) The bill of lading is made in complete set. If any part is missing, an explanation should be obtained and the collecting bank must be advised accordingly.

(c) Goods should not be dispatched direct to the address of a bank or consigned to a bank without prior agreement on the part of the bank. That means, the consignee of bill of lading cannot be made to the banks without his agreement. Under collection, the bank has no obligations to take delivery of the goods, which remain at the risk and responsibility of the party dispatching the goods.

(d) If the bill of lading is made out to order, it must be endorsed blank by the shipper.

(e) The draft is correctly drawn. The drawee of the draft will always be the importer to indicate that collection is under trader's credit.

(f) Ensure that the amount of the bill agrees with the invoice and collection order if available.

(g) Ensure that shipping marks appear on all the relevant documents.

(h) If the invoice shows an applicable incoterm, check that the documents conform to it,

e. g. with FOB, the bill of lading must be marked "freight collect"; with CIF, the bill of lading should be marked "freight prepaid" and an insurance document should also be presented.

(i) Make sure that the instructions on the collection order are logical and consistent with each other, e. g. D/A must be accompanied by a time draft.

(j) Check the banker's reference book to see if there are any special documentary requirements in the importer's country. Failure to fulfil these requirements could mean that the goods are physically present in the importer's country, but the importer cannot obtain possession. In this case, the exporter has lost physical possession of the goods and will not be paid for them.

(k) Ensure that the customer/exporter signs the collection order.

On the other hand, the escaping clauses will specify that banks will not be responsible for the consequences arising from:

(a) delay and/or loss in transit of any messages, letters or documents unless the bank itself is in fault;

(b) delay, mutilation or other errors arising in the transmission of cables, telegrams or telexes, nor for errors in translation or interpretation of technical terms;

(c) natural disaster;

(d) the act of another bank involved in the collection.

Section Four　Finance under Documentary Collection

Under payment methods, bank financing can be provided in two ways. First is for the bank to make payments/negotiation before and on behalf of the importer so that the exporter can obtain payment beforehand and the importer can defer the time of payment. Second, a bank can lend its credit worthiness to a trader so that he could obtain funds from a discounting house. Under documentary collection, both the importer and the exporter can get financed through these two methods.

1. For the Exporter

(1) Negotiation – Outward Bill Purchased

Collection bills purchased means that the remitting bank, under a general letter of hypothecation as a pledge from the exporter, buys the exporter's bill drawn on the importer and the documents attached at the time when the collection items are sent abroad. It is also called negotiation. The exporter is financed under negotiation because he can obtain funds in advance, prior to the payment made by the importer. Of course, the amount the exporter has obtained would be less than the face amount of the draft, and the differences between them is the discount interest and other bank charges which represent the remitting bank's profits in this operation.

After negotiation, the remitting bank becomes the holder in due course, it can recover the funds when it receives funds from the collecting bank. In the event that the importer dishonors the draft by non-payment, the remitting bank will exercise right of recourse against its prior party, the exporter. When this happens, the credit standing of the exporter is of vital importance and the remitting bank is at a risk in recovering of its funds, though, the letter of hypothecation will minimize the remitting bank's risk in negotiation.

（2）Advance against Collection

An advance against collection means that the remitting bank may lend to its principal a portion of the amount for each bill presented, leaving the balance to be collected through the normal collection procedure. Therefore, an advance against collection can be described as being equivalent to partial negotiation and partial collection.

（3）Accommodation under Collection

Accommodation under collection means that the exporter draws an accommodating bill on the remitting bank against his collection bill. The collection bill will be used as a security so that an accommodating bill can be drawn. Under an accommodating bill, the exporter will obtain payment before he collects the proceeds under the collection bill. In practice, an Acceptance Credit Agreement should usually be concluded between the exporter and the remitting bank beforehand.

The amount under the accommodating bill should be slightly smaller than that of the collecting bill so that the financed amount and bank charges can be covered by that of the collection bill. On the other hand, the tenor of the accommodating bill should be a little longer than that of the collection bill so that there is time to allow the exporter provides funds to the remitting bank with the proceeds he receives from the collecting bill. Thus, the remitting bank can honor the accommodating bill at maturity. The differences between the accommodating bill and the collection bill will be summarized as follows:

Collection bill		Accommodating bill	
Drawer	The exporter	Drawer	The exporter
Drawee	The importer	Drawee	The remitting bank
Payee	The exporter/The remitting bank /The collecting bank	Payee	The exporter
Tenor	Suppose 60 days sight	Tenor	70 days
Amount	Suppose USD16,000	Amount	USD15,000

The procedure of the accommodation will be shown as follows:

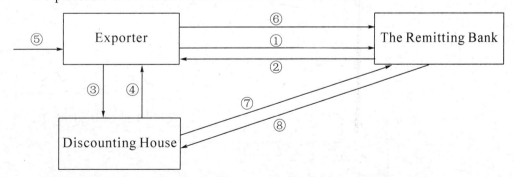

① The exporter draws an accommodating bill on the remitting bank with the tenor slightly longer and the amount slightly smaller than those of the collection bill.

② The remitting bank accepts the bill and returns it to the exporter.

③ Before maturity of the accommodating bill, the exporter discounts the banker's accepted bill in a discount market.

④ The discount house discounts (buys) the accommodating bill and pays the proceeds to the exporter.

⑤ At maturity of the collection bill, the exporter obtains payments against the collection bill.

⑥ Slightly before the maturity of the accommodating bill, the exporter provides funds to the remitting bank.

⑦ At maturity of the accommodating bill, the discount house presents the bill to the remitting bank for payment.

⑧ The remitting bank makes payment to the discount house and the accommodating bill is discharged.

The risk for the remitting bank is that it should make payment to the discount house at maturity no matter the exporter provides the funds to him or not. For this reason, the remitting bank must make careful consideration before arranging the said accommodation.

2. **For the Importer**

(1) D/P after Sight against Trust Receipt (D/P, T/R)

Against T/R with his banker (the collecting bank), the importer can obtain goods before he makes payment. In this way, the importer is financed.

When the collecting bank arranges T/R with the importer, the collecting bank is under the risk that in the event of default by the importer, the collecting bank should make payment to the exporter by himself. The importer's credit standing is of vital importance when the collecting bank makes such an arrangement. However, the exporter can also instruct the banks to arrange D/P T/R to his overseas trade partner. In this case, the risk of non-payment is borne by the exporter and it does not concern the collecting bank.

(2) Accommodation under D/P Sight

The importer can also draw an accommodating bill to get financed. With title documents from abroad as a pledge, the importer can draw such a bill on the collecting bank payable to himself. The funds obtained this way are to be remitted immediately through the collecting bank to the overseas exporter. The importer is financed because he can obtain goods and his own payment is deferred. In practice, usually an Acceptance Credit Agreement should be concluded between the importer and the collecting bank beforehand.

The procedure of the accommodating for the importer is as follows:

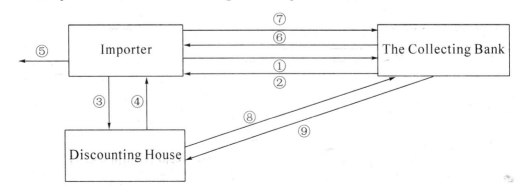

① The importer draws an accommodating bill on the collecting bank with the amount being slightly larger than that of the sales contract. The tenor will depend on how long the importer wishes to be financed.

② The collecting bank accepts the bill and returns it to the importer.

③ The importer discounts the banker's accepted bill in a discount market.

④ The discount house discounts (buys) the accommodating bill and pays the proceeds to the importer.

⑤ The importer remits the proceeds through the collecting bank to the overseas exporter.

⑥ The collecting bank releases title documents to the importer against his payment.

⑦ Slightly before the maturity of the accommodating bill, the importer provides funds to the collecting bank.

⑧ At maturity of the accommodating bill, the discount house presents the bill to the collecting bank for payment.

⑨ The collecting bank makes payment to the discount house and the accommodating bill is discharged.

Similar to the risk borne by the remitting bank under accommodation, the collecting bank should make payment to the discount house at maturity no matter the importer pays or not. Although the collecting bank has title documents as a security and could recover the funds by selling the goods in the event of default by the importer, the purpose of accommodation is to provide finance rather than to deal with the physical goods. For this reason, the collecting bank must make careful consideration before arranging the said accommodation.

Chapter Eight　Payment Methods(Ⅲ)
－ International Factoring

Section One　Introduction

1. Definition

Factoring refers to the purchase of claim by a financial institution (the factor) from a business entity (its client, the exporter) who has sold goods or provided services abroad to his trade debtor (the client's customer, namely the importer) whereby the factor purchases his client's (the exporter's) account receivables, normally without recourse, controls the credit extended to importer and administers his client's bookkeeping and collections. In simple words, factoring refers to the purchase of claim by a financial institution from the exporter in order to ensure payment from the importer. The factor will provide a package of financial services including export trade finance, maintenance of the exporter's sales ledger, collection of receivables and evaluation of the importer's credit standing.

The fierce competition has made the world market mostly the buyer's market. In order to be competitive, as an alternative to quality improvement and price reduction, the exporter may look for favorable payment methods to attract business. The favorable payment methods are open account (O/A) under remittance and documents against acceptance (D/A) under collection. However, because both O/A and D/A are on trader's credit, it is obvious that these two methods will place the exporter under a great risk of non-payment. As a result, the exporter will worry about the safety of payments under these methods. This disadvantage of O/A and D/ A can be overcome by factoring in which a package of services will be provided by a financial institution. Thus, the trader's credit of O/A and D/A has been transformed to banker's credit of factoring in the sense that the payment undertaking will come from a bank. As a result, the exporter can offer O/A or D/A to the importer so as to maintain his competitiveness, on the other hand, he is freed from the worry of non-payment.

2. Parties to International Factoring

There are four parties in international factoring. They are:

(1) The Exporter

The exporter is the factor's client who invoices on the importer for the supply of goods or the provision of services and whose accounts of receivables is factored by the factor. In simple words, the exporter will invoice the importer and sell the invoice to the factor. The invoice represents the exporter's account receivables or, in other words, his claim on the importer.

(2) The Importer

The importer is liable for making payment for the account receivables arising from his purchase of goods or services.

(3) The Export Factor

The export factor will factor (buy) the exporter's account receivables under an agreement to that effect. The export factor is normally the exporter's bank.

(4) The Import Factor

The import factor agrees to collect the account receivables invoiced by the exporter which is consigned to him from the export factor. He is bound to pay such accounts receivable assigned to him for which he has assumed the credit risk.

3. **Services Offered by the Factors**

The services in the service package offered by the factors are closely related to one another. They are to minimize the risks on the part of the factors in the process.

(1) Evaluation of the Importer's Credit Standing

The factor should evaluate the importer's credit standing and conclude a Preliminary Credit Assessment. Based on it, the factors can set a Credit Approval for a certain period of time for each order prior to its shipment. Credit Approval means the amount for each transaction should be kept within the approved credit line and any such approved amount will be called Approved Account Receivables by which the factor will assume the responsibility of payment. Any transaction beyond the Credit Approval will become unapproved receivables and the risk of bad debts will be borne by the exporter himself. This method can protect the factors from the risk of the importer's non-payment.

(2) Export Trade Finance

It is up to the exporter whether or not to apply for trade finance from the export factor. If the exporter chooses to do so and if a transaction is within the credit approval, the export factor may grant finance to the exporter prior to the maturity of the invoice by buying without recourse the latter's account receivables. The payment is advanced and the exporter's turnover is speeded up. When the account receivables are assigned to the factor, the ownership to the goods will also be transferred to him.

(3) Maintenance of Sales Ledger

Once the invoice is sent to a factor, he will set up corresponding sales ledger in his computer record system if the exporter is a new customer, or he will update the sales ledger for his old clients. Professional services such as book keeping, calculation and making statements will be carried out by the factor.

(4) Collection of Receivables

At maturity of the invoice, the import factor will collect payment from the importer. The proceeds will be credited to the exporter if they have not been advanced to the exporter. In the event that the importer fails to make payment on due date and if the payment is not advanced, the import factor will make payments to the exporter, plus doubled interest calculated from the due date to the date of the actual payment.

According to Article 1 Sub – Article 2, Section 6 of *Convention on International Factoring*, factors must perform at least two of the above functions.

4. Factors Chain International (FCI)

FCI is the largest organization of factors in the world with over a 100 factors from 40 different countries. China has become one of its member countries in 1993. FCI has completed the *Convention on International Factoring* (CIF), a set of rules and regulations which should be followed and observed in the conclusion of the Export Factoring Agreement between the exporter and the export factor and the Correspondent Contract between the export factor and import factor.

Section Two　Types and Procedures of Factoring

1. Types of International Factoring

International factoring takes two forms: single factor system and two-factor system.

(1) Single Factor System

Under a single factor system, the exporter's bank is not a factor but only an intermediary. No factoring agreement is made between the exporter and the exporter's bank. There are only three parties to a single factor system, namely, the exporter, the importer and the import factor.

Being an intermediary, the exporter's bank will only assist the import factor in the process of forwarding documents and transferring funds. As the factoring agreement is made between the exporter and the import factor, a single factoring system has the following disadvantages:

(A) There will be communication problems between the exporter and the import factor because they are located in two different countries.

(B) The exporter's bank acts only as an intermediary and he assumes no responsibility and liability in the factoring operation.

(C) The exporter can not be financed under a single factor system as export trade finance is provided by the exporter's bank to the exporter.

(D) Without the involvement of the exporter's bank, it will be difficult for the import factor to make a complete assessment of the exporter. As a result, the exporter's performance will not be guaranteed.

(2) Two-factor System

Under a two-factor system, an export factoring agreement will be established between the exporter and the export factor and a correspondent contract will be signed between the export factor and the import factor. Therefore, there are four parties to a two-factor system, namely the exporter, the export factor, the importer and the import factor. The major advantages of this system are:

(A) There will be no communication problems when the exporter can contact a foreign bank through his own bank.

(B) Upon request, the export factor can provide finance to the exporter as well as other financial services.

(C) The correspondent contract between the export factor and the import factor will be subject to the *International Factoring Customs* (IFC) by which the rights and obligations of the two factors are clearly stated. The IFC will ensure a smooth operation and through which any dispute can be settled more easily.

(D) Under a two-factor system, the exporter will be better protected because the importer's overdue invoices will also be chased by the export factor.

A two-factor system can be further classified into maturity factoring and discount factoring.

(A) Maturity factoring.

Maturity factoring means that the exporter will not draw funds till the maturity date of the account receivables. It is an non-financed factoring and payment will be collected on the following two bases:

＊ Collect funds basis

Proceeds are to be remitted on a pay-as-paid basis. That is to say, the factor will collect payment before he pays the exporter.

＊ Average due-date basis

Funds are to be remitted to the client on a fixed date based upon previous collection experience with each account. This method of settlement is adjusted regularly on the basis of performance.

(B) Financed factoring.

Financed factoring is also referred to as discount factoring. It means that the exporter will apply for trade finance and the export factor will provide funds to him prior to the maturity date of the account receivables.

2. Export Factoring Agreement

The export factoring agreement is concluded between the exporter and the export factor. It is a basic document and serves as a guideline in a factoring operation between the exporter and the export factor. It mainly includes: general rules; a detailed information about the two parties; the application range; the application for a credit approval; notification and coming into effect; the credit line reduced or cancelled; the documents to be submitted; the transfer of receivables; statements of the accounts; payment; finance; disputes settlement; factoring charges; the period of validity of the agreement and the modification of the agreement, etc. After signed by the two parties concerned, the agreement will take effect.

3. Application for a Credit Approval

After export factoring agreement is concluded and before each transaction is made between the exporter and the importer, the exporter should fill in an application for credit approval and submit it to factors so that they can carry out an assessment on the credit standing of the importer and determine a credit line for the transaction. The exporter should furnish in the application the detailed information of both the exporter and the importer, with the major items including the names, addresses, their bankers and account numbers, payment methods as well as the past history of sales volumes and payment performances, etc. Any transaction within the credit line will be a covered transaction and will have a payment undertaking from the factors.

4. Notification and Transfer of Receivables

A notification and transfer of receivables should be filled in and signed by the exporter when the account receivables is transferred to the export factor. The following wordings should also be clearly indicated in the notification:

"Pursuant to the agreement between us, we hereby notify you of transactions entered into by us with our debtors as represented by the attached copies of invoice. We hereby also transfer to you all right, title and interest in and to all the debts as specified on the copy attached."

5. Procedure of Two-factors System

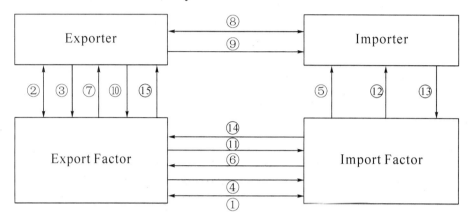

① A correspondent agreement is concluded between the export factor and the import factor.

② An Export Factoring Agreement is established between the exporter and the export factor.

③ Exporter applies for a credit approval.

④ Export factor transmits the application for a credit approval.

⑤ Import factor appraises importer's credit standing.

⑥ Advise export factor of import factor's approval of credit line.

⑦ Advise exporter of the import factor's approval of credit line.

⑧ Sales contract is established between the exporter and the importer within the approved credit line and with the payment terms as either O/A or D/A.

⑨ Exporter delivers goods for shipment.

⑩ The exporter fills in and signs the "Notification and Transfer of Receivables" and submits it to the export factor. Both the original and/or the duplicated copies of the invoice and other shipping documents may be submitted together with the notification to the export factor. The exporter may also apply for finance at this stage.

⑪ Invoices and other shipping documents are transmitted by the export factor to the import factor.

⑫ Deliver documents to the importer and ask for payment.

⑬ At maturity, the importer effects payment to the import factor.

⑭ Proceeds are remitted by the import factor to the export factor.

⑮ Proceeds are credited by the export factor to the exporter's account. If the exporter has obtained finance by partial advance, discount charges should be deducted before the balance is credited to the exporter's account.

Section Three   Characteristics of International Factoring

1. Advantages of International Factoring

(A) Full payment is secured within the approved credit line. If an exporter enters into a relationship with a factor, the latter will conduct preliminary credit assessment on the importer and determines a credit line for the exporter. The factor will undertake to buy without recourse the former's claims within this limit. That is to say, the exporter has the factor's undertaking to make payment.

(B) Proceeds will be obtained within maturity. Provided that the exporter makes shipment on time, the factor will assume the responsibility for managing and controlling the exporter's sales ledger and press the importer for any payment due.

(C) Finance to the exporter is available under a two-factor system. The exporter may get financed at the time when he submits his invoices and other documents to the export factor. As a result, his turnover will be speeded up or his financial difficulties can be tied over.

(D) The exporter will be free from the risks under O/A and D/A. O/A and D/A are based on trader's credit but with the financial institutions' involvement as factors, trader's credit is transformed to banker's credit. Factoring enables the exporter to sell to his overseas importer on O/A and D/A terms, competitive against local suppliers while fully protected against bad debt losses.

(E) The exporter saves the cost of maintaining his won administrative department because the factor will take full administrative control of the exporter's sales ledger. The exporter can get assistance from the factors through a service package offered by the latter, which ranges from an assessment of the creditworthiness of the overseas buyers to credit protection and collection services.

2. Comparison of Factoring and Other Payment Methods

(1) Compared with Letter of Credit (L/C)

The procedure under L/C is more complicated than that under factoring and L/C is a more expensive payment method. When under L/C, the importer has to bear L/C issuing charges and a deposit margin is required to be placed with the issuing bank. The deposit margin equals to a certain percentage of L/C amount and this means that part of his capital is tied up. Additional charges will occur when the exporter does not accept some of the terms and conditions under a given L/C. Amendment of L/C is also time consuming. Whereas under factoring, there is no issuing charges for the importer and he dose not need to place a deposit margin into the bank. On the other hand, when Under L/C, exporter will obtain payments only after the documents are in strict compliance with the L/C stipulations as well as with each other. Whereas under factoring, if the exporter makes the shipment on time, he will be sure to be paid and there is no requirement that the documents he submits have been found in strict compliance with the credit.

(2) Compared with O/A and D/A

The additional advantages under factoring can be understood from payment chasing. Under

D/A and O/A, the exporter himself should chase the payment. Being located in a different country, the exporter can only chase payment through letters, faxes or telexes which are less effective. As a result, O/A and D/A may be done with the result that large amounts of debts will become overdue and some of them will even become bad debts. This will greatly affect the exporter's turn over and future performances. Whereas under factoring, payment chase from the factors can be more convenient, professional and effective on the following grounds: the import factor resides in the same country as that of the importer. As a financial institution, it has a thorough understanding of importer as well as the laws and regulations of the said country. In addition, there would be no language barriers between the import factor and the importer. All these make factoring an ideal guarantee to O/A and D/A.

Chapter Nine   Payment Methods（IV）
- Letter of Credit

Section One   Introduction

Payment in advance, open account, collection and letter of credit are the four most commonly used methods of payment in international settlement. Based on our previous discussion we should know that payment in advance is favorable to the exporter while placing the importer at the greatest risk of non-delivery. In contrast, open account will be favorable to the importer while placing the exporter at the greatest risk of non-payment. Collection, as a compromise between payment in advance and open account, provides a certain degree of protection for both the exporter and the importer. But collection is also based on trader's credit in the sense that there is no payment undertaking from banks. Still, generally speaking, collection is more in favor of the importer because the exporter should always make the shipment first, without any promise that the payment will be forthcoming. In order to obtain a better protection from banks, letter of credit is evolved to be a payment method based on banker's credit.

1. Definition

The International Chamber of Commerce publication No. 415 has defined letter of credit as follows: A letter of credit is a written undertaking issued by a bank (the issuing bank) given to the seller (the beneficiary) at the request and in accordance with the instructions of the buyer (the applicant) to effect payment at sight or at a determinable future time up to a stated sum of money and against stipulated documents which are complied with the terms and conditions of the credit.

In simple terms, a letter of credit is a conditional undertaking of payment by a bank. Here, the word "conditional" means that the beneficiary should submit stipulated documents within a designated time limit and against any stipulated terms and conditions. The phrase "effect payment" means that the payment under L/C can be effected by payment, acceptance and negotiation.

Letter of credit can be issued by airmail or by cable/telex/SWIFT. If it is issued by an airmail, it ought to be authenticated by signatures and by test key or SAK if it is issued by cable/telex/SWIFT.

2. Immediate Parties to a Documentary Credit

There are four immediate parties to a documentary credit:
(1) Applicant or Opener

The applicant of a L/C is always the importer. When a sales contract stipulates that the settlement is under L/C, the importer will fill in and sign a L/C application form by which he is making a request to his bank to issue a letter of credit in favor of the exporter. It is his duty and responsibility to ensure that the credit will be issued in strict compliance with the sales contract. Because once issued, L/C will become a separate document independent of the sales contract despite the fact that the former is issued based on the latter. The applicant can also be called the consignee, account party or the principal.

(2) Beneficiary

The beneficiary is always the exporter. He is so called because the credit is issued in his favor. He should check the terms and conditions in the credit against the sales contract. Once the exporter accepts the credit, he should arrange production and shipment accordingly and make sure that the documents he supplies would be in strict compliance with the L/C stipulations. The beneficiary is also called the shipper because he will arrange the delivery of goods and the drawer because he will draw a draft on a bank.

(3) The Issuing Bank

The issuing bank is one which issues a letter of credit at the request of an applicant to the beneficiary. It is usually the importer's bank. When a bank issues a L/C, it must do it with the clear understanding that it assumes the full responsibility of payment undertaking upon itself. That means, in the event of default on the part of the importer, the issuing bank itself will make payments to the exporter. For this reason, L/C is a payment method based on banker's credit. The issuing bank is supposed to be a first-class bank.

(4) The Advising Bank and the Transmitting Bank

The advising bank is the correspondent bank of the issuing bank or its head office/ branch or subsidiary located in the exporter's country. It is to advise the credit to the beneficiary. The transmitting bank plays the same role as that of the advising bank. If the addressee of the credit is an overseas bank, this bank will be called an advising bank who can advise the credit in its own form. On the other hand, if the addressee of the credit is the beneficiary, then this bank will be called a transmitting bank who will transmit the original L/C to the exporter.

No matter which is the way to advise the credit, neither the advising bank nor the transmitting bank assumes any payment undertaking upon itself. However, both of these two banks should take reasonable care to check the apparent authenticity of the credit before it advises.

However, it is of vital importance for the exporter to have an inward L/C advised through a local bank before the exporter relies or acts on the "documentary credit". As in practice, unfortunately, fraudulent documentary credits issued by a foreign fictitious non-existing "bank" are a fact in real life situations. Therefore, it is necessary that the authenticity of both the issuing bank and the credit itself are checked by a local bank (the advising or the transmitting bank).

3. The Three Contractual Arrangements under L/C

The three contractual arrangements under a L/C operation refer to the sales contract between the exporter and the importer, the L/C application between the importer and the issuing bank and letter of credit between the issuing bank and the exporter. They are related to one another in the sense that L/C is issued based on the application which in turn is on the sales contract. However, they should be dealt with and guided by the "Independence and Abstraction Principle" from the legal point of view.

The principle means that each arrangement has its binding power only on the two parties concerned. Three points will help to understand its implications:

(A) Letter of credit is separate from sales contract. Although credit is established according to the L/C application form which is also based on the sales contract, the credit is separate from the sales contract as is the L/C application independent from the sales contract. That is to say, banks in the L/C operation will be bound by the credit only.

(B) Documents are separate from the physical goods. Banks would not be bound by the sales contract. As a result, in L/C operation, banks deal with the required documents stipulated in the L/C only and do not concern whether the goods are of the right quality and quantity described in the sales contract.

(C) When the terms and conditions are complied with by the exporter, the issuing bank should fulfil its independent payment undertaking under the credit and it does not concern whether or not the actual sales contract has been performed by the exporter.

4. **Other Parties to the L/C**

In order to facilitate the operation of the documentary credit, other banks may also be involved in the process. These banks include the confirming bank and nominated banks such as the negotiating bank, the paying bank, the accepting bank and the reimbursing bank. These banks are referred to as other parties to the L/C.

(1) The Confirming Bank

When an advising bank or a transmitting bank has been authorized or requested by the issuing bank to add its own confirmation and it is prepared to do so, it will state so on its advice to the beneficiary and then become a confirming bank. Such a confirmation constitutes its commitment to pay or to accept without recourse to the beneficiary provided all the documents stipulated in the documentary credit are presented in order and that the terms and conditions of the documentary credit are complied with.

When the L/C is confirmed, the beneficiary has two independent payment undertakings against one credit, one from the issuing bank and the other from the confirming bank. The payment by the confirming bank is effected without recourse against the exporter.

(2) The Negotiating Bank

The negotiating bank will negotiate (buy) the sight drafts and /or documents presented by the exporter. The advising bank will normally become the negotiating bank. In the case when a credit is available by negotiation, a negotiating bank will be needed. A bank may become a negotiating bank either as a result of being specially nominated in the credit or as a result of simply being any bank when the credit is a freely negotiable credit.

After negotiation, the negotiating bank becomes the holder in due course. He has the right to claim payment from the drawee and will obtain the right of recourse against the exporter in the event of dishonor by non - payment.

(3) The Paying Bank and the Accepting Bank

In the case of a credit available by payment at sight, the draft should be a sight draft and a paying bank should be nominated by the issuing bank. The paying bank should be the drawee bank of the sight draft and must effect payment to the exporter without recourse provided all the documents stipulated in the documentary credit are presented in order and that the terms and conditions of the documentary credit are complied with. The advising bank will normally become the paying bank.

In the case of a credit available by acceptance, the draft should be a time draft and a bank should be nominated by the issuing bank to be the drawee bank which accepts the time draft. The accepting bank must then effect payment to the exporter without recourse at maturity provided all the documents stipulated in the documentary credit are presented in order and that the terms and conditions of the documentary credit are complied with. The advising bank will normally become the accepting bank.

(4) Reimbursing Bank

Reimbursing bank is nominated by the issuing bank to honor the claim from the negotiating bank, the paying bank or the accepting bank on behalf of the issuing bank. When claiming a reimbursement, the negotiating bank, paying bank or the accepting bank who claims reimbursement after making payments to the exporter becomes the claiming bank. The reimbursing bank is to facilitate the funds transfer and thus is always located either in the exporter's country or in a clearing center. The reimbursing bank is usually the issuing bank's head office/branch or its correspondent bank located in that country.

When nominating a reimbursement bank in the credit, the issuing bank should also give proper instructions to it. When payment is effected, the claiming bank will forward the documents to the issuing bank while claiming reimbursement from the reimbursing bank.

The reimbursement made by the reimbursing bank is not a final payment. That is to say, the issuing bank can reclaim the funds from the claiming bank, once the issuing bank finds any discrepancies between the documents and the credit. In other words, it means that when payment is effected by the claiming bank, it should check the compliance of the documents.

It should be noted that the different names of the banks only indicate the different roles the banks play in a L/C operation. The distinction is not a clear-cut and one bank can simultaneously assume different roles in a single process.

5. Drafts under L/C

It should make a clear distinction between the draft under collection and that under L/C. Drafts under collection is based on trader's credit thus it is drawn on a trader, whereas drafts under L/C should be drawn on a bank from which the payment undertaking is given. However, as both the collection and L/C are reverse remittance, drafts under both methods should be drawn by the exporter. The following comparison will make the matter clear:

Draft under Collection		Draft Under L/C	
Drawer	Exporter	Drawer	Exporter
Drawee	Importer	Drawee	Drawee Bank
Payee	Exporter / Remitting Bank / Collecting Bank	Payee	Exporter / Exporter's Banker

6. **UCP** 500

The *Uniform Customs and Practices for Documentary Credit*, ICC publication No. 500 is the governing rule concerning documentary credit. The bank's obligation is conditioned on total compliance with its terms and conditions and subject to UCP 500. Any issued L/C should indicate clearly that the said L/C is "subject to the *Uniform Customs and Practice for Documentary Credits* (1993 revision, International Chamber of Commerce, Paris, France, Publication No. 500)."

Section Two   The Contents and Procedure of L/C

1. The Contents of a L/C

Though L/C has different types, their contents are in the main the same. The International Chamber of Commerce has drafted "the Guidance Notes and Standard Forms for Banks, Noted Irrevocable Documentary Credit Form (Advice for the beneficiary and for the advising bank)". Based on this, we will illustrate the major items under L/C:

(1) Type of the Credit

The standard documentary form has been drafted for the issuance of an irrevocable documentary credit. If the form is used for the issuance of a revocable credit, the word: "irrevocable" should be replaced by the word "revocable".

(2) Credit Number

The credit number is the running number of the credit opened by the issuing bank. This number is to be indicated and it will tie up all the relevant documents.

(3) Place and Date of Issue

The place of issue is where the issuing bank is located. The date of issue is the date when the L/C is issued by the issuing bank.

(4) Date and Place of Expiry

All credits must stipulate a definite date, not a period, as an expiry date for presentation of documents for payment, acceptance or negotiation.

The place where the documents have to be presented on or before such an expiry date is the place of expiry. It will usually be inserted as a city or a country so that "date and place of expiry" will read as:

200X December 17 at London

The ISO sequence is Year, Month, Day. When indicating the time, it is recommended to express the name of the month in order to avoid confusion.

The place of expiry should be chosen in keeping with the location of the issuing bank, the nominated bank, or a third bank. The third bank is usually a clearing bank in a major currency clearing center in the world.

(5) Name and Address of the Applicant

(6) Name and Address of the Beneficiary

(7) Advising Bank

Here is to be inserted the name and address of the bank which is to advise the credit.

"Ref. No. " is for the use of the advising bank and nothing should be inserted by the issuing bank. If the advising bank is also to be the nominated bank, its name and place will also to be inserted under the heading "credit available with nominated bank" in item (9).

(8) Amount of the Credit and Its Currency

The amount should be expressed both in figures and in words. Any changes should be made authorized by a stamp of the authorized person. If the amount is preceded by "about", "approximately" or "circa", the credit will allow 10% tolerance.

The currency should be indicated in the ISO Currency Code, eg. USD, GBP, etc. If there is no such indication, it is the currency of the country where the issuing bank is located.

(9) Credit Available with Nominated Bank

A credit will nominate a bank to effect payment to the beneficiary. A credit will also stipulate the way the credit amount is made available to the beneficiary by that nominated bank.

Three kinds of bank can be nominated:

(A) Credit available with the issuing bank.

This means that the issuing bank nominates itself to effect payment upon receipt of documents together with a draft "drawn on us". Here the word "us" refers to the issuing bank itself. In other words, this means that the credit will be expired at the counter of the issuing bank and the documents should be presented to the issuing bank within the validity of the credit. No other bank can effect payment and it can only act as an intermediary bank to remit or forward the documents to the issuing bank but not to effect payment in the process.

This type of credit is unfavorable to the beneficiary because he will not receive payment until the issuing bank pays and he will be responsible for the documents to reach the issuing bank within the validity of the credit. Any delay or loss in the transit of documents may hinder the exporter in his obtaining of payments.

(B) Credit available with the Exporter's bank.

The issuing bank may nominate the Exporter's bank to be the paying bank, accepting bank or negotiating bank. When Exporter's bank becomes the nominated bank, it will effect payment upon receipt of documents together with a draft either "drawn on the exporter's bank when it is nominated as the paying or accepting bank or a draft "drawn on the issuing bank" when the exporter's bank is nominated as the negotiating bank. As the nominated bank is the exporter's bank, so the credit is to be expired at the exporter's country. This type of credit is favorable to the exporter as there is no need for him to forward the documents to a foreign bank.

(C) Credit available with a third bank.

This third bank is normally a clearing bank in a major currency clearing center in the world. When credit is available this way, documents must be presented to this clearing bank within the validity of credit and it is the beneficiary who is responsible for any delay in presentation.

There are four ways to effect payment under L/C:

(A) Credit available by sight payment.

Under this condition, the payment should be effected against a sight draft. Therefore, the small box preceding "and Beneficiary's draft (s)" should be cross-marked and the blank following "drawn on" should be inserted with the name of either the issuing bank or the paying bank accordingly. Sometimes, However, no draft is required under sight payment.

(B) Credit available by deferred payment.

Under this condition, payment should be effected on a specific future date but no draft is required. Therefore, the small box preceding "and Beneficiary's draft (s) " should be left blank and the blank following "drawn on" should also be left blank.

(C) Credit available by acceptance.

Under this condition, payment should be effected by acceptance and payment at maturity against a time draft on the accepting bank. Therefore, the small box preceding "and Beneficiary's draft (s) " should be cross-marked and the blank following "drawn on" should be inserted with the name of either the issuing bank or the accepting bank accordingly.

(D) Credit available by negotiation.

Under this condition, payment should be effected by negotiation against a sight draft on the issuing bank. Therefore, the small box preceding "and Beneficiary's draft (s) " should be cross-marked and the blank following "drawn on" should be inserted with the name of the issuing bank, but not the negotiating bank.

In summary, the availability of a credit should take into consideration both the bank and the method of effecting payment. That is to say, these small boxes should be marked accordingly so that they will make a logical combination.

(10) Partial Shipment

Although partial shipment is allowed by UCP 500, it is necessary to indicate clearly in the credit and cross-mark the box "allowed" or "not allowed" according to each individual shipment under a given L/C.

(11) Transhipment

Although transhipment is allowed by UCP 500, it is necessary to indicate clearly in the credit and cross-mark the box "allowed" or "not allowed" according to each individual shipment under a given L/C.

(12) Insurance Covered by the Buyer

This box should only be cross-marked when the credit does not require the presentation of an insurance document. For example, when the incoterm is either FOB or C&F, etc, or when the applicant has indicated that he has insured or will insure the goods, this box will be cross-marked.

(13) Port of Shipment and Port of Discharge

After the word "from", the port of shipment should be inserted. After the phrase "for transportation to" , the port of discharge/destination should be indicated. Both ports should avoid abbreviations to express country's name like UK or PRC and avoid vague expressions, such as Main Ports, Middle East Ports to express the port's name.

The latest date for shipment is also to be indicated by inserting the period of shipment after the phrase "not later than". Date term is to be understood or constructed as follows:

(A) "To", "until", "from" will be understood to include the date mentioned.

(B) The word "after" will be understood to exclude the date mentioned.

(C) The terms "first half", "second half" of a month should be constructed as the 1st to the 15th and the 16th to the last day of the month respectively.

(D) The term "beginning", "middle" or "end" of a month should be understood respectively as the 1st to the 10th, the 11th to the 20th, and the 21st to the last day of such month.

(14) Description of Goods

Description of goods in the credit should be made in a general term because a detailed description will be provided in the invoice. In practice, the normal way is to make the description as "as per invoice No. xx" and be placed under the word "covering".

(15) ~ (20) Stipulate Documents

Documents here refer to the commercial documents and they should be logically chosen to be consistent with other L/C stipulations and are normally listed in the following order:

Commercial Invoice

Transport Documents

Insurance Documents

Certificate of Origin

Certificate of Inspection

Packing List / Weight List

The number of copies, either in original form or in duplicated form should also be clearly indicated. In practice, the name of the maker, the order and other detailed stipulations should also be made clear, such as in the case of a Certificate of Inspection or Bills of Lading.

(21) Presentation Period

Every credit will call for documents to be presented at a stipulated time period after the date of shipment but within the validity of the credit. In practice, this stipulated time period can be 14 or 21 days after the date of shipment.

Normally, the credit issuing date, the last date for shipment and the expiry date should be made distant enough so that there is enough time to allow the exporter to make production, shipment and presentation. On the other hand, when determining the last date for presentation, it should take both the last date for shipment, and the expiry date and the presentation period into consideration. When the stipulated presentation period falls within the expiry date, then the last day of the said presentation period should be the last date for document presentment. However, when the former falls beyond the expiry date, then the expiry date should be the last date for presentment. For example:

L/C issuing date	Jan. 1, 2002,
The last date for shipment	May 10, 2002,
L/C expiry date	May 30, 2002,
Presentation period	Documents to be presented within 14 days after the date of shipment but within the validity of the credit

If the B/L date is made on May 10, 2002, the last date for presentment should be on May 24, 2002 instead of May 30. If the last date for shipment is extended to May 20, then the last date for presentment should be on May 30, 2002 instead of June 3, 2002. In simple words, the last date for presentment should fall on the earlier date.

(22) Instructions to the Advising Bank

The issuing bank may instruct the advising bank of the credit in the following three ways:

"Without adding your confirmation". It means that the advising bank simply advises the credit without adding his own confirmation to the credit. In this way, the advising bank takes no payment undertaking upon itself.

"With adding your confirmation". It means that the advising bank is authorized to be the confirming bank when advising the credit and assumes an independent payment undertaking upon itself once it chooses to be the confirming bank. However, the advising bank may also choose not to be the confirming bank.

"Adding your confirmation if requested by the beneficiary". It means that the advising bank advises the credit without its confirmation. But if the beneficiary subsequently requests the credit to be confirmed, then the nominated bank is authorized to add its confirmation and becomes a confirming bank of the credit.

(23) Bank to Bank Instructions

The issuing bank is to indicate to the nominated bank as the paying, accepting or negotiating bank the method of reimbursement as to where, how and when they will obtain funds. The reimbursement can be made by the issuing bank or by another bank acting as the reimbursing bank. The reimbursement instructions will be read as follows:

Debit our account on your books, or

Credit your account on our books, or

Claim reimbursement from (the name of the reimbursing bank)

(24) Number of Pages

The issuing bank should always indicate in how many pages the credit is issued.

(25) The Signature of the Issuing Bank

The signature of the issuing bank is required to validate the advice both for the beneficiary and for the advising bank. The sample advice will be shown as follows:

GUIDANCE NOTES AND STANDARD FORMS FOR BANKS

Noted Irrevocable Documentary Credit Form (Advice for the Beneficiary)

Advice for the Beneficiary

Name of Issuing Bank:	**Irrevocable Documentary Credit** ① Number ②
Place and Date of Issue: ③	**Expiry Date and Place for Presentation of Documents**
Applicant: ⑤	Expiry Date Place for Presentation ④
	Beneficiary: ⑥
Advising Bank:　　　　Reference No. ⑦	**Amount:** ⑧

Partial shipments ☐ allowed ☐ not allowed ⑩	**Credit available with Nominated Bank:**
Transhipment ☐ allowed ☐ not allowed ⑪	☐ by payment at sight ☐ by deferred payment at ☐ by acceptance of drafts at ☐ by negotiation ⑨
☐ Insurance covered by buyers ⑫	
Shipment as defined in UCP 500 Article 46 From: For transportation to Not later than: ⑬	Against the documents detailed herein: ☐ and Beneficiary's draft(s) drawn on.

Covering ⑭

⑮-⑳

Documents to be presented within ☐ days after the date of shipment but within the validity of the Credit. ㉑

We hereby issue the irrevocable Documentary Credit in your favour. It is subject to the Uniform Customs and Practice for Documentary Credits (1993 Revision, International Chamber of Commerce, Paris, France, Publication No. 500) and engages us in accordance with the terms thereof. The number and the date of the Credit and the name of our bank must be quoted on all drafts required. If the Credit is available by negotiation, each presentation must be noted on the reverse side of this advice by the bank where the Credit is available.

㉔ This document consists of ☐ signed page(s).

㉕ Name and signature of the Issuing Bank

GUIDANCE NOTES AND STANDARD FORMS FOR BANKS

Noted Irrevocable Documentary Credit Form (Advice for the Advising Bank)

Applicant:	**Irrevocable Documentary Credit**　　Number
Place and Date of Issue: **Applicant:**	**Expiry Date and Place for Presentation of Documents** Expiry Date Place for Presentation **Beneficiary:**
Advising Bank:　　　　Reference No	**Amount:**
Partial shipments ☐ allowed ☐ not allowed Transhipment ☐ allowed ☐ not allowed ☐ Insurance covered by buyers **Shipment as defined in UCP 500 Article 46** From: For transportation to: Not later than:	**Credit available with** ☐ by payment at sight ☐ by deferred payment at: ☐ by acceptance of drafts at: ☐ by negotiation Against the documents detailed herein: ☐ and Beneficiary's draft(s) drawn on:

Advice for the Advising Bank

Documents to be presented within ☐ days after the date of shipment but within the validity of the Credit.

We have issued the Irrevocable Documentary Credit as detailed above. It is subject to the Uniform Customs and Practice for Documentary Credits(1993 Revision, International Chamber of Commerce. Paris, France, Publication No. 500). We request you to advise the Beneficiary.

☐ without adding your confirmation ☐ adding your confirmation ☐ adding your confirmation, if requested by the Beneficiary ㉒

Bank-to-Bank Instructions ㉓

This document consists of ☐ signed page(s)

Name and signature of the issuing Bank

2. Documentary Credit Application

Documentary credit application is to be filled in and signed by the applicant / the importer. It is a contract between the applicant and the issuing bank. With the knowledge of the contents of the credit, it is easier to understand the items in the application.

① The full name and address of the beneficiary.

② The amount of the documentary credit and its ISO currency code.

③ The type of documentary credit, whether revocable or irrevocable, or irrevocable with the added information whether the nominated bank is authorized to add its confirmation to the credit.

④ The credit availability.

⑤ The drawee and the tenor of the draft.

⑥ A general description of the goods, indicating its price term, e. g. CIF, CFR, FOB or other incoterms.

⑦ Details of the documents required.

⑧ The place where the goods are to be dispatched, taken in charge, or loaded on board, as the case may be, and the place of final destination, or the port of discharge.

⑨ Whether the freight is to be prepaid or to be collected. This item should be made consistent with the given incoterm.

⑩ Whether transhipment is allowed or not.

⑪ Whether partial shipment is prohibited or not.

⑫ The latest date for shipment. This is not applicable when the credit is to cover the payment of services.

⑬ The presentment period.

⑭ The date and place of expiry of the documentary credit.

⑮ Whether the documentary credit is to be a transferable one.

⑯ How the documentary credit is to be advised, i. e. by mail or by tele-transmission. In practice, the bank may also hold the credit for the beneficiary's own collection if they are located in the same country.

The sample documentary credit application form will be shown below:

Irrevocable Documentary Credit Application

③ **Irrevocable Documentary Credit Application**

Applicant:	**Issuing Bank:**

Date of Application:

☐ Issue by (air) mail ☐ with brief advice by teletransmission (see UCP 500 Article 11) ⑯

☐ Issue by teletransmission (see UCP 500 Article 11)

☐ Transferable Credit-as per UCP 500 Article 48 ⑮

Expiry Date and Place for Presentation of Documents ⑭
Expiry Date
Place for Presentation

Beneficiary: ①

Confirmation of the Credit: ③

☐ not requested ☐ requested ☐ authorised if requested by Beneficiary

Amount in figures and words (Please use ISO Currency Codes) ②

Partial shipments ☐ allowed ☐ not allowed ⑪

Transhipments ☐ allowed ☐ not allowed ⑩
Please refer to UCP 500 transport Articles for exceptions to this condition

☐ Insurance will be covered by us

Credit available with Nominated Bank:

☐ by payment at sight
☐ by deferred payment at ④
☐ by acceptance of drafts at
☐ by negotiation

Shipment as defined in UCP 500 Article 46
From

For transportation to ⑧

Not later than ⑫

Against the documents detailed herein:

☐ and Beneficiary's draft(s) drawn on ⑤

Goods (Brief description without excessive details - See UCP 500 Article 5): ⑥

Terms:
☐ FAS ☐ CIF ⑥
☐ FOB ☐ Other terms
☐ CFR ☐ as per INCOTERMS

Commercial invoice ☐ signed original and ☐ copies

Transport Document:
☐ Multimodal Transport Document; covering at least two different modes of transport ⑦
☐ Marine/Ocean Bill of Lading covering a port-to-port shipment
☐ Non-Negotiable Sea Waybill covering a port-to-port shipment
☐ Air Waybill original for the consignor
☐ Other transport document
☐ to the order of
☐ endorsed in blank
☐ marked freight ☐ prepaid ☐ payable at destination ⑨
☐ notify

Insurance Document:
☐ Policy ☐ Certificate ☐ Declaration under an open cover Covering the following risks

Certificates:
☐ Origin
☐ Analysis
☐ Health
☐ Other

Other Documents:
☐ Packing List
☐ Weight List

Documents to be presented within ☐ days after the date of shipment but within the validity of the Credit ⑬

Additional Instructions: ③

We request you to issue on our behalf and for our account your Irrevocable Credit in accordance with the above instructions (marked (x) where appropriate).
This Credit will be subject to the Uniform Customs and Practice for Documentary Credits (1993 Revision, Publication No. 500 of the International Chamber of Commerce, Paris, France), insofar as they are applicable

Name and signature of the Applicant

Consult the Issuing Bank for guidance if the completion of this form should raise any question

To **Malayan Banking Berhad**   Date _____

Application For Irrevocable Documentary Credit

	Issuing Bank's No.	Approved by:
Beneficiary: Full name and Address	Amount: Figures & Words (including currency)	
	Expiry Date for negotiation in beneficiary's country	

We request you to establish

☐ by registered airmail　　☐ by registered airmail with　　☐ by full SWIFT/Telex　　☐ by courier
　　　　　　　　　　　　　　pre-advice by SWIFT/Telex　　　(operative credit instrument)　　service

an **IRREVOCABLE DOCUMENTARY CREDIT**

available by beneficiary's drafts in duplicate at　　　　　　sight drawn on Malayan Banking Berhad for invoice value
accompanied by the following documents (in duplicate unless otherwise specified):-

☐　　Signed commercial invoices in quadruplicate.

☐　　Full set of clean on board marine Bills of Lading made out to the order of Malayan Banking Berhad, notify applicant and marked
　　　'Freight Prepaid'/Collect.

☐　　Insurance policies (or certificate) endorsed in blank, for invoice value of the goods plus 10% covering Marine and War Risks,
　　　including Institute Cargo Clauses A　　　　Institute War Clauses (Cargo) and Institute Strikes Clauses (Cargo).

　　　Claims payable at

☐　　Certificate of　　　　　　　　　　　　　　　origin

☐

☐

　　　Covering

　　　　　　　　　　　　　　　　　　　　　　　　　　　(please specify price basis CIF/CFR/FOB/C & I/etc.)

SHIPMENT/DELIVERY FROM		TO	
LATEST SHIPMENT/DELIVERY DATE	Partial Shipment ☐ Permitted　☐ Prohibited		Transhipment ☐ Permitted　☐ Prohibited

SPECIAL CONDITIONS:

The documents must be presented not later than　　　　　　days after the date of issuance of the transport documents.
Nevertheless such presentation must not be after the expiry of the credit. All bank charges outside Singapore are for beneficiary's
account.

WE AGREE TO BE BOUND BY THE GENERAL CONDITIONS APPEARING ON THE REVERSE HEREOF.

_____
Authorised Signature of Applicant

Address:

All alterations and additions to this application must be initialed by the applicant. Please indicate your requirements by placing X in the applicable check boxes.

Malayan Banking Berhad
Form IE 28a (1/2)

APPLICATION FOR IRREVOCABLE DOCUMENTARY CREDIT

ORIGINAL   1

TO:

_____ LIMITED

HHHH

A MEMBER OF THE UNITED OVERSEAS BANK GROUP

WE HEREBY REQUEST YOU TO OPEN AN IRREVOCABLE DOCUMENTARY CREDIT
ON THE FOLLOWING TERMS AND CONDITIONS:
PLEASE MARK [X] IN THE RELEVANT BOX.

DATE :

CREDIT NO.:

APPLICANT FULL NAME AND ADDRESS	AMOUNT IN FIGURES AND WORDS
	EXPIRY DATE

A/C NO.	TEL NO.
CONTACT PERSON	FAX NO.

CREDIT IS AVAILABLE AGAINST DOCUMENTS DETAILED HEREIN ACCOMPANIED BY BENEFICIARY'S

DRAFT AT _____ SIGHT FOR 100% OF INVOICE VALUE

(If the L/C is issued at sight, it will be made available by negotiation or payment at your discretion)

BENEFICIARY FULL NAME AND ADDRESS

CREDIT TO BE SENT BY

☐ AIRMAIL   ☐ AIRMAIL WITH BRIEF TELETRANSMISSION

☐ FULL TELETRANSMISSION   ☐ COURIER

(The Credit will be advised through UOB Group Offices or correspondents)

☐ FOR LOCAL LC HOLD ORIGINAL FOR BENEFICIARY COLLECTION

FOR CUSTOMER'S COPY   ☐ MAIL   ☐ HOLD FOR COLLECTION

FAX NO.	TEL NO.

SHIPMENT FROM	TRANSHIPMENT ALLOWED
	☐ YES ☐ NO
T O	PARTIAL SHIPMENT ALLOWED
LATEST SHIPMENT DATE	☐ YES ☐ NO

INCOTERMS

☐ CIF / CIP *   ☐ CFR / CPT *   ☐ Others _____

☐ FOB / FCA *   ☐ EX-WORK / EX-WAREHOUSE / EX-FACTORY *

DOCUMENTS REQUIRED (IN TRIPLICATE UNLESS OTHERWISE STATED)

INVOICES AND OTHER DOCUMENTS

☐ SIGNED COMMERCIAL INVOICE   ☐ WEIGHT LIST

☐ PACKING LIST   ☐ CERTIFICATE OF _____ ORIGIN

☐   ☐

INSURANCE

☐ INSURANCE *POLICY/CERTIFICATE
BLANK ENDORSED FOR 110% OF INVOICE VALUE COVERING
INSTITUTE CARGO CLAUSES *(A / B / C / AIR),
INSTITUTE WAR CLAUSES (CARGO), _____

_____ WITH CLAIMS PAYABLE AT SINGAPORE

☐ INSURANCE TO BE COVERED BY *BUYER/ULTIMATE BUYER

COVER NO.

INSURANCE CO

TRANSPORT DOCS

☐ FULL SET OF 3/3 CLEAN ON BOARD OCEAN BILLS OF LADING

☐ AIR WAYBILL

☐ DELIVERY ORDER COUNTERSIGNED BY APPLICANT

☐

(All transport docs are to be made out to your order unless otherwise stated)

MARKED, IF NECESSARY,   ☐ FREIGHT PREPAID   ☐ FREIGHT COLLECT

NOTIFYING, IF ANY,   ☐ APPLICANT   ☐

SPECIAL INSTRUCTIONS

ALL OTHER BANK'S CHARGES INCLUDING CONFIRMATION CHARGES IF ANY FOR ACCOUNT OF

☐ BENEFICIARY

☐ US

BRIEF DESCRIPTION OF GOODS

FOR BANK USE ONLY

WE HEREBY AGREE TO THE GENERAL CONDITIONS APPEARING ON
THE REVERSE SIDE HEREOF :

FOR BANK'S USE ONLY		
SIGNATURE(S) VERIFIED	APPROVED BY BM/CMD	APPROVED BY ITSR

AUTHORISED SIGNATURE(S) & COMPANY STAMP
*DELETE INAPPLICABLE

FRN-8.1 (R3.97) (6.97)

GENERAL CONDITIONS

In consideration of your issuing a Letter of Credit ("the Credit") in accordance with the particulars overleaf and your agent negotiating the draft or drafts under the credit, I/we hereby agree:

1. To accept on presentation and pay at maturity the full amount drawn together with interest, commission and all customary bank charges.

2. To admit and recognise that all goods and all Bills of Lading, Warrants, Delivery Orders, Documents of Title and securities whatsoever which have been or shall be hereafter delivered into your possession or that of your agents as a result of opening or in connection with transactions under the Credit, are and shall be pledged to you as security for all payments made or which may be made by you or your agents under the Credit.

3. To hold you and your agents harmless and free from any responsibility whatsoever for any delay, mistake or omission that may happen in the transmission of instructions by mail or cable, or for the loss or delay in the forwarding of the documents, or for the validity, regularity or genuineness of the documents if apparently in order or for the description, quality, quantity or value of the property represented by such documents.

4. To authorise you to dispose of the property in whole or in part by public or private sale at your discretion without notice to me/us whenever I/we fail to pay the said drafts at maturity or to discharge my/our liabilities and obligations.

5. Where the Credit calls for the insurance to be effected by the buyers, to keep the property covered by insurance in the joint names of yourself and myself/ourselves or to transfer or assign the Insurance Policy or Certificate to you in a manner satisfactory to you, and in case of the expiry of any insurance, you are at liberty to insure for my/our account until such time as deemed necessary.

6. That the Credit is subject to the usual terms and conditions followed in the area where the Credit is to be established.

7. If a satisfactory marginal deposit has not been made against the Credit, that you may earmark or charge my/our account at your absolute discretion with all moneys so paid or for which you are liable under the Credit. And it is agreed and understood that I/we shall not be entitled to claim the refund or the release of the funds earmarked in my/our account until and unless the draft or drafts drawn under the Credit and all other moneys which may be due to you shall have been paid in full.

8. That the delivery of the documents of title to the goods with or without the draft or drafts by you to me/us against a Trust Receipt or other form of security affecting the merchandise contained therein or without security as the case may be, shall not release me/us from my/our undertakings and obligations under these conditions which you may enforce independently of or in conjunction with the rights conferred on you by the security given.

9. To admit and regard all promises, agreements and undertakings contained herein notwithstanding any amendment, extension, renewal, revision or modification of any kind in the terms of the Credit which you may have caused to be done at my/our request. And in the event of this Application being signed by two or more parties whether as partners or in the name of the firm or in any other capacity, each and all such parties signing shall be deemed JOINTLY and SEVERALLY liable hereunder.

10. This Application and the Credit shall be subject to the Uniform Customs and Practice for Documentary Credits (1993 revision), International Chamber of Commerce Publication No. 500 and shall be governed by and construed in accordance with Singapore law. In the event of inconsistency, the laws of Singapore shall prevail. I/We irrevocably submit to the non-exclusive jurisdiction of the Singapore courts.

11. You may at your discretion and without giving notice to me/us convert into Singapore dollars equivalent all drafts and documents negotiated under the Credit at your then prevailing rate of exchange at any time after the receipt of advice of negotiation of the respective drafts and documents.

GUARANTEE

IN CONSIDERATION OF YOUR ISSUING THE CREDIT IN ACCORDANCE WITH THE PARTICULARS OVERLEAF, I/we hereby jointly and severally guarantee the fulfillment of the promises and agreements, contained herein, including extensions, renewals and modifications and in the event of default promise to make good and pay on demand any loss or damage suffered by yourselves and to waive hereby expressly any defence that may be interposed to any claim or action thereon or hereon, especially also as to the order in which you shall choose to reimburse yourselves.

Dated this   day of   19   .

Witness:

Signature   Signature

Name: Name:

Address: NRIC No.:

☐ Self Collection   ☐ Mail

BANK OF CHINA,
SINGAPORE

Date

DEAR SIRS
I/WE HEREBY REQUEST YOU TO OPEN BY
☐ **FULL TELEX** ☐ **BRIEF TELEX** ☐ **AIRMAIL** ☐ **COURIER SERVICE**
AN IRREVOCABLE DOCUMENTARY CREDIT ON THE
FOLLOWING TERMS AND CONDITIONS

APPLICATION FOR IRREVOCABLE
DOCUMENTARY CREDIT

EXPIRY DATE

Number

(BANK USE ONLY)

IN THE BENEFICIARY S COUNTRY

Advising Bank (BANK USE ONLY)	Beneficiary (Full name & address)
Applicant (Full name & address)	
Current A/C No.	Amount (in figures & in words)
Tel. No. Person to contact.	

Partial shipments	Transhipment
☐ allowed ☐ not allowed	☐ allowed ☐ not allowed

Shipment/dispatch/taking in charge from/at

to

LATEST

Credit available
against presentation of the document detailed herein and
draft(s) at _____ sight
drawn on issuing bank for full invoice value.

Documents required are marked with an "X" **(in three fold unless otherwise specified)**

☐ Signed Commercial Invoice

☐ Signed Weight/Packing List
☐ Certificate of _____ Origin
☐ Insurance policy or certificate, endorsed in blank covering: War, _____
   for 110% CIF value.

☐ Air Waybills/Parcel Post Receipt/Full set of clean 'on board' ocean bills of lading, made out to order of Bank of China, Singapore/
   endorsed in blank, and marked Freight Prepaid/To collect and notify applicant.

Evidencing shipment of:

Other terms and conditions: **(Please mark "x" if applicable)**
☒ All banking charges including reimbursement charges outside Singapore are for account of beneficiary.

☐ Freight forwarder's transport document is not acceptable.

──────── (BANK USE ONLY) ────────

@ .... = S$ a/c No. _____

Margin   % :   Bills No. _____
Comm.   % :
Postage/Cable   : _____
Total: S$ _____

WE AGREE TO THE DOCUMENTARY CREDIT AGREEMENT
APPEARING ON THE REVERSE HEREOF

_____
AUTHORISED SIGNATURE(S) OF APPLICANT

THIS APPLICATION IS WHOLLY GUARANTEED BY

	Date		
Approved	Recorded	Checked	Signature Verified

_____
AUTHORISED SIGNATURE(S) FOR AND ON
BEHALF OF THE GUARANTOR

BI-13(1)

3. **The Procedure of a Documentary Credit**

① Sales contract is established between the exporter and the importer, agreeing to settle the payment by L/C.

② Based on the sales contract, the importer (the applicant) fills in an application form and requests his banker (the issuing bank) to issue a credit in favor of the exporter (the beneficiary). It is the importer's duty to make the application form consistent with the sales contract.

③ The importer's bank will examine the creditworthiness of the buyer before it considers issuing the documentary credit. If the applicant is a new customer to the bank, he may need to pay a deposit margin up to 20% of the credit amount. Having been issued, the credit is then passed on to the exporter's bank who represents the beneficiary in his country.

④ The exporter's bank is expected to pass the documentary credit to the beneficiary after verification of the genuineness of the credit as:

* Advising bank / Transmitting bank – When the exporter's bank assumes no payment undertaking upon himself. Or

* Confirming bank – When the bank adds his own confirmation on the credit while advising or transmitting the credit at the authorization or request of the issuing bank.

⑤ On receiving the documentary credit, the exporter should check the terms and conditions of the credit against the sales contract to ensure that everything agrees with the credit requirement. If there is a discrepancy, the beneficiary may have the option to accept it as it stands or to persuade the applicant to have it amended so as to be in line with the contract, for these two documents are independent of each other from the legal point of view.

After shipment is made and shipping documents are obtained, the exporter will prepare other documents according the L/C requirements. If the credit stipulates that the credit is available with exporter's bank, then the exporter's bank becomes the nominated bank. The exporter should make presentation to his own bank who will effect payment to him as :

* The negotiating bank – If the credit is a negotiable L/C, payment should be effected to the beneficiary by negotiation. Or

* The paying bank - If the credit is a payment credit, payment should be effected to the beneficiary by either sight or deferred payment. Or

* The accepting bank - If the credit is an accepting credit, payment should be effected by acceptance and payment at maturity.

⑥ After receiving the documents from the beneficiary, the negotiating bank / paying bank / accepting bank will check the documents against the terms and conditions of the credit. If all are proper, the above said bank will effect payment by negotiation / payment / acceptance.

⑦ After payment is effected, the negotiating bank/ paying bank / accepting bank will forward the documents to the reimbursing bank to claim reimbursement. If no reimbursing bank is nominated in the credit or the reimbursing bank fails to make the compensation, the reimbursement will be effected by the issuing bank.

⑧ Having received the documents forwarded from the overseas nominated bank, the reimbursing bank or the issuing bank will make reimbursement. Although the reimbursing bank is not required to make reimbursement against correct documents, the issuing bank will check the documents when making compensation.

⑨ The issuing bank will notify the importer of the arrival of documents and require the latter to get ready to make payments.

⑩ Documents will be released to the importer against his payment.

Section Three　Types of Letter of Credit under UCP 500

According to UCP 500, Letter of Credit can be classified into the following types: clean or documentary credit; revocable or irrevocable credit; confirmed or unconfirmed credit, sight payment credit, deferred payment credit, accepting credit or negotiable credit; sight credit or time credit. As these types are made to serve common commercial purposes of the traders, they are considered to be the normal ones.

In practice, the issuing bank can also add some special terms and conditions in the credit to serve different purposes of the customers provided that they are not against the stipulations of UCP 500. For these special purposes, the credit can also take the forms of buyer's usance credit; transferable credit; revolving credit; red clause credit and back to back credit. These types are considered to be special ones.

1. Normal Types of Credit under UCP 500

(1) According to the Attachment of Commercial Documents

(A) Clean credit.

A clean credit is one under which payment will be effected only against a draft without any commercial documents attached thereto or sometimes against a draft with an invoice alone attached thereto.

Clean credit does not necessarily mean that there are no shipping documents under the sales transaction, only that the title documents, if any, are directly sent to the importer. One purpose of clean credit is to enable the beneficiary to receive payments before the shipment is made. On other occasions, clean credit is used when the shipping documents are not available, such as the payments for commissions, down-payments or service transactions. Traveler's letter of credit and stand-by credit are two examples of clean credit, which will be introduced in separate sections.

(B) Documentary credit.

A documentary credit is one which payment will be made against title documents either with a draft attached or not. It is an important form of credit and against which other types of documentary credit will be made possible.

(2) According to the Revocability of a Credit

(A) Irrevocable credit.

An irrevocable credit constitutes a definite undertaking of the issuing bank provided that the stipulated documents are presented to the nominated bank or to the issuing bank and that terms and conditions of the documentary credit are complied with, to pay or to accept drafts and/or document(s) presented under the documentary credit. The definite undertaking of the issuing bank will be expressed clearly in the "undertaking clause" which appears at the end of the credit. Its typical expressions are as follows:

" We (Issuing bank) hereby undertake that daft(s) drawn and in compliance with the terms of the credit shall be duly honored on due presentation. " Or

"We (Issuing bank) hereby engage with drawers (beneficiary) and/or bona fide holder (Nominated bank) that drafts drawn and negotiated in conformity with the terms of this credit will be duly honored on presentation and that drafts accepted within the terms of this credit will be duly honored at maturity. " Or

" We (Issuing bank) hereby issue the irrevocable documentary credit in your favor. It is subject to the *Uniform Customs and Practices for Documentary Credit* (1993 Revision, International Chamber of Commerce, Paris, France, Publication No. 500) and engage us in accordance with the terms thereof, and especially in accordance with the terms of Article 9a thereof. "

An irrevocable documentary credit gives the beneficiary greater assurance of payment, though he remains dependent on an undertaking of a foreign issuing bank. The irrevocable documentary credit cannot be cancelled or modified without the express consent from the issuing bank, the confirming bank (if any) and the beneficiary.

An irrevocable credit normally should first be a documentary credit. The combination of a documentary and irrevocable credit makes the most popular form of credit and it is a requisite based on which other types of documentary credit are made possible.

Every credit should clearly indicate its revocability. In the absence of such indication, the credit will be deemed to be irrevocable.

(B) Revocable credit.

A revocable credit is one which can be modified or cancelled at any moment by the issuing bank without the beneficiary's consent or even without prior notice to the beneficiary.

The revocable documentary credit is less favorable to the exporter than the irrevocable documentary one. It involves risks to the beneficiary since the credit may be modified or cancelled while the goods are sent to shipment, or before the documents are presented, or, although documents may have been presented, before payment has been effected. The exporter then faces the problem of obtaining payment directly from the importer without the issuing bank's payment undertaking. A revocable credit should bear such clauses to indicate clearly its revocability, the absence of such clear indications will make the credit an irrevocable one:

" This credit is subject to revocation or modification at any time without notice to you, conveys no engagement on our part, and is simply for your guidance in preparing and presenting drafts and documents. " Or

" We hereby undertake to reimburse you for all drafts honored by you in accordance with the terms of this credit prior to your receiving notice of cancellation. "

Revocable credit is not a popular one. It is normally accepted as usage between affiliated parties or subsidiary companies.

(3) According to the Adding of Confirmation

(A) Irrevocable confirmed documentary credit.

An confirmation of an irrevocable documentary credit by a bank (the Confirming Bank) upon the authorization or request of the issuing bank constitutes a definite undertaking of the confirming bank in addition to that of the issuing bank provided that the stipulated documents are presented to the confirming bank or any other nominated bank on or before the expiry date and the terms and conditions of the documentary credit are complied with, to pay or to accept draft(s).

When the confirmation is authorized or requested by the issuing bank, the issuing bank will cross-mark the box preceding "adding your confirmation" in its "advice for the Advising Bank". The confirmation is normally added by the advising bank or any other nominated bank when the credit is advised to the beneficiary. If a bank is not prepared to add its confirmation, it can advise the credit as unconfirmed and should inform the issuing bank of this immediately. When a bank confirms a credit, it usually writes a clause as follows:

" As requested by our correspondent bank, we hereby confirm the above mentioned credit. " Or

" We confirm the credit and hereby undertake that all drafts drawn and presented to us as above specified in compliance with the terms of this credit will be duly honored by us. " Or

" As the request of our correspondent, we confirm this credit and engage with you that all drafts drawn under and in compliance with the terms and conditions of this credit will be duly honored by us. "

Confirmation usually adds to an irrevocable and documentary credit. A confirmed irrevocable documentary credit gives the beneficiary double assurances of payment, since it represents both the undertaking of the issuing bank and that of the confirming bank.

Normally, a beneficiary will consider the classification of the credit and the financial standing of the issuing bank before the credit is to be confirmed. If an issuing bank is considered to be the first class bank, there may not be any need to have its documentary credit confirmed by another bank. However, if an issuing bank is a smaller bank or if it is located in a country of both politically and economically unstable, the beneficiary may desire that the credit be guaranteed by a bank located in his own country in order to have an additional payment undertaking from a local bank.

(B) Unconfirmed credit.

The issuing bank's credit is simply advised through an advising bank. The advising bank acts as an agent of the issuing bank and does not assume any responsibility to the beneficiary under the documentary credit except for taking reasonable care to check the apparent authenticity of the documentary credit which it advises. Such a credit is an irrevocable unconfirmed credit.

The issuing bank will cross the box preceding "without adding your confirmation" in its "advice for the Advising Bank". The advising bank will inform the beneficiary that it is passing on the issuing bank's credit and will add to this advice the following:

" This notification and the enclosed advice are sent to you without any engagement on our part", or words of similar intent.

(4) According to the Availability of Payment

(A) Irrevocable documentary sight payment credit.

A sight payment credit is one available by sight payment, under which a bank nominated therein is authorized to pay against shipping documents with or without a sight draft presented in conformity with the terms of the credit.

The nominated paying bank in the credit may be the issuing bank, the exporter's bank or a third bank. That is to say, if the draft, if required, is drawn on the issuing bank, then the issuing bank is the paying bank, or if the draft is drawn on the exporter's bank or a third bank, the exporter's bank or the third bank is the paying bank. The sight payment effected by the paying bank is final.

The issuing bank's undertaking clause will read as:

" We hereby engage that payment will be duly made against sight draft and documents or documents presented in conformity with the terms of this credit. "

Sight payment credit also includes straight credit. Under an irrevocable straight documentary credit, the obligation of the issuing bank is extended only to the beneficiary in honoring draft(s)/document(s) and the credit usually expires at the counter of the issuing bank. This kind of documentary credit conveys no commitment or obligation on the part of the issuing bank to persons other than the named beneficiary. When other banks choose to purchase the beneficiary's drafts / documents, their purchase should be done with the understanding that they acquire no rights against the issuing bank under the credit. That is to say, this kind of credit conveys no engagement on the issuing bank to protect such purchasers of drafts/ documents. The purchaser only has the right to present the drafts/documents on behalf of the beneficiary. This kind of credit is less favorable to the exporter since he will not obtain payment until the issuing bank pays, and at the same time, he should be responsible for the drafts/documents to be presented to the counter of the issuing bank within the validity of the credit.

The engagement of the issuing bank under straight credit is normally indicated in the credit as:

" Credit available by payment with the issuing bank and expiry place for presentation of documents being at the office of the issuing bank. " Or, the engagement of the issuing bank may be stated more explicitly as follows:

" We hereby agree with the beneficiary that all drafts drawn under and /or documents presented hereunder will be duly honored by us provided the terms and conditions of the credit are complied with and that presentation is made at this office on or before the expiry date. "

When payment is made by the paying bank, it is final and without recourse against the beneficiary.

(B) Irrevocable documentary deferred payment credit.

Deferred payment credit is one that payment is to be deferred to a specified future date provided that the presented documents are in agreement with the terms and conditions of the credit. No draft is required for this credit.

The nominated paying bank may be the issuing bank, the exporter's bank or a third bank. The payment effected by the paying bank at maturity is final.

The determinable future date would be expressed as xx days after presentation of documents, or xx days after the date of shipment or a fixed future date. The undertaking clause of the issuing bank will read as follows:

" We hereby engage that payment will be duly made at maturity against the documents presented in conformity with the terms of the credit. "

(C) Irrevocable documentary acceptance credit.

An irrevocable documentary acceptance credit constitutes the issuing bank's undertaking that the time draft will be accepted upon presentation and paid at maturity, provided that the drafts / documents are in compliance with the terms and conditions of the credit.

The nominated accepting bank may be the exporter's bank or a third bank who becomes the drawee of the time draft. Accepting bank accepts the time draft upon presentation and pays at maturity. Payment made by the accepting bank on due date is final, without recourse to the beneficiary.

The undertaking clause of the issuing bank will be read as follows:

" We hereby engage that drafts drawn in conformity with the terms of this credit will be duly accepted on presentation to drawee bank and duly honored on maturity. "

(D) Irrevocable negotiation documentary credit.

Under the irrevocable negotiation documentary credit, the issuing bank's engagement is extended to third party who negotiates or purchases the beneficiary's draft(s) /document(s) under the documentary credit. This assures anyone who is authorized to negotiate draft (s) /document(s) that these draft(s) /document(s) will be duly honored by the issuing bank provided the terms and conditions of the documentary credit are complied with. A bank which effectively negotiates(buys) draft(s) and/or document(s) from the beneficiary, thereby becomes a holder in due course.

The nominated negotiating bank can be the exporter's bank or a third bank, or, in the case of a freely negotiable credit, any bank of the beneficiary's choice becomes the negotiating bank.

Negotiation means giving value for draft and documents by the bank authorized to negotiate. After negotiation, the negotiating bank becomes the holder in due course who can exercise right of recourse against the beneficiary in the event that the reimbursement is not forthcoming from the Issuing bank. Therefore, payment by the negotiating bank is not final.

The draft under negotiation is a sight draft with the drawee to be made on the issuing bank. It needs to point out that the draft of a negotiation credit can never be drawn on the negotiating bank.

The undertaking clause under a negotiation credit is always written as:

" We hereby engage with the drawers, endorsers and/or bona fide holders that drafts drawn and negotiated in conformity with the terms of this credit will be duly honored on presentation. "

A negotiation credit can be further divided into restrictive and freely negotiable credit. If the credit stipulates that this credit is available by negotiation with a nominated bank, it is a restricted negotiation credit. It means that the negotiation is restricted by the bank nominated therein and the beneficiary must present his documents to the bank so nominated. In this case, if the credit is negotiated by a bank other than the nominated one, this bank negotiates the beneficiary's drafts/ documents at its own risk, without any legal protection and payment undertaking from the issuing bank. The issuing bank's undertaking clause will state clearly that the credit is a restricted one:

" We engage with you that all drafts drawn under and in compliance with the terms of this credit will be duly honored on presentation to the nominated bank. " Or

" The negotiation under this credit is restricted to the nominated Bank only. "

If the credit is available by negotiation with any bank, it is a freely negotiable credit, and the beneficiary may present documents to and receive money from any bank of his choice. In practice, however, a freely negotiable credit may be freely negotiated within a city or a country, as to make any bank in the world to be the negotiation bank will incur great risk to the issuing bank.

Let's compare the above mentioned credits in the following table:

(5) According to the Time of Credit Availability

(A) Sight/Demand credit.

Sight credit means that the credit amount is available to the beneficiary at sight. From the above chart, it will easily make the conclusion that when payment is effected by sight payment or by negotiation, the credit will be a sight one.

(B) Time/Usance credit.

Time credit means that the credit amount is available to the beneficiary at a future time. From the above chart, it will easily make the conclusion that when payment is effected by deferred payment or by acceptance, the credit will be a time one.

In summary, the classification of credits is not a clear cut in the sense that one credit can take several types. Another point to note is that only "irrevocable" and "documentary" credits will be clearly indicated in the box of type of credit and other types are determined by the wordings stated in the various parts of the credit. Therefore, careful reading of the credit is necessary to have a correct understanding of the types for a credit.

Type / Condition	Sight Payment L/C	Deferred Payment L/C	Acceptance L/C	Negotiation L/C	Freely Negotiable L/C
Draft and tenor	Sight draft or no draft	NA	Time draft	Sight draft	Sight draft
Drawee	The nominated paying bank: the issuing bank, the exporter's bank, or a third bank	NA	The nominated accepting bank: the issuing bank, the exporter's bank or a third bank.	The issuing bank but not the nominated negotiating bank	The issuing bank but not the negotiating bank
Payment effecting time	Sight payment	Time payment	Time payment	Sight payment	Sight payment
Credit available with	The issuing bank or the nominated paying bank	The issuing bank or the nominated paying bank	The nominated accepting bank	The nominated negotiating bank	Any freely chosen negotiating bank by the beneficiary
Right of recourse against the beneficiary	No	No	No	Yes	Yes
Due date calculated from	NA	The date of shipment, the date of presentment, etc.	The accepting date	NA	NA

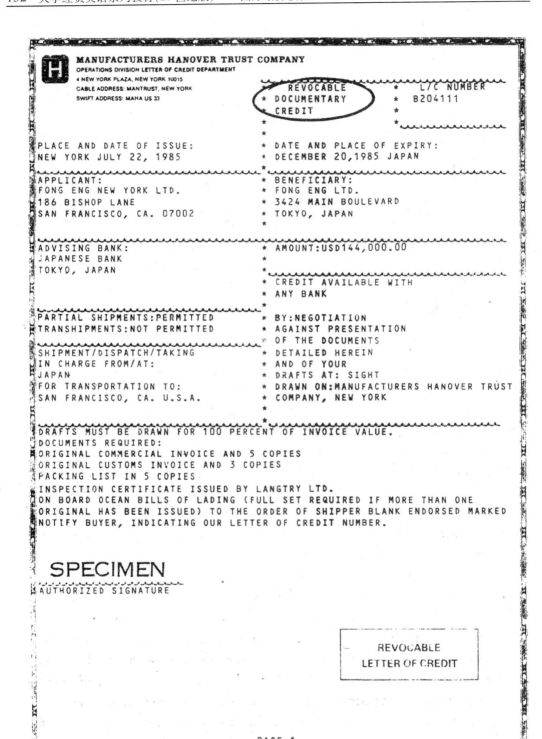

Revocable Letter of Credit (1)

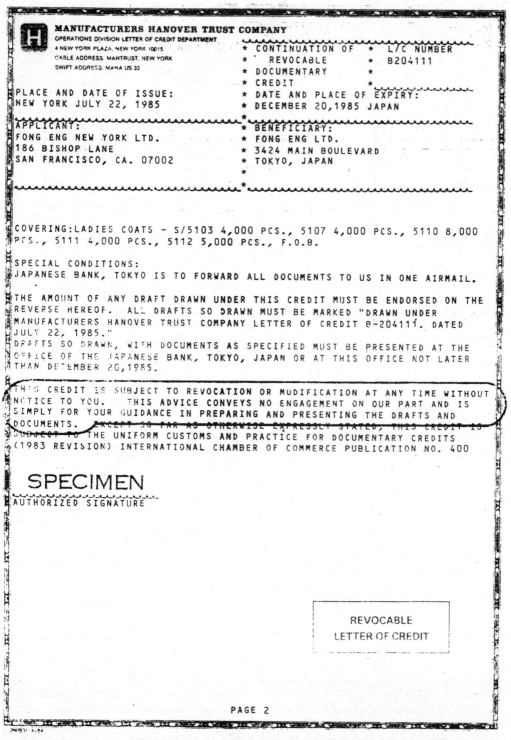

MANUFACTURERS HANOVER TRUST COMPANY
OPERATIONS DIVISION LETTER OF CREDIT DEPARTMENT
4 NEW YORK PLAZA, NEW YORK 10015
CABLE ADDRESS, MANTRUST, NEW YORK
SWIFT ADDRESS: MAHA US 33

```
* CONTINUATION OF  *  L/C NUMBER
*   REVOCABLE      *  B204111
* DOCUMENTARY      *
* CREDIT           *
```

PLACE AND DATE OF ISSUE:
NEW YORK JULY 22, 1985

```
* DATE AND PLACE OF EXPIRY:
* DECEMBER 20,1985 JAPAN
```

APPLICANT:
FONG ENG NEW YORK LTD.
186 BISHOP LANE
SAN FRANCISCO, CA. 07002

```
* BENEFICIARY:
* FONG ENG LTD.
* 3424 MAIN BOULEVARD
* TOKYO, JAPAN
*
```

COVERING:LADIES COATS - S/5103 4,000 PCS., 5107 4,000 PCS., 5110 8,000
PCS., 5111 4,000 PCS., 5112 5,000 PCS., F.O.B.

SPECIAL CONDITIONS:
JAPANESE BANK, TOKYO IS TO FORWARD ALL DOCUMENTS TO US IN ONE AIRMAIL.

THE AMOUNT OF ANY DRAFT DRAWN UNDER THIS CREDIT MUST BE ENDORSED ON THE
REVERSE HEREOF. ALL DRAFTS SO DRAWN MUST BE MARKED "DRAWN UNDER
MANUFACTURERS HANOVER TRUST COMPANY LETTER OF CREDIT B-204111. DATED
JULY 22, 1985."
DRAFTS SO DRAWN, WITH DOCUMENTS AS SPECIFIED MUST BE PRESENTED AT THE
OFFICE OF THE JAPANESE BANK, TOKYO, JAPAN OR AT THIS OFFICE NOT LATER
THAN DECEMBER 20,1985.

THIS CREDIT IS SUBJECT TO REVOCATION OR MODIFICATION AT ANY TIME WITHOUT
NOTICE TO YOU.   THIS ADVICE CONVEYS NO ENGAGEMENT ON OUR PART AND IS
SIMPLY FOR YOUR GUIDANCE IN PREPARING AND PRESENTING THE DRAFTS AND
DOCUMENTS. EXCEPT SO FAR AS OTHERWISE EXPRESSLY STATED, THIS CREDIT IS
SUBJECT TO THE UNIFORM CUSTOMS AND PRACTICE FOR DOCUMENTARY CREDITS
(1983 REVISION) INTERNATIONAL CHAMBER OF COMMERCE PUBLICATION NO. 400

SPECIMEN
AUTHORIZED SIGNATURE

```
REVOCABLE
LETTER OF CREDIT
```

PAGE 2

79091) 4-84

This exhibit is fictitious and is provided only as an example. The information contained therein reflects the terms and conditions
of the Uniform Customs and Practice per International Chamber of Commerce publication #400 in effect as of October 1984.

Revocable Letter of Credit (2)

Irrevocable Confirmed Documentary Credit

Name of the Issuing Bank	Irrevocable Documentary Credit	Number 12345
The French Issuing Bank 38 rue François 1er 75008 Paris, France		

Place and Date of Issue Paris, 1 January 1994	Expiry Date and place for presentation of Documents
Applicant The French Importer Co. 89 rue du Commerce Paris, France	Expiry Date: May 29, 1994 Place for Presentation: The American Advising Bank, Tampa
	Beneficiary The American Exporter Co. Inc. 17 Main Street Tampa, Florida
Advising Bank Reference. No The American Advising Bank 456 Commerce Avenue Tampa, Florida	**Amount** US$100,000.- one hundred thousand U.S.Dollars
Partial shipments [X] allowed [ ] not allowed Transhipment [X] allowed [ ] not allowed [ ] Insurance covered by buyers	Credit available with nominated Bank: The American Advising Bank, Tampa [X] by payment at sight [ ] by deferred payment at [ ] by acceptance of drafts at [ ] by negotiation
shipment as defined in UCP 500 Article 46 From: Tampa, Florida For transportation to: Paris, France Not later than: May 15, 1994	Against the documents detailed herein: [X] and Beneticiary's draft(s) drawn on The American Advising Bank.

Commercial Invoice, one original and 3 copies

Multimodal Transport Document issued to the order of the French Importer Co. marked freight prepaid and notify XYZ Custom House Broker Inc

Insurance Certificate covering the Institute Cargo Clauses and the Institute War and Strike Clauses for 110% of the invoice value endorsed to The French Importer Co.

Certificate of Origin evidence goods to be of U.S.A. Origin

Packing List

Covering: Machinerie and spare parts as per pro-forma invoice number 657 dated December 17, 1993 - CIP INCOTERMS 1990

Documents to be presented within [14] days after the date of shipment but within the validity of the credit

We hereby issue the irrevocable Documentary credit in your favour. It is subject to the Uniform Customs and Practice for Documentary Credits (1993 Revision,International)Chamber of Commerce, Paris France,Publication No.500) and engages us in accordance with the terms thereof. The number and the date of the credit and the name of our bank must be quoted on all drafts required. If the credit is available by negotiaton, each presentation must be noted on the reversed side of this advice by the bank where the credit is available.

This document consists of [1] signed page(s)   The French Issuing Bank

Irrevocable Confirmed Documentary Credit Advise

Name of Advising Bank The American Advising Bank 456 Commerce Avenue Tampa, Florida	**Notification of Irrevocable Documentary Credit**
Reference Number of Advising Bank: 2417 **Place and date of Notification:** January 14, 1994, Tampa	
Issuing Bank: The French Issuing Bank 38 rue François 1er Paris, France	**Beneficiary:** The American Exporter Co. Inc 17 Main Street Tampa, Florida
Reference Number of the Issuing Bank: 12345	**Amount:** US$100,000.- One hundred thousand U.S. Dollars

We have been informed by the above-mentioned Issuing Bank that the above-mentioned Documentary Credit has been issued in your favour.
Please find enclosed the advice intended for you.

Check the Credit terms and conditions carefully. In the event you do not agree with the terms and conditions, or if you feel unable to comply with any of those terms and conditions, kindly arrange an amendment of the Credit through your contracting party (the Applicant).

Other information:

☐ This notification and the enclosed advice are sent to you without any engagement on our part

☒ As requested by the Issuing Bank, we hereby add our confirmation to this Credit in accordance with the stipulations under UCP 500 Article 9

The American Advising Bank

Irrevocable Documentary Credit (Unconfirmed)

Name of Issuing Bank: The French Issuing Bank 38 rue François 1er 75008 Paris, France	**Irrevocable Documentary Credit** Number 12345
Place and Date of Issue: Paris, 1 January 1994	**Expiry Date and Place for Presentation of Documents** Expiry Date: May 29, 1994 Place for Presentation: The American Advising Bank, Tampa

Applicant:
 	
The French Importer Co.
89 rue du Commerce
Paris, France
	Beneficiary:
	     The American Exporter Co. Inc.
	     17 Main Street
	     Tampa, Florida

Advising Bank: Reference. No The American Advising Bank 456 Commerce Avenue Tampa, Florida	**Amount:** US$100,000.- one hundred thousand U.S.Dollars
Partial shipments [X] allowed [ ] not allowed Transhipment [X] allowed [ ] not allowed [ ] Insurance covered by buyers	**Credit available with Nominated Bank:** The American Advising Bank [ ] by payment at sight [ ] by deferred payment at: [ ] by acceptance of drafts at: [X] by negotiation
Shipment as defined in UCP 500 Article 46 From: Tampa, Florida For transportation to: Paris, France Not later than: May 15, 1994	Against the documents detailed herein: [X] and Beneficiary's draft(s) drawn on: The French Issuing Bank, Paris, France

Commercial Invoice, one original and 3 copies

Multimodal Transport Document issued to the order of the French Importer Co.
marked freight prepaid and notify XYZ Custom House Broker Inc.

Insurance Certificate covering the Institute Cargo Clauses and the Institute War
and Strike Clauses for 110% of the invoice value endorsed to The French Importer Co.

Certificate of Origin evidencing goods to be of U.S.A. Origin

Packing List

Covering: Machinery and spare parts as per pro-forma invoice number 657
dated December 17, 1993 - CIP INCOTERMS 1990

Documents to be presented within [14] days after the date of shipment but within the validity of the Credit.

We hereby issue the Irrevocable Documentary Credit in your favour. It is subject to the Uniform Customs and Practice for Documentary Credits (1993 Revision, International Chamber of Commerce, Paris, France, Pubication No. 500) and engages us in accordance with the terms thereof. The number and the date of the Credit and the name of our bank must be quoted on all drafts required. If the Credit is available by negotiation, each presentation must be noted on the reverse side of this advice by the bank where the Credit is available.

This document consists of [1] signed page(s)   The French Issuing Bank

Irrevocable Documentary Credit (Unconfirmed) Advice

Name of Advising Bank The American Advising Bank 456 Commerce Avenue Tampa, Florida	**Notification of Irrevocable Documentary Credit**
Reference Number of Advising Bank: 2417 **Place and date of Notification:** January 14, 1994, Tampa	

Issuing Bank: The French Issuing Bank 38 rue François 1er Paris, France	**Beneficiary:** The American Exporter Co. Inc 17 Main Strret Tampa, Florida
Reference Number of the Issuing Bank: 12345	**Amount:** US$100,000.- One hundred thousand U.S. Dollars

We have been informed by the above-mentioned Issuing Bank that the above-mentioned Documentary Credit has been issued in your favour.
Please find enclosed the advice intended for you

Check the Credit terms and conditions carefully. In the event you do not agree with the terms and conditions, or if you feel unable to comply with
any of those terms and conditions, kindly arrange an amendment of the Credit through your contracting party (the Applicant).

Other information:

[X] This notification and the enclosed advice are sent to you without any engagement on our part.

[ ] As requested by the Issuing Bank, we hereby add our confirmation to this Credit in accordance with the stipulations under UCP 500 Article 9.

The American Advising Bank

Irrevocable Straight Documentary Credit

Name of Issuing Bank: The French Issuing Bank 38 rue François 1er 75008 Paris, France	**Irrevocable Documentary Credit**	Number 12345

Place and Date of Issue: Paris, 1 January 1994	**Expiry Date and Place for Presentation of Documents** Expiry Date: May 29, 1994 Place for Presentation: The French Issuing Bank, Paris, France
Applicant: The French Importer Co. 89 rue du Commerce Paris, France	**Beneficiary:** The American Exporter Co. Inc. 17 Main Street Tampa, Florida
Advising Bank: Reference. No The American Advising Bank 456 Commerce Avenue Tampa, Florida	**Amount:** US$100,000.- one hundred thousand U.S.Dollars
Partial shipments [X] allowed [ ] not allowed Transhipment [X] allowed [ ] not allowed [ ] Insurance covered by buyers	**Credit available with Nominated Bank:** The French Issuing Bank [X] by payment at sight [ ] by deferred payment at: [ ] by acceptance of drafts at: [ ] by negotiation
Shipment as defined in UCP 500 Article 46 From: Tampa, Florida For transportation to: Paris, France Not later than: May 15, 1994	Against the documents detailed herein: [X] and Beneficiary's draft(s) drawn on: The French Issuing Bank, Paris, France

Commercial Invoice, one original and 3 copies

Multimodal Transport Document issued to the order of the French Importer Co.
marked freight prepaid and notify XYZ Custom House Broker Inc.

Insurance Certificate covering the Institute Cargo Clauses and the Institute War
and Strike Clauses for 110% of the invoice value endorsed to The French Importer Co.

Certificate of Origin evidencing goods to be of U.S.A. Origin

Packing List

Covering: Machinery and spare parts as per pro-forma invoice number 657
dated December 17, 1993 - CIP INCOTERMS 1990

Documents to be presented within [14] days after the date of shipment but within the validity of the Credit.

This document consists of [1] signed page(s)

The French Issuing Bank

Advice for the Beneficiary

© Copyright 1993, International Chamber of Commerce / Chambre de Commerce Internationale

Irrevocable Negotiation Documentary Credit

Name of Issuing Bank: The French Issuing Bank 38 rue françois 1er 75008 Paris, France	**Irrevocable Documentary Credit** Number 12345

Place and Date of Issue: Paris, 1 January 1994	**Expiry Date and Place for Presentation of Documents** Expiry Date: May 29, 1994 Place for Presentation: The American Advising Bank, Tampa
Applicant: The French Importer Co. 89 rue du Commerce Paris, France	**Beneficiary:** The American Exporter Co. Inc. 17 Main Street Tampa, Florida
Advising Bank: Reference. No The American Advising Bank 456 Commerce Avenue Tampa, Florida	**Amount:** US$100,000.- one hundred thousand U.S.Dollars
Partial shipments [X] allowed [ ] not allowed Transhipment [X] allowed [ ] not allowed [ ] Insurance covered by buyers	**Credit available with Nominated Bank:** The American Advising Bank [ ] by payment at sight [ ] by deferred payment at: [ ] by acceptance of drafts at: [X] by negotiation
Shipment as defined in UCP 500 Article 46 From: Tampa, Florida For transportation to: Paris, France Not later than: May 15, 1994	Against the documents detailed herein: [X] and Beneficiary's draft(s) drawn on: The French Issuing Bank, Paris, France

Commercial Invoice, one original and 3 copies

Multimodal Transport Document issued to the order of the French Importer Co.
marked freight prepaid and notify XYZ Custom House Broker Inc.

Insurance Certificate covering the Institute Cargo Clauses and the Institute War
and Strike Clauses for 110% of the invoice value endorsed to The French Importer Co.

Certificate of Origin evidencing goods to be of U.S.A. Origin

Packing List

Covering: Machinery and spare parts as per pro-forma invoice number 657
dated December 17, 1993 - CIP INCOTERMS 1990

Documents to be presented within [14] days after the date of shipment but within the validity of the Credit.

We hereby issue the Irrevocable Documentary Credit in your favour. It is subject to the Uniform Customs and Practice for Documentary Credits (1993 Revision, International Chamber of Commerce, Paris, France, Publication No. 500) and engages us in accordance with the terms thereof. The number and the date of the Credit and the name of our bank must be quoted on all drafts required. If the Credit is available by negotiation, each presentation must be noted on the reverse side of this advice by the bank where the Credit is available.

This document consists of [1] signed page(s)   The French Issuing Bank

```
+*
+*                                        REIMBURSING BANK'S CHARGES
+*                                        OUTSIDE TAIWAN ARE FOR
+*                                        BENEFICIARY'S ACCOUNT
+* :48 /period for presentation          :. DOCUMENTS TO BE PRESENTED WITHIN
+*                                        15 DAYS AFTER THE DATE OF SHIPMENT
+*                                        BUT WITHIN THE VALIDITY OF THIS
+*                                        CREDIT.
+* :49 /confirmation instructions        :WITHOUT
+* :53A/reimbursement bank - BIC         :FCBKSGSG
+*                                        FIRST COMMERCIAL BANK
+*                                        SINGAPORE
+* :78 /instructions to pay/acc/neg bk:
+*      THE NEGOTIATING BANK IS AUTHORIZED TO DRAW AT SIGHT AGAINST THEIR
+*      CERTIFICATE CERTIFYING THAT ALL TERMS AND CONDITIONS OF THIS
+*      CREDIT HAVE BEEN COMPLIED WITH ON REIMBURSING BANK.
+*      NEGOTIATING BANK MUST FORWARD TO US ALL DOCUMENTS REQUIRED
+*      BY REGISTERED AIRMAIL IN ONE COVER.
+*      THIS CREDIT IS SUBJECT TO ICC PUBLICATION NO.500 1993 REVISION
+*      REIMBURSEMENT IS SUBJECT TO ICC URR525.
+* :57D/advise thru bank - name/addr  :PLS ADVISE THROUGH
+*                                      MALAYAN BANKING BERHAD
+*                                      TEXTILE CENTRE BRANCH
+* -
+*-----------------------------------------------------------------------
+* :MAC /Message Authentication Code:295394E2
+* :CHK /Checksum Result             :E0E06B37CAD0
+*-----------------------------------------------------------------------
+* :SAC /Authenticated with current key:
+*
+*------------------------- ACKNOWLEDGEMENT ------------------------------
+*
+* :177 /date and time               :961108 17:10
+* :451 /acceptance/rejection        :accepted
+*
+*------- SNAPSHOT GENERATED BY SWSERV ON PMT7 ON 08-NOV-96 AT 17:10:20 -------
+*
+* Entry    : SWSERV Date:961108 Time:17:10:18
+*
+*================================= CMT7/00024791/12-NOV-96/09:01:13 = P 2/2 =
```

OF SGD35.00 / SGD25.00

RECEIVED = issue of a documentary credit FM700 ================ S-COPY 0002 =
*
* DESTINATION   FCBKSGSGAXXX   SW19961108FS000000009400
* SESS   2097   DATE RCVD 08-NOV-96 17:10
* SEQU 154575
*---
* ORIGINATOR   FCBKTWTPAXXX   FROM SWIFT
* SESS   2307   FIRST COMMERCIAL BANK   DATE SENT 08-NOV-96 17:10
* SEQU 374328   TAIPEI
*
*--------------------------------- NORMAL --------------------------------
*
* :27 /sequence of total   :1 / 1
* :40A/form of documentary credit :IRREVOCABLE
* :20 /documentary credit number   : 6NF2/00508/1163
* :31C/date of issue   :08/11/96
* :31D/date and place of expiry   :15/12/96 SINGAPORE
* :50 /applicant   :   INDUSTRIAL CORP
*   P.O. BOX 8 - 52
*   TAIPEI TAIWAN ROC
* :59 /beneficiary   :.   INTERNATIONAL PTE LTD.
*   14 WOODLANDS INDUSTRIAL PARK
*   SINGAPORE 277
* :32B/currency code amount   :USD 17660,00
* 1D/available with/by-name,addr :AVAILABLE WITH ANY BANK
*   BY NEGOTIATION
* :42C/drafts at   :DRAFTS AT SIGHT
*   FOR FULL INVOICE VALUE
* :42D/drawee - name and addr   :DRAWN ON US
* :43P/partial shipments   :PROHIBITED
* :43T/transshipment   :PROHIBITED
* :44A/on board/disp/taking charge :SINGAPORE
* :44B/for transportation to   :KAOHSIUNG
* :44D/latest date of shipment   :30/11/96
* :45A/descr goods and/or services :FOB SINGAPORE
*   BUILDING MATERIALS
*   MORTAC SEALER, CEMENTITIOUS STUCCO AND STUCCO SPRAY GUN
* :46A/documents required   :
*   . SIGNED COMMERCIAL INVOICE IN 6 COPIES INDICATING THIS
*   CREDIT NUMBER.
*   . FULL SET LESS ONE OF CLEAN ON BOARD MARINE BILLS OF LADING
*   MADE OUT TO THE ORDER OF FIRST COMMERCIAL BANK
*   NOTIFY APPLICANT, MARKED ''FREIGHT COLLECT'' AND INDICATING
*   THIS CREDIT NUMBER.
*   . PACKING LIST IN 3 COPIES SIGNED BY BENEFICIARY.
*   . BENEFICIARY'S CERTIFICATE STATING THAT ONE SET OF SHIPPING
*   DOCUMENTS, INCLUDING: 1/3 CLEAN ORIGINAL ON BOARD OCEAN
*   BILL OF LADING HAS BEEN SENT TO THE APPLICANT.
*   . CERTIFICATE OF ORIGIN OF SINGAPORE.
* :47A/additional conditions   :
*   . THE NUMBER AND THE DATE OF THE CREDIT AND THE NAME OF OUR BANK
*   MUST BE QUOTED ON ALL DRAFTS.
* :71B/charges   :ALL BANKING CHARGES INCLUDING
*
*= = = = = = = = = = = = = = = = CMT7/00024791/12-NOV-96/09:01:13 = P 1/2 =

FIRST COMMERCIAL BANK
SINGAPORE BRANCH
No. 6696-3116

Section Four　Types of Credit for Special Purposes

1. Buyer's Usance Credit

Buyer's usance credit is issued for the purpose of financing the importer and is used when the transaction is conducted on a sight basis.

We have already discussed acceptance credit in the previous section. The acceptance credit is a normal usance credit and it is issued when the sales contract is made on a time basis with the agreement that the exporter will obtain payment in a determinable future time. In this case, if the exporter wants to obtain advance payment, as a beneficiary under the usance credit, he can discount the time draft(s) under the credit and the discounting interest and acceptance commissions will be borne by the exporter. This kind of normal acceptance credit is called the seller's usance credit.

When a sales contract is concluded on a sight basis, the seller is supposed to obtain payment at sight. But if only an usance credit can be established, the importer may require it to be a special usance credit to finance himself by enabling the exporter to obtain payment at sight. The goal is realized by discounting the time draft(s) under the credit and the discounting interest and acceptance commissions are to be borne by the importer/applicant rather than by the exporter/beneficiary. In effect, usance credit is payable at sight to the exporter. This kind of usance credit is called the buyer's usance credit.

The following clause will be found in the buyer's usance credit:

" Credit available with ourselves by acceptance against presentation of the documents and drafts at 90 days sight drawn on ourselves. Accepted draft will be paid by us on sight basis, interest charges being for the applicant's account. " Or

" Please pay beneficiary on a sight basis. Discount charges and stamp duties (if any) are for the buyer's account in excess of the credit amount. " Or

" Usance drafts will be negotiated at sight basis. "

2. Revolving Documentary Credit

A revolving documentary credit is issued to facilitate the importer's continuous and repeated purchases from the same supplier under which the issuing charges and the deposit margins on the part of the applicant can be saved.

A revolving documentary credit is one by which, under the terms and conditions thereof, the amount is renewed or reinstated without specific amendments to the documentary credit being issued. A revolving documentary credit may be revocable or irrevocable, and may revolve in relation to time or value.

(A) In the case of a documentary credit that revolves in relation to time, the credit is available for a fixed amount over a given period.

A credit of this nature can be culmulative or non-culmulative. If it is culmulative, any amount of the credit available for a fixed period that is used during that period may be used in the subsequent period. If it is non-culmulative any amount. If there is no indication whether the amount is colmulative or non-culmulative, it will be deemed as a non-culmulative one. For example:

"This is a monthly revolving credit which is available up to the amount of USD10,000 per month, and the full credit amount will be automatically renewed on the 1st day of each succeeding calendar month. Our maximum liability under this revolving credit does not exceed USD60,000 being the aggregate value of six months. The unused balance of each month is non-cumulative to the succeeding month. "

(B) In the case of a documentary credit that revolves in relation to value, the amount is reinstated upon utilization within a given overall period of validity until the total amount is used up. For example:

"This credit is revolving for six shipments only. The amount of each shipment is not exceeding USD10,000. The total value of the this revolving credit does not exceed USD60,000. It must be remembered that under a revolving credit and as shown in the above example, the obligations of the issuing bank would be USD60,000. While the face value of the documentary credit is made at USD10,000, the total undertaking of the issuing bank is for the aggregate amount that might be drawn.

The revolving of the credit can be effected in the following three different ways according to the stipulation in the credit:

* Automatic

The amount of the credit shall be reinstated immediately after its drawing has been made. For example:

" The amount paid under this credit shall be again available to you automatically until the total payment reaches USD30,000. "

* Semi-automatic

The amount of the credit shall be reinstated if no advice to stop renewal is sent from the issuing bank within a specified period as mentioned in the credit. For example:

" This credit will be automatically restored to the face amount unless the advising bank is advised by the contrary within two weeks after a drawing is presented for payment. "

* Non-automatic

The amount of the credit shall be renewed only upon receipt of issuing bank's notice of renewal as mentioned in the credit. For example:

" The amount of drawings paid under this credit becomes available to you again upon your receipt from us of the advice to the effect. "

In summary, the revolving documentary credit is not in common use because it can involve an incalculable liability to the issuing bank who is held liable for the aggregate amount that might be drawn under the credit. If a revolving documentary credit is to be issued, it is important for the issuing bank to maintain a certain degree of control by specifying the aggregate amount and that such an amount should be decided by the importer and the exporter to meet their sales requirements and should be agreed by the issuing bank.

3. Transferable Documentary Credit

A transferable documentary credit is normally issued when the first beneficiary is the middle man who does not supply the merchandise himself. The actual supplier is the second beneficiary.

A transferable documentary credit is one under which the beneficiary (the first beneficiary) may request the bank authorized to pay, incur a deferred payment undertaking, accept or negotiate (the transferring bank), or in the event of a freely negotiable credit, the bank specially authorized in the credit as a transferring bank to make documentary credit available in whole or in part to one or more other beneficiaries (the second beneficiary).

Only an irrevocable documentary credit can be transferred and it can be transferred only once. It is necessary to consider both the original part and the transferred part of the credit.

The Original Part		The Transferred Part	
Applicant	The Importer	Applicant	
Beneficiary	The Middle Man (The 1st Beneficiary)	Beneficiary	The Exporter (The 2nd Beneficiary)
The Issuing Bank	The Importer's Bank	The Issuing Bank	
		The Transferring Bank	The Middle Man's Bank

It should be noted that a transferable credit is made at the authorization of the issuing bank and the transfer must be effected in accordance with the terms and conditions of the credit, subject to the following exceptions:

* The 1st beneficiary of the original part becomes the applicant of the transferred part. His interest is protected by such a credit since neither the actual buyer nor the actual supplier may know each other.

* The amount of the transferred part and the unit price may be reduced. The difference between the two parts represents the profits of the middle man.

* The percentage of the insurance cover may be increased for the transferred part to match the amount insured under the original part.

* The last shipment date, the expiry date and the last date for presentation of the transferred part may be shortened in order to enable the middle man to exchange documents within the validity of the credit.

* The transferable credit allows the 1st beneficiary to substitute his invoice(s) and draft(s) for those presented by the second beneficiary.

The transferable credit will undergo the following procedure:

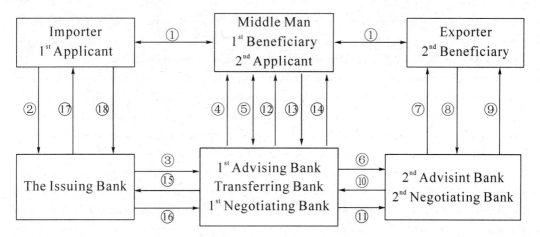

① 1st sales contract is established between the importer and the middle man and 2nd sales contract between the middle man and the exporter.

② Importer applies for the issuance of an irrevocable documentary transferable credit.

③ The issuing bank issues an irrevocable documentary transferable credit in favor of the middle man (1st beneficiary) and forwards it to the middle man's bank.

④ The middle man's bank, acting as the 1st advising bank, advises the credit to the middle man (1st beneficiary).

⑤ The 1st beneficiary gives instruction to his bank to transfer the credit in favor of the exporter. He will request his bank to make necessary changes regarding the names of the applicant and the beneficiary, the credit amount, the percentage of the insurance cover, the last date of shipment, the last date for the presentation of documents and the expiry date of the transferred part.

⑥ The 1st advising bank transfers the credit accordingly and forwards the transferred part to the exporter's bank.

⑦ The exporter's bank, acting as the 2nd advising bank, advises the transferred part to the exporter (the 2nd beneficiary).

⑧ After shipment is made, the 2nd beneficiary presents the draft(s) and document(s) to his bank for payment.

⑨ The exporter's bank effects payment to the 2nd beneficiary by negotiation.

⑩ The exporter's bank forwards the draft(s)/document(s) to the transferring bank for reimbursement.

⑪ The transferring bank makes reimbursement to the exporter's bank.

⑫ The transferring bank notifies the 1st beneficiary to supply his invoice(s) and draft(s) to replace those presented by the 2nd beneficiary.

⑬ The 1st beneficiary presents the draft(s) and documents with the necessary changes to the transferring bank for payment.

⑭ The transferring bank effects payments to the 1st beneficiary by negotiation. The payment at this stage is only the difference between the 2 invoices.

⑮ After payment is effected, the transferring bank forwards the draft(s) and document(s) to the issuing bank for reimbursement.

⑯ The issuing bank makes reimbursement to the transferring bank.

⑰ The issuing bank notifies the importer (1st applicant) to make payment to retire documents.

⑱ The Importer (1st applicant) makes payment and retires documents.

Although a transferable documentary credit can facilitate the transactions through a middle man, it can incur additional risks to both the importer and the exporter. For the importer, he should know that the exporter under the transferable credit is only a middle man. Therefore, he may suffer a loss in the event that the goods shipped do not agree with those mentioned in the sales contract while having to make payments against correct documents.

For the exporter, as the beneficiary under the transferred part, he may also suffer a loss in the event that drafts/documents presented by the middle man do not comply with the terms of the transferable credit. The risk is that he may not receive payments no matter how fully other documents presented by him do comply with the transferred part of the credit. For this reason, it is recommended that the transferred credit will be confirmed by the transferring bank.

4. Back-to-Back Credit

A back-to-back credit may be used when the credit issued in favor of the middle man is not transferable or, although transferable, cannot meet the commercial requirements of transfer in accordance with UCP500 conditions. The beneficiary, that is the middle man, who may not be able to supply goods and should purchase them from and make payment to another supplier may desire to use a back to back credit.

The definition of a back-to-back credit reads as follows: "The benefit of an irrevocable documentary credit (the original credit) may be made available to a third party (the exporter) where the 1st beneficiary (the middle man) uses the documentary credit as security to obtain another documentary credit (the new credit) in favor of the actual supplier (the exporter)."

A back to back credit involves two legally independent credits: one opened in favor of the middle man and the other in favor of the exporter. The two credits are put back to back against each other and it is necessary to consider the details of them:

The Original Credit		The New Credit	
Applicant	The Importer	Applicant	The Middle Man
Beneficiary	The Middle Man (The 1st Beneficiary)	Beneficiary	The Exporter (The 2nd Beneficiary)
The Issuing Bank	The Importer's Bank	The Issuing Bank	The Middle Man's Bank

With the middle man's bank becoming the second issuing bank, it assumes payment undertaking to the exporter (the 2nd beneficiary). That is to say, it must make reimbursement to the exporter's bank. While at the same time, as a negotiating bank under the original credit, whether it can get reimbursement from the 1st issuing bank must depend on the correct presentation of drafts/documents on the part of the middle man.

The two credits are identical as regards to the documentary requirements as well as the credit terms except for a price difference as shown in the invoice and the draft, the names of the applicant and the beneficiary, the latest date of shipment, the latest date for presentation of documents and the time validity.

As back to back credit resembles transferable credit in may aspects, it is necessary to make a comparison between them and point out their differences.

Transferable credit	Back to back Credit
A transferable credit is one credit only and the tranferred part is an extension of the original credit, under which the original issuing bank undertakes to pay.	The back credit is an independent credit from the original credit, though the back credit is issued based on the first one.
The issuing bank of the transferable part is the original issuing bank.	The issuing bank of the back credit is not the original issuing bank. It is the middle man's bank.
The 1st issuing bank's payment undertaking is extended to the 2nd beneficiary.	The 1st issuing bank's payment undertaking can not be extended to the 2nd beneficiary.
The 2nd beneficiary can not have the payment undertaking from the middle man's bank. If the issuing bank refuses to pay, the transferring bank has no obligation to effect payment.	The 2nd beneficiary is sure to have the payment undertaking from the middle man's bank which is the 2nd issuing bank. The 2nd issuing bank should effect payment against correct documents no matter whether the 1st issuing bank pays or not.
The prescribed contents of a transferable credit are subject to UCP500 Article No. 48.	A back credit has no such bindings.

For the Procedure of a back to back credit, please turn to corresponding procedure under a transferable credit for reference.

5. Irrevocable Documentary Reciprocal/Counter Credit

A reciprocal credit is used mainly for the barter system with two underlying transactions, one being an import and the other an export. It is in all respects similar to an ordinary commercial credit except the applicant of the primary credit takes the position of the beneficiary of the reciprocal/counter credit, while the beneficiary of the primary credit becomes the applicant of the reciprocal credit. The amounts under the two credits will be made roughly equal with each other. The relationship of the two credits is illustrated as follows:

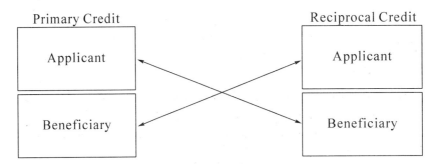

In order to protect the interest of all parties involved, the primary credit will incorporate in it a special clause as follows:

" This credit shall not be available /operative/effective unless and until the reciprocal credit in favor of (the original applicant) for account of (the original beneficiary) is established by (the original beneficiary's bank). "

When the reciprocal credit is established in response to the primary credit, it will normally incorporate a special clause as follows:

" This is a reciprocal credit against (the primary issuing bank) credit No. _____ in favor of (the original applicant) covering the shipment of _____. "

6. Anticipatory/Red Clause Credit

A red clause credit is often used when the importer wants to extend finance to his reliable supplier(the exporter) by providing him the funds prior to shipment.

A red clause credit is a credit with a special condition incorporated into it that authorizes the confirming bank or any other nominated bank to make advances to the beneficiary before presentation of the documents. A red clause credit is so called because this clause was originally written in red ink to draw attention to the unique nature of this credit. The special clause is incorporated at the specific request of the applicant, and the wording is upon his requirements.

The clause specifies that the amount of the advance authorized may be for a partial or full amount of the credit. When advance payment is made by the confirming bank or other nominated bank, the confirming bank or the nominated bank will get repayment for the advances plus interest from the proceeds to be paid to the beneficiary when goods are shipped and documents are presented in compliance with the terms of the credit.

In the event that the beneficiary fails to ship goods, the confirming bank or any other nominated bank will have a right of recourse against the issuing bank, which will in turn have the similar right of recourse against the applicant/importer to demand repayment plus interest and other charges incurred. Therefore, this kind of advance arrangement is made at the risk of the applicant.

The undertaking clause of the issuing bank will read as follows:

" We (the issuing bank) hereby authorize you (the nominated bank) at your discretion to grant to the beneficiary an advance or advances to the extent to AUD20,000, being 80% of the credit amount, any interest accrued thereon should be charged to the beneficiary from the date of each advance to the date of repayment at the current rate of interest in Australia. The proceeds of any drafts negotiated under this credit may at your discretion be applied by you in the repayment to you of such advances together with interest as aforesaid. In consideration of your bank making such advances to the beneficiary who will eventually fail to effect shipment covered by the credit, we guarantee repayment and undertake to pay you on demand any sum owed by the beneficiary in respect of such advances together with interest thereon. "

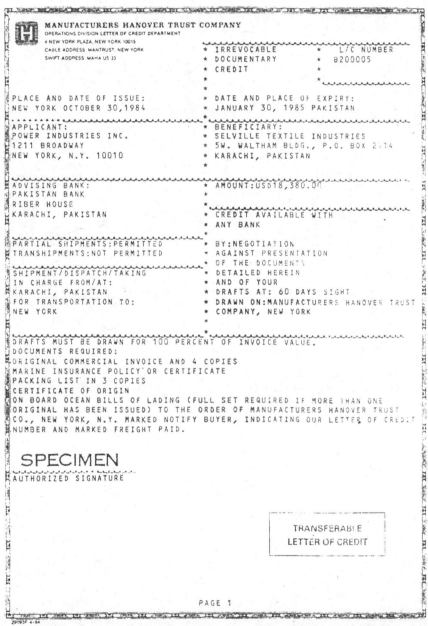

Transferable Letter of Credit (1)

```
MANUFACTURERS HANOVER TRUST COMPANY
OPERATIONS DIVISION LETTER OF CREDIT DEPARTMENT
4 NEW YORK PLAZA, NEW YORK 10015            * CONTINUATION OF  * L/C NUMBER
C/BLE ADDRESS: MANTRUST, NEW YORK           * IRREVOCABLE       * B200005
SWIFT ADDRESS: MAHA US 33                   * DOCUMENTARY       *
                                            * CREDIT            *
PLACE AND DATE OF ISSUE:                    * DATE AND PLACE OF EXPIRY:
NEW YORK OCTOBER 30,1984                    * JANUARY 30, 1985 PAKISTAN

APPLICANT:                                  * BENEFICIARY:
POWER INDUSTRIES INC.                       * SELVILLE TEXTILE INDUSTRIES
1211 BROADWAY                               * 5W. WALTHAM BLDG., P.O. BOX 2114
NEW YORK, N.Y. 10010                        * KARACHI, PAKISTAN

COVERING:20X40 TERRY TOWELS-HERCULES QUALITY AT U.S.$9.19 PER DOZEN,
CONTRACT NO. RG 8/640 CIF NEW YORK

SPECIAL CONDITIONS:
THIS LETTER OF CREDIT IS TRANSFERABLE.
IN CASE OF ANY TRANSFER:
1.THE TRANSFERRING BANK MUST ENDORSE THE FACT OF SUCH TRANSFER ON THIS
LETTER OF CREDIT.
2. A LETTER FROM THE ORIGINAL BENEFICIARY ADDRESSED TO US CONFIRMING
SUCH TRANSFER MUST ACCOMPANY THE FIRST DRAFT DRAWN BY EACH TRANSFEREE.
3.THIS CREDIT MAY NOT BE TRANSFERRED TO ANY DESIGNATED NATIONALS AS
DEFINED IN THE U.S. FOREIGN ASSET CONTROL REGULATIONS AND THE U.S. CUBAN
ASSETS CONTROL REGULATIONS.

THE AMOUNT OF ANY DRAFT DRAWN MUST BE ENDORSED ON THE REVERSE OF THE
ORIGINAL CREDIT. ALL DRAFTS MUST BE MARKED "DRAWN UNDER MANUFACTURERS
HANOVER TRUST COMPANY LETTER OF CREDIT NUMBER B-200005 DATED OCTOBER 30,
1984."

EXCEPT SO FAR AS OTHERWISE EXPRESSLY STATED,  THIS CREDIT IS SUBJECT TO
THE UNIFORM CUSTOMS AND PRACTICE FOR DOCUMENTARY CREDIT (1983 REVISION)
INTERNATIONAL CHAMBER OF COMMERCE PUBLICATION NO. 400
WE HEREBY AGREE WITH THE DRAWERS, ENDORSERS AND BONAFIDE HOLDERS OF
DRAFTS DRAWN UNDER AND IN COMPLIANCE WITH THE TERMS OF THIS CREDIT THAT
SUCH DRAFTS WILL BE DULY HONORED ON DUE PRESENTATION TO THE DRAWEE IF
NEGOTIATED ON OR BEFORE THE EXPIRATION DATE OR PRESENTED TO THE DRAWEES
TOGETHER WITH THIS LETTER OF CREDIT ON OR BEFORE THIS DATE.

SPECIMEN
AUTHORIZED SIGNATURE

                        TRANSFERABLE
                        LETTER OF CREDIT

                        PAGE 2
```

This exhibit is fictitious and is provided only as an example. The information contained therein reflects the terms and conditions of the Uniform Customs and Practice per International Chamber of Commerce publication #400 in effect as of October 1984.

Transferable Letter of Credit (2)

BANK OF CHINA HONGKONG PLACE and date of issue HONG KONG 1983-11-3	IRREVOCABLE DOCUMENTARY CREDIT	NUMBER 375-83-8990
	Date and place of expiry 1984-05-20 in China	

Applicant Hang Seng Bank Ltd., Kowloon Main Branch a/c The Yardley Garment Factory Ltd., Hongkong. (Ref. KHS340379EX)	Beneficiary China National Textiles I/E Corp., Shanghai Branch, 27 Chungsnan Rd., E. 1. Shanghai.

Advising Bank Ref. No. Bank of China Shanghai	Amount US$252,685.00 (Say, U.S. Dollars Two Hundred Fifty Two Thousand Six Hundred Eighty Five Only)

Partial Shipments	Transhipment	Credit available
[x] allowed [ ] not allowed	[ ] allowed [x] not allowed	by [ ] Payment [ ] Acceptance [x] Negotiation against presentation of the documents detailed herein and of your draft(s)
Shipment from Shangnai to Penang . Latest May 10, 1984		at sight in duplicate drawn on Hang Seng Bank Ltd., Kowloon Main Branch a/c The Yardley Garment Factory Ltd., H.K. (Ref.KHS340379EX) for full invoice value.

List of documents to be presented:

Signed Commercial invoice(s) in duplicate.

Covering shipment of:

...... (.... Hundred Thousand) yards of 100% Cotton Yarn Dyed Woven Flannel in Check Designs, 2-sides brushed, Washable colours, width: 34/35" presnrunk. Packing: in export bale packing. @USD0.xxx per yard, as per beneficiary's Sales Confirmation No. 32HA101S.   C.I.F. Penang, Malaysia.

Other terms and conditions:

Full set of at least three signed original Clean "On Board" Ocean Bills of Lading showing beneficiary as shipper, made out to order of shipper and endorsed in blank marked "Freight Prepaid" and "Notify Penang Textile Sdn. Bhd., No. 37 Hamilton Rd., Penang, Malaysia "evidencing Shipment from Shanghai to Penang, Malaysia not later than May 10, 1984 required.

Insurance Policies or Certificates in negotiable form, in duplicate and endorsed in blank, covering Ocean Marine Cargo Clauses (W.A.) Ocean Marine Cargo War Risks Clauses of the P.I.C.C. for full invoice value plus at least 10% with claims payable at destination in the currency of drafts irrespective of percentage required. In case of container shipment, insurance policies or certificate must state that the risks of jettison and/or washing overboard have been included.

Beneficiary's certificate to the effect thatone set of non-negotiable copies of shipping documents has been airmailed direct to The Yardley Garment Factory Ltd., 479 Castle Park Rd., 4th Floor, Kowloon, Hongkong immediately after shipment required.

All documents must be sent by one registered airmail.
Combined transport Bills of Lading not acceptable.
Invoice to snow a deduction of 3% discount.
Certificate of Chinese Origin in duplicate required.
Insurance also to include T.P.N.D. Clauses.

On board notation on B/L must be signed/initialled by the carrier or its agent.

The Ref. No. KMS340379EX of Hang Seng Bank Ltd., L/C No. and value of the goods must not be snown on all documents other than draft and invoice.

Documents in combined form not acceptable.

We hereby issue this Documentary Credit in your favour, it is subject to the Uniform Customs and Practice for Documentary Credits (1974 Revision International Chamber of Commerce, Paris, France, Publication No. 290).·

For Bank of China, Hong Kong
SIGNATURE

Back to Back Letter of Credit

```
    MANUFACTURERS HANOVER TRUST COMPANY
[H] OPERATIONS DIVISION LETTER OF CREDIT DEPARTMENT
    4 NEW YORK PLAZA NEW YORK 10015
    CABLE ADDRESS MANTRUST, NEW YORK
    SWIFT ADDRESS MAHA US 33

                                 *  IRREVOCABLE        *  L/C NUMBER
                                 *  DOCUMENTARY        *  B200762
                                 *  CREDIT             *
                                 *
PLACE AND DATE OF ISSUE:         *  DATE AND PLACE OF EXPIRY:
NEW YORK AUGUST 29, 1985         *  OCTOBER 23,1985 BRAZIL

APPLICANT:                       *  BENEFICIARY:
MARLBORO LEATHERS INC.           *  SANTIAGO RUIZ LTD.
16 WEST 19TH STREET              *  P.O. BOX 6311, SANTA CRUZ
NEW YORK, N.Y. 10011             *  BRAZIL

ADVISING BANK:                   *  AMOUNT:USD17,000.00
BRAZILIAN BANK S.A.              *
SANTA CRUZ                       *
BRAZIL                           *  CREDIT AVAILABLE WITH
                                 *  ANY BANK

PARTIAL SHIPMENTS:NOT PERMITTED  *  BY:NEGOTIATION
TRANSHIPMENTS:NOT PERMITTED      *  AGAINST PRESENTATION
                                 *  OF THE DOCUMENTS
SHIPMENT/DISPATCH/TAKING         *  DETAILED HEREIN
IN CHARGE FROM/AT:               *  AND OF YOUR
BRAZILIAN AIRPORT                *  DRAFTS AT: SIGHT
FOR TRANSPORTATION TO:           *  DRAWN ON:MANUFACTURERS HANOVER TRUST
NEW YORK                         *  COMPANY, NEW YORK
                                 *
DRAFTS MUST BE DRAWN FOR 100 PERCENT OF INVOICE VALUE.
DOCUMENTS REQUIRED:
ORIGINAL COMMERCIAL INVOICE AND 5 COPIES
CUSTOMS INVOICE IN 3 COPIES
PACKING LIST
AIRWAY BILL CONSIGNED TO MARLBORO LEATHERS INC., NEW YORK, N.Y. MARKED
NOTIFY GOTHIC INT'L., J.F.K. INT'L., AIRPORT, CARGO BLDG., NO. 124,
JAMAICA, NEW YORK INDICATING MANUFACTURERS HANOVER TRUST LETTER OF
CREDIT NUMBER B-200762

SPECIMEN
AUTHORIZED SIGNATURE

                                          RED CLAUSE
                                          LETTER OF CREDIT

                         PAGE 1
```

This exhibit is fictitious and is provided only as an example. The information contained therein reflects the terms and conditions of the Uniform Customs and Practice per International Chamber of Commerce publication #400 in effect as of October 1984.

Red Clause Letter of Credit（1）

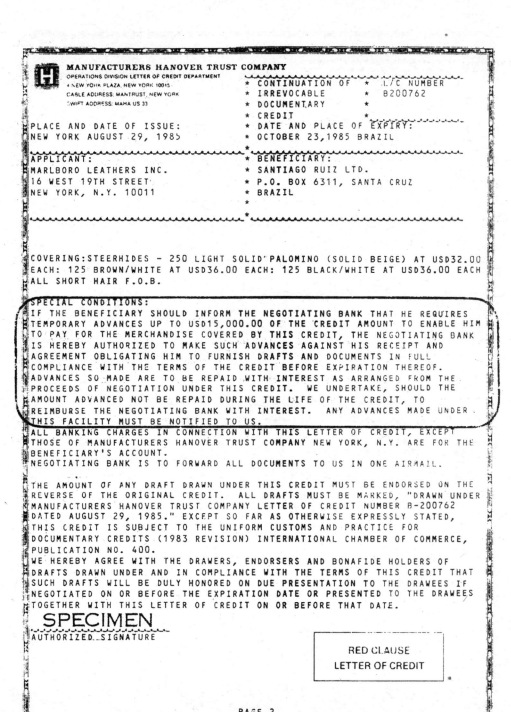

MANUFACTURERS HANOVER TRUST COMPANY
OPERATIONS DIVISION LETTER OF CREDIT DEPARTMENT
4 NEW YORK PLAZA, NEW YORK 10015
CABLE ADDRESS: MANTRUST, NEW YORK
SWIFT ADDRESS: MAHA US 33

* CONTINUATION OF * L/C NUMBER
* IRREVOCABLE   * B200762
* DOCUMENTARY   *
* CREDIT   *

PLACE AND DATE OF ISSUE: * DATE AND PLACE OF EXPIRY:
NEW YORK AUGUST 29, 1985   * OCTOBER 23,1985 BRAZIL

APPLICANT: * BENEFICIARY:
MARLBORO LEATHERS INC.   * SANTIAGO RUIZ LTD.
16 WEST 19TH STREET   * P.O. BOX 6311, SANTA CRUZ
NEW YORK, N.Y. 10011   * BRAZIL
                                *

COVERING:STEERHIDES - 250 LIGHT SOLID PALOMINO (SOLID BEIGE) AT USD32.00
EACH: 125 BROWN/WHITE AT USD36.00 EACH: 125 BLACK/WHITE AT USD36.00 EACH
ALL SHORT HAIR F.O.B.

SPECIAL CONDITIONS:
IF THE BENEFICIARY SHOULD INFORM THE NEGOTIATING BANK THAT HE REQUIRES
TEMPORARY ADVANCES UP TO USD15,000.00 OF THE CREDIT AMOUNT TO ENABLE HIM
TO PAY FOR THE MERCHANDISE COVERED BY THIS CREDIT, THE NEGOTIATING BANK
IS HEREBY AUTHORIZED TO MAKE SUCH ADVANCES AGAINST HIS RECEIPT AND
AGREEMENT OBLIGATING HIM TO FURNISH DRAFTS AND DOCUMENTS IN FULL
COMPLIANCE WITH THE TERMS OF THE CREDIT BEFORE EXPIRATION THEREOF.
ADVANCES SO MADE ARE TO BE REPAID WITH INTEREST AS ARRANGED FROM THE
PROCEEDS OF NEGOTIATION UNDER THIS CREDIT. WE UNDERTAKE, SHOULD THE
AMOUNT ADVANCED NOT BE REPAID DURING THE LIFE OF THE CREDIT, TO
REIMBURSE THE NEGOTIATING BANK WITH INTEREST. ANY ADVANCES MADE UNDER
THIS FACILITY MUST BE NOTIFIED TO US.
ALL BANKING CHARGES IN CONNECTION WITH THIS LETTER OF CREDIT, EXCEPT
THOSE OF MANUFACTURERS HANOVER TRUST COMPANY NEW YORK, N.Y. ARE FOR THE
BENEFICIARY'S ACCOUNT.
NEGOTIATING BANK IS TO FORWARD ALL DOCUMENTS TO US IN ONE AIRMAIL.

THE AMOUNT OF ANY DRAFT DRAWN UNDER THIS CREDIT MUST BE ENDORSED ON THE
REVERSE OF THE ORIGINAL CREDIT. ALL DRAFTS MUST BE MARKED, "DRAWN UNDER
MANUFACTURERS HANOVER TRUST COMPANY LETTER OF CREDIT NUMBER B-200762
DATED AUGUST 29, 1985." EXCEPT SO FAR AS OTHERWISE EXPRESSLY STATED,
THIS CREDIT IS SUBJECT TO THE UNIFORM CUSTOMS AND PRACTICE FOR
DOCUMENTARY CREDITS (1983 REVISION) INTERNATIONAL CHAMBER OF COMMERCE,
PUBLICATION NO. 400.
WE HEREBY AGREE WITH THE DRAWERS, ENDORSERS AND BONAFIDE HOLDERS OF
DRAFTS DRAWN UNDER AND IN COMPLIANCE WITH THE TERMS OF THIS CREDIT THAT
SUCH DRAFTS WILL BE DULY HONORED ON DUE PRESENTATION TO THE DRAWEES IF
NEGOTIATED ON OR BEFORE THE EXPIRATION DATE OR PRESENTED TO THE DRAWEES
TOGETHER WITH THIS LETTER OF CREDIT ON OR BEFORE THAT DATE.

SPECIMEN
AUTHORIZED SIGNATURE

RED CLAUSE
LETTER OF CREDIT

PAGE 2

2093F 4-84
This exhibit is fictitious and is provided only as an example. The information contained therein reflects the terms and conditions
of the Uniform Customs and Practice per International Chamber of Commerce publication #400 in effect as of October 1984.

Red Clause Letter of Credit (2)

```
MANUFACTURERS HANOVER TRUST COMPANY
OPERATIONS DIVISION LETTER OF CREDIT DEPARTMENT
4 NEW YORK PLAZA, NEW YORK 10015
CABLE ADDRESS: MANTRUST, NEW YORK
SWIFT ADDRESS: MAHA US 33

* IRREVOCABLE          *  L/C NUMBER
* DOCUMENTARY          *  B104321
* CREDIT               *
*                      *

PLACE AND DATE OF ISSUE:      * DATE AND PLACE OF EXPIRY:
NEW YORK MAY 6,1985           * NOVEMBER 6, 1985 THAILAND
                              *
APPLICANT:                    * BENEFICIARY:
INTERNATIONAL PIGMENT CO.     * AHMED PRODUCT COMPANY
214 MADISON AVENUE            * 629 SRIPUVANART ROAD
NEW YORK, N.Y. 10010          * SONGKAI, THAILAND

ADVISING BANK:                * AMOUNT:USD300,000.00
THAILAND TRUST BANK LTD.      * SEE BELOW X
HATYAI BRANCH
BANGKOK, THAILAND             * CREDIT AVAILABLE WITH
                              * ANY BANK

PARTIAL SHIPMENTS:SEE BELOW XX  * BY:NEGOTIATION
TRANSHIPMENTS:NOT PERMITTED     * AGAINST PRESENTATION
                                * OF THE DOCUMENTS
SHIPMENT/DISPATCH/TAKING        * DETAILED HEREIN
IN CHARGE FROM/AT:              * AND OF YOUR
THAILAND                        * DRAFTS AT: SIGHT
FOR TRANSPORTATION TO:          * DRAWN ON:MANUFACTURERS HANOVER TRUST
U.S.A. PORT                     * COMPANY, NEW YORK
                                *

DRAFTS MUST BE DRAWN FOR 100 PERCENT OF INVOICE VALUE.
X AMOUNT: REVOLVING MONTHLY NON-CUMULATIVE COMMENCING MAY 6,1985
XX PARTIAL SHIPMENT PERMITTED WITHIN EACH MONTH
DOCUMENTS REQUIRED:
COMMERCIAL INVOICE IN 5 COPIES
CUSTOMS INVOICE
CERTIFICATE OF ORIGIN IN 3 COPIES
PACKING LIST IN 3 COPIES
ON BOARD MARINE BILL OF LADING (FULL SET REQUIRED IF MORE THAN ONE
ORIGINAL HAS BEEN ISSUED) TO THE ORDER OF MANUFACTURERS HANOVER TRUST
CO., NEW YORK, N.Y. MARKED NOTIFY BUYER, INDICATING OUR LETTER OF CREDIT
NUMBER MARKED FREIGHT COLLECT.

SPECIMEN
AUTHORIZED SIGNATURE

                          REVOLVING
                          LETTER OF CREDIT

                    PAGE 1
```

Revolving Letter of Credit (1)

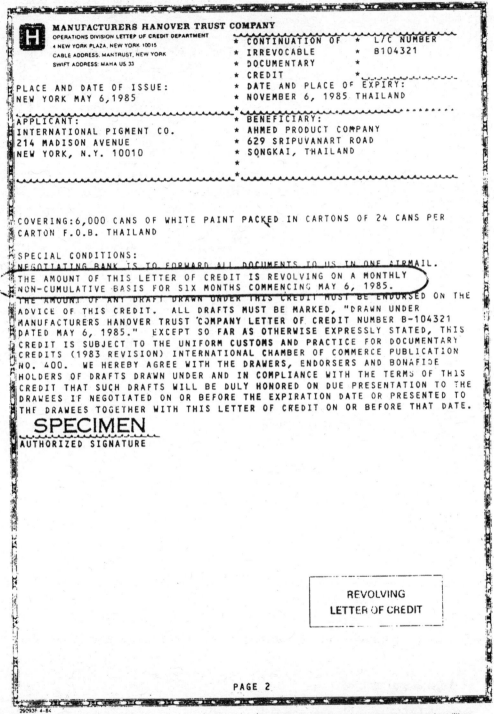

MANUFACTURERS HANOVER TRUST COMPANY
OPERATIONS DIVISION LETTER OF CREDIT DEPARTMENT
4 NEW YORK PLAZA, NEW YORK 10015
CABLE ADDRESS: MANTRUST, NEW YORK
SWIFT ADDRESS: MAHA US 33

```
* CONTINUATION OF  *  L/C NUMBER
* IRREVOCABLE       *  B104321
* DOCUMENTARY       *
* CREDIT            *
```

PLACE AND DATE OF ISSUE:
NEW YORK MAY 6,1985

```
* DATE AND PLACE OF EXPIRY:
* NOVEMBER 6, 1985 THAILAND
```

APPLICANT:
INTERNATIONAL PIGMENT CO.
214 MADISON AVENUE
NEW YORK, N.Y. 10010

```
* BENEFICIARY:
* AHMED PRODUCT COMPANY
* 629 SRIPUVANART ROAD
* SONGKAI, THAILAND
```

COVERING:6,000 CANS OF WHITE PAINT PACKED IN CARTONS OF 24 CANS PER CARTON F.O.B. THAILAND

SPECIAL CONDITIONS:
NEGOTIATING BANK IS TO FORWARD ALL DOCUMENTS TO US IN ONE AIRMAIL.
THE AMOUNT OF THIS LETTER OF CREDIT IS REVOLVING ON A MONTHLY NON-CUMULATIVE BASIS FOR SIX MONTHS COMMENCING MAY 6, 1985.
THE AMOUNT OF ANY DRAFT DRAWN UNDER THIS CREDIT MUST BE ENDORSED ON THE ADVICE OF THIS CREDIT. ALL DRAFTS MUST BE MARKED, "DRAWN UNDER MANUFACTURERS HANOVER TRUST COMPANY LETTER OF CREDIT NUMBER B-104321 DATED MAY 6, 1985." EXCEPT SO FAR AS OTHERWISE EXPRESSLY STATED, THIS CREDIT IS SUBJECT TO THE UNIFORM CUSTOMS AND PRACTICE FOR DOCUMENTARY CREDITS (1983 REVISION) INTERNATIONAL CHAMBER OF COMMERCE PUBLICATION NO. 400. WE HEREBY AGREE WITH THE DRAWERS, ENDORSERS AND BONAFIDE HOLDERS OF DRAFTS DRAWN UNDER AND IN COMPLIANCE WITH THE TERMS OF THIS CREDIT THAT SUCH DRAFTS WILL BE DULY HONORED ON DUE PRESENTATION TO THE DRAWEES IF NEGOTIATED ON OR BEFORE THE EXPIRATION DATE OR PRESENTED TO THE DRAWEES TOGETHER WITH THIS LETTER OF CREDIT ON OR BEFORE THAT DATE.

SPECIMEN
AUTHORIZED SIGNATURE

REVOLVING
LETTER OF CREDIT

PAGE 2

Revolving Letter of Credit (2)

It will be helpful to consider the following table to clarify the confusing items concerning some credits:

Item \ Type	Ordinary L/C	Confirmed L/C	Transferable L/C	Back to Back L/C	Reciprocal L/C
No. of underlying sales transactions	1	1	1	1	2
No. of sales contracts	1	1	2 Imp. - Midm. Midm. - Exp.	2 Imp. - Midm Midm. - Exp.	2 Imp. - Exp. Exp. - Imp.
No. of credits	1	1	1 Original + Extension	2 Original + Back credit	2 Original + counter credit
No. of issuing bank	1	1	1	2 Imp. 's bank + Midm. 's Bank	2 Imp. 's bank + Exp. 's Bank
No. of undertakings	1	2 Issuing bank + confirming bank	1	2 Imp. 's bank + Midm. 's Bank	2 Imp. 's bank + Exp. 's Bank
No. of beneficiaries	1	1	2 Midm. + Exp.	2 Midm. + Exp.	2 Exp. + Imp.
No. of applicants	1	1	2 Imp. + Midm.	2 Imp. + Midm.	2 Imp. + Exp.

Notes: Imp. = Importer; Exp. = Exporter; Midm. = Middle man.

Section Five   Amendment, Characteristics, Advantages and Risks of L/C

1. Amendment of L/C

Although L/C is issued based on the sales contract, it is a separate document independent from the sales contract once issued. Any discrepancies between the two documents mentioned above may lead to the amendment of the credit.

For the exporter/beneficiary, if he finds the terms and conditions in the credit are not in line with those mentioned in the sales contract, he may either accept it as it is or request the applicant to amend the credit through the issuing bank. On the other hand, if the amendment is initiated by the applicant, it must be issued by the issuing bank, and, in the case of an irrevocable credit, the amendment should also obtain consent from the beneficiary and the confirming bank, if any. The issuing bank will charge a fee for such amendments to the account of the applicant.

When the issuing bank issues an amendment, the items amended should be attached to the original copy and to replace the corresponding items in the original L/C and have a legal binding on all parties concerned, such as the applicant, the beneficiary and the confirming bank, if any.

For the issuing bank, the amendment takes effect on the issuing date of the amendment; for the beneficiary, the effective date should be deemed either on the date of his formal certificate of acceptance or when he presents the documents in agreement with the amendment. In order to make sure whether or not the amendment is accepted by the beneficiary, the issuing bank may incorporate in the credit an additional document requirement as:

" Beneficiary's certificate confirming their acceptance or non-acceptance of the amendment dated _____ made under this credit quoting the relevant amendment number (Such certificate is not required if this credit has not been amended). "

Or, the issuing bank may request the advising bank to do the job on his behalf by a special instruction to the advising bank:

" Please advise this amendment to the beneficiary and inform us promptly by tele-transmission of his acceptance or rejection thereof within 21 days (calendar day) after our issuing date of amendment. "

2. **Characteristics of the Credit**

(A) Letter of credit is a payment method based on banker's credit in the sense that the bank assumes the payment undertaking on behalf of the importer. Compared with collection, which is made on trader's credit, the importer will be required to make payments and/or acceptance to retire documents under both payment methods. However, before the exporter makes shipment, he has already obtained a payment undertaking from the issuing bank. Therefore, L/C is more favorable to the exporter rather than to the importer.

(B) Under L/C, banks deal with documents rather than physical goods, services or other performances to which the documents may relate. Banks effect payment only against the doctrine of strict compliance, that is, the documents presented must comply with the terms of the credit on one hand and the documents themselves ought to be consistent with each other.

(C) Even dealing with documents, banks will enjoy the following escaping clauses:

* Banks assume no liability or responsibility for the form, sufficiency, accuracy, genuineness, falsification or legal effect of any documents presented. Banks are only to examine that documents are on the face to be in compliance with the L/C.

* Banks assume no responsibility for the acts of a third party taking part in one way or another in the credit operation or the acts of their correspondent banks to which they have instructed to carry out the operation.

* Banks are not responsible for delays in the transmission of information over which they have no control.

3. Advantages under L/C

(1) For the Exporter

(A) The most outstanding benefit to the exporter is that he is freed from the worry of non-payment. He can rely on the bank's undertaking for payment provided the shipping documents are in line with the terms of the credit. Through various methods of financing available under the credit, he can obtain payment immediately after the shipment or even before the shipment is made. Thus his turnover is speeded up.

(B) The exporter can be freed from the worry of funds transfer to him or the prohibition of his goods from being imported because the importer must have obtained the foreign exchange permit and import license before the credit is issued.

(2) For the Importer

(A) When applying for L/C, the applicant may be requested to place a deposit margin with the issuing bank, and sometimes even no deposit margin is required by the issuing bank. This brings benefits to the importer because occupancy of his own flowing funds is reduced and deferred till the time when the issuing bank makes payment on his behalf.

(B) The importer can exercise certain control over the quality, quantity and the time of delivery of goods through the terms and conditions under the credit. For example, the credit stipulates the latest shipment date to control the time of delivery of goods. The credit may call for an inspection certificates to control the quality and the quantity of the covered goods.

(C) He is freed from the problem of non-delivery. He can obtain title documents immediately after he makes payment. With various methods of finance available under the credit, the importer can obtain documents before he makes payment.

(3) For the Issuing Bank

(A) The issuing bank can earn a commission by opening the credit. An additional advantage for him is that from the time the credit is opened till the time the draft(s)/document(s) are presented for reimbursement, only its name and creditworthiness are lent out, no actual funds are granted.

(B) Before the importer makes payment, the title documents are in the hands of the issuing bank. With the ownership over the goods through the documents, the bank can sell the goods to recover the loss in the event that the importer fails to fulfil his obligations.

(4) For the Negotiating Bank

(A) The negotiation of the negotiating bank is done with the definite payment undertaking of the issuing bank. The negotiating bank is willing to negotiate the draft(s)/document(s) under the credit to gain profits through examining documents charges and discounting charges.

(B) An additional benefit to the negotiating bank is to obtain foreign exchange by converting the proceeds into the local currency.

(5) For Other Banks in the L/C Operation

They will make a profit and earn a commission for every service they have provided in the operation.

4. Risks under L/C

Because the operation of credit lays great emphasis on the documents to be on the face in consistence with the credit, the integrity of the contracting parties, namely the importer, the exporter, and the credit standing of the issuing bank are of vital importance. Any deficiency in this respect may incur risks to the other parties concerned.

(1) For the Exporter

The exporter may suffer a loss if a L/C is a false L/C opened by a fictitious bank or a dishonest bank who might declare bankruptcy after shipment is made but before payment is obtained.

(2) For the Importer

He may suffer a loss if a dishonest exporter ships the inferior goods quite different from those described in the sales contract.

(3) For the Issuing Bank

The issuing bank can be cheated into issuing credit when the exporter and importer make "correct" documents to cover the false goods. For example, the importer may purposely refuse to make payment to retire the documents after the issuing bank fulfils his payment undertaking to the exporter against "correct" documents.

Section Six   Finance under Letter of Credit

Letter of credit is not only a payment method, but also an instrument of finance to facilitate international trade. The case in point is buyer's usance credit and red clause credit. In this section, however, the focus is on how finance can be granted to the traders against a credit through the L/C procedure.

1. **To the Exporter**

(1) Packing Loan

It is a finance extended to the exporter by the exporter's bank against the original credit received from overseas banker together with the sales contract. In other words, the original credit and sales contract are used as security for the exporter to obtain the said loan. It is so called because the loan is extended at the stage of production and packing and it enables the exporter to obtain payment before shipment is made.

The amount under this loan will usually up to 80% of the credit amount with the time limit with 3 months or no longer than 21 days after the expiry date of the credit.

(2) Outward Bill Purchased – Negotiation

The bank authorized or chosen to negotiate gives value to the draft(s) drawn on the issuing bank at the time when the exporter presents the documents to him.

Similar to negotiation under collection, the negotiation bank will become the holder in due course who has the right of recourse against the exporter when the draft is dishonored by the drawee.

However, under the credit, the drawee is a bank rather than a trader (the importer). Therefore, the negotiating bank is more secured to get compensation in the sense that he has a payment undertaking from the issuing bank rather than from a trader (the importer) under collection. Another difference is that under collection, the exporter will not get the said finance if the bank decides not to negotiate. While under a negotiable credit, the exporter is entitled to obtain the said finance.

2. **To the Importer**

(1) Deposit Margin for Issuing a Credit

It is a kind of finance extended by the issuing bank to the importer. At the time of applying for the issuance of a credit, the deposit margin required to place with the issuing bank is just a certain percentage of the credit amount, and normally it is around 20%. This means that the importer can utilize the full credit amount against a partial margin. The importer is financed in the sense that the occupancy of his flow of funds is greatly reduced. And in some cases, the importer may enjoy greater benefits when no margin is required on the part of the importer when the credit is issued at his request.

(2) L/C against Trust Receipt (T/R)

This kind of finance is extended to the importer by the issuing bank at the time when the importer is supposed to make payment to retire documents but faces some financial difficulties, or when under a time credit where the physical goods are at the seaport long before the maturity of the documents.

After the arrangement, the bank will release the documents to the importer against T/R under which he will clear the goods as a "trustee" of his bank. Thus, payment is deferred and the importer will obtain goods at once.

(3) Inward Bill Purchased

This kind of finance is extended to the importer by the issuing bank at the time when the issuing bank receives documents sent from the exporter or his banker. The importer is financed because the payment is made by the issuing bank on his behalf.

The importer is entitled to obtain the said finance which reflects the most important characteristic of the credit: a credit is the payment undertaking from a bank on behalf of the importer. After payment is effected, the issuing bank will look for the importer for compensation.

(4) Shipping Guarantee under Credit

It is always possible that the arrival of physical goods will be ahead of the arrival of the documents because they are going through different routes. In this case, the importer may request his bank to arrange a shipping guarantee with the shipping company against his T/R with the bank. Shipping Guarantee is a contract of indemnity between the issuing bank and the shipping company against which the bank requires the shipping company to release the physical goods to the importer under the bank's promise to surrender the original Bill of lading to him upon arrival. Only the surrendered original B/L will cancel the shipping guarantee and discharge the liability of the bank to the shipping company.

It is clearly shown in the above mentioned methods that finance is present throughout the L/C procedure. They can be selected to better serve the different purposes of the traders. Readers may turn back to the L/C procedure to have a better understanding of the above-mentioned methods of finance.

Chapter Ten   Payment Methods (V)
− Letter of Guarantee and Stand-by Credit

Section One   Introduction to Letter of Guarantee

In international trade, both the contracting parties will seek ways to protect himself from the breach of the other party. Various payment methods provide different degrees of protection for the either party against the problems of non-payment or non-delivery. For example, with a bank's payment undertaking under a documentary credit, the exporter is protected against the importer's non-payment and the importer is protected against the exporter's non-delivery.

The international economic transactions cover a much wider area than international trade where the obligations for the two contracting parties will go beyond payment and delivery to a greater extent where the problem of non-performance may occur. For example, in international bidding, the party inviting tender will suffer a loss if the tenderer refuses to take the bid upon awarded. Even under a documentary credit, the importer can not be protected in the event that the exporter fails to make shipment after the credit is established in his favor. These are just two examples of non-performance in economic transactions, which are beyond the protection of the payment methods we have discussed in the previous chapters. This limitation can be overcome by another payment method − letter of guarantee where the contracting parties, be it the exporter or the importer, be the owner or the contractor, etc. , will be protected in the sense that contractual obligations will be performed or the breached obligations will be compensated for under a letter of guarantee.

1. Definition

A letter of guarantee (L/G) is a written promise by a bank at the request of its customer (the principal/applicant), undertaking to make payment to the beneficiary within the limits of a stated sum of money in the event of non-performance of the contractual obligations by the principal. It is also called a bank guarantee or a bond in distinction from other types of guarantee issued by other institutions such as the insurance company, the trust company, etc.

The definition tells us that one obvious difference between an issuing bank's payment undertaking under a documentary credit and that under a bank guarantee lies in the conditions to effect payment. Under a documentary credit, the issuing bank will effect payment against the beneficiary's performance. While under a bank guarantee, the issuing bank will effect payment against the principal's non-performance.

2. Parties to a Bank Guarantee

There are three parties to a bank guarantee.

(1) Principal/Applicant

The principal is the person at whose request the guarantee is issued. In the event that he fails to fulfill his contractual obligations, the principal will be claimed after the payment being effected by the guarantor. The amount to be claimed will include the face value of the guarantee and the relevant interest. He may be required to place a partial or a full margin with the guarantor at the time of applying for a L/G.

(2) The Beneficiary

The beneficiary is the person in whose favor the guarantee is issued. In the event of default by the principal, he is entitled to obtain payment upon presentment of correct documents against the bond with the guarantor.

(3) The Guarantor

The guarantor is the issuing bank of a bank guarantee. He is a bank located in the applicant's country. He is responsible to issue a bond in agreement with the application form. Once a guarantee is established, the bank is under the obligation to make payment to the beneficiary under the terms stipulated in the bond. The bank has the right to claim compensation from the applicant to cover the funds outlay to the beneficiary.

In practice, there will be a bank in the beneficiary's country acting as an advising bank to be authorized or requested by the guarantor to advise the bond to the beneficiary.

3. **Conditional Guarantee and "(On) Demand" Guarantee**

(1) Conditional Guarantee/Bond

The International Chamber of Commerce in Paris issued *"Uniform Rules for Contract Guarantee"* in 1978 in its publication No. 325. It stipulates the conditions under which a beneficiary can claim compensation from the guarantor. Conditional guarantee requires documentary evidence which gives maximum protection to the principal(applicant) to be presented by the beneficiary when demanding payment. To attest the non-performance of the principal, the beneficiary should present such documentary evidence as a court decision, an arbitrary award or an approval to the claim from the principal in writing. Such stipulations are unfavorable to the beneficiary since it is time consuming to get a judgement from a court or an arbitrary tribunal when there is a dispute. In addition, the applicant will be reluctant to issue such an approval to the beneficiary's claim. As a result, conditional bond is often found unagreeable to the beneficiary.

(2) "(On) Demand" Guarantee

A new rule governing the letter of guarantee operation, the *"Uniform Rules for Demand Guarantee"*, was published by the International Chamber of Commerce in 1992 in its publication No. 458. Under the new rule, the guarantee can be called "on demand" at the sole discretion of the beneficiary. In other words, the bank must pay if called upon to do so by simply a written demand from the beneficiary without a written proof from a neutral third party or from the principal himself, even in circumstances that the claim is wholly unjustified. Compared with conditional guarantee, this "on demand" bond is sometimes referred to as an "unconditional" guarantee. It is more favorable to the beneficiary and has gained general acceptance from prevailing banking and commercial practices.

It is necessary to consider the nature of a demand guarantee:

(A) In the event of default by the principal, the guarantor must make compensation in the form of monetary payment. It can never be made by the fulfillment of the guarantor himself on behalf of the principal.

（B）Compensation will be made against correct documents rather than the actual condition of the non-performance. It must be stressed that bank should never be involved in contractual disputes. If payment is called for by documents which conform to the terms of the bond, the bank must pay. This means that the guarantor is not concerned with the fact of default or actual default by the principal in the underlying transaction but concerned only with the documents. Payment will not be made by the guarantor only when documents do not appear on their face to conform with the terms of the guarantee or appear on their face to be inconsistent with other documents.

（C）Letter of guarantee and contract are two legally independent documents. Although L/ G may be issued based on contract, only L/G has the legal binding upon guarantors who are in no way concerned with or bound by such contract. That is to say, the obligations of the guarantor do not relate to the underlying contract.

4. **Direct Guarantee and Indirect Guarantee**

（1）Direct Guarantee

A direct guarantee means that the guarantee is issued directly by a foreign guarantor to the beneficiary.

The operation of a direct guarantee mainly involves three parties, namely the guarantor, the applicant and the beneficiary. When any local bank in the beneficiary's country is involved, he acts no more than an advising bank to advise the bond to the beneficiary or to forward required documents. The procedure of a direct guarantee is as follows:

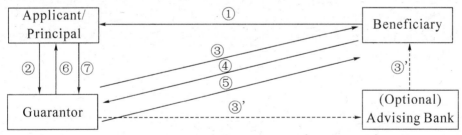

① A contract is established between the two parties.

② One contracting party will apply to his bank for issuing a guarantee directly to the other contracting party in a foreign country. This party becomes the applicant and the other party becomes the beneficiary under the direct guarantee. The guarantee will be issued against a counter indemnity contract or a reimbursement contract between the guarantor and the applicant.

③ After the direct guarantee is issued, either the guarantor himself or he will request or authorize another bank in the country of the beneficiary （represented by the dotted line）to advise the guarantee to the beneficiary.

④ In the event of performance by the principal, the guarantee will be expired at an expiry date or by an expiry event. The expired guarantee will be returned to the guarantor without any compensation being made by him and the whole procedure may end here. Or, in the event of non-performance by the principal, the beneficiary will claim compensation from the guarantor against the L/G and the stipulated documents under the L/G.

⑤ The guarantor will make compensation against correct documents. The L/G expires.

⑥ The guarantor will claim compensation from the principal against the counter indemnity contract or reimbursement contract.

⑦ The principal will make compensation to the guarantor.

(2) Indirect Guarantee

In certain countries, notably in the Middle East, local laws or customs prevent beneficiary from accepting bond issued directly by a foreign bank. Under this circumstance, the foreign bank will instruct a bank domiciled in the beneficiary's locality to issue a bond against the foreign bank's own indemnity - a counter guarantee. Therefore, when the issue of a guarantee is based on a counter guarantee where two banks in two different countries get involved, it is an indirect guarantee. As a result, there are four parties in the process of an indirect guarantee.

* The Principal

The principal is the person at whose request a guarantee is issued. He is under the same obligations as under a direct guarantee.

* The Beneficiary

The beneficiary is the person in whose favor a guarantee is issued. His rights and obligations will be similar to those under a direct guarantee.

* The Guarantor

The guarantor is the bank who issues a guarantee to make payment undertaking to the beneficiary. Unlike direct guarantee, the guarantor under indirect guarantee would be a bank domiciled in the beneficiary's locality who issues the guarantee against a counter guarantee in his favor from a foreign bank. Under indirect guarantee, the guarantor assumes double identities, both as a guarantor under the guarantee and as the beneficiary under the counter guarantee.

* The Instructing Party

The instructing party is a bank who issues a counter guarantee at the request of the applicant in favor of the guarantor of a guarantee. A counter guarantee is a guarantee which represents the instructing party's payment undertaking to its beneficiary, the guarantor on presentation of correct documents and against which the instructing party instructs its beneficiary to issue a guarantee on behalf of its principal in favor of a specified party named therein.

The procedure of the indirect guarantee is as follows:

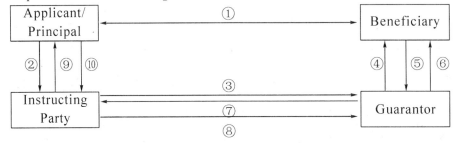

① A contract is established between the two parties.

② One contracting party (the applicant) will apply to his bank to issue a guarantee in favor of the other contracting party (the beneficiary) in a foreign country. The guarantee will be issued against a counter indemnity contract or a reimbursement contract between the guarantor and the applicant.

③ The applicant's bank issues a guarantee in favor of another bank domiciled in the beneficiary's country and instructs the latter to issue a new guarantee on behalf of its client in favor of a specified party named therein. The first guarantee is a counter guarantee, and it is so called because the new guarantee is issued against it. The applicant's bank becomes the instructing party because the new guarantee is established against his request and instruction.

④ The bank domiciled in the beneficiary's locality issues a guarantee at the request of the instructing party on behalf of the latter's principal to the beneficiary. The bank becomes the guarantor.

⑤ In the event of performance by the principal, the guarantee will be expired at an expiry date or by an expiry event. The expired guarantee will be returned to the guarantor without any compensation being made by him, so will the counter guarantee and the whole procedure may end here. Or, in the event of non－performance by the principal, the beneficiary will claim compensation from the guarantor against the L/G and the stipulated documents under the L/G.

⑥ The guarantor will make compensation against correct documents. The L/G expires.

⑦ The guarantor will claim compensation from the instructing party against the counter guarantee.

⑧ The instructing party makes compensation/reimbursement to the guarantor against the guarantor's correct documents under the counter guarantee. The counter guarantee expires.

⑨ The instructing party will claim compensation from the principal against the counter indemnity contract or reimbursement contract.

⑩ The principal makes compensation to the instructing party.

5. The Characteristics of the Contract, the Guarantee and the Counter Guarantee

Although they are related to each other, the contract, the guarantee and the counter guarantee are separate documents and have the binding only upon the relevant parties concerned. For example, the contract concerns the applicant and the beneficiary only but the banks are in no way bound by it.

In this connection, it is also necessary to consider and compare the parties of the two independent guarantees under indirect guarantee.

	Guarantee	Counter Guarantee
Applicant	Applicant	Applicant
Guarantor	Beneficiary's Bank	Applicant's Bank（The Instructing Party)
Beneficiary	Beneficiary	Beneficiary's Bank

It is clearly shown in the table that the beneficiary's bank has played double roles in an indirect guarantee. Governed by the principle of independence, the guarantor will be responsible to his beneficiary only whenever there is a default by the principal. That means, the beneficiary of the guarantee can not have the payment undertaking from the applicant's bank whose beneficiary is the beneficiary's bank. On the other hand, when the beneficiary's bank effects payment to the beneficiary, he may be exposed to the risk of non-payment by the instructing party if they hold different opinions regarding the documents because from the legal point of view, the guarantee and the counter guarantee are two independent documents.

6. Contents of a Letter of Guarantee

A letter of guarantee should be made clear, specific and accurate and not too much in detail. A L/G should include:

(a) The principal/applicant.

(b) The beneficiary.

(c) The guarantor bank.

(d) The advising bank(optional).

(e) General information of the underlying transaction, such as the contract No., the date, the name of the goods/services/projects and the relevant quantity, quality or performance requirements.

(f) The name and the amount of the guarantee and its currency.

(g) The expiry date and/or the expiry event of the guarantee.

According to ICC publication No. 458, expiry date shall be on a specified calendar date or on presentation to the guarantor of the documents specified for the purpose of expiry. If both an expiry date and an expiry event are specified, the guarantee shall be expired on whichever occurs first.

(h) The terms for effecting payment.

A guarantee should specify the documents to be produced in support of a claim. If the terms follow ICC publication No. 325, the guarantee is a conditional guarantee and is less favorable to the beneficiary. Or the guarantee can be an "on demand" guarantee following ICC publication No. 458 and is more favorable to the beneficiary.

(i) Any other provisions such as the reduction of the amount, the governing law and jurisdiction.

Section Two   Types of Guarantee

The classification of a guarantee is made according to the request of the contracting parties to serve their varied purposes in their economic transactions. According to *Uniform Rules for Contract Guarantees*, the major types of a bank guarantee are tender bond, performance bond, repayment guarantee, payment guarantee and loan guarantee.

1. Tender Guarantee / Tender Bond / Bid Bond

A tender guarantee is an undertaking given by a bank at the request of a tenderer(bidder) in favor of a party inviting tenders abroad, whereby the guarantor undertakes, in the event of non-performance by the principal in the obligations resulting from the submission of tender documents(bid documents), to make payment to the beneficiary within the time limits for a stated sum of money.

There are three immediate parties to a tender guarantee:

(1) The Principal

The principal is the tenderer/bidder who submits his tender documents (bid documents).

(2) The Beneficiary

The beneficiary is the party inviting tenders.

(3) The Guarantor

The guarantor is the bank who will effect payment if the principal fails to meet his obligations resulting from his submission of tender documents.

When tender documents are submitted, it would be taken as obligations for the tenderer that:

* The tender not to be modified and withdrawn before the expiry date.

* The tenderer undertakes to sign the contract if the tender is awarded to him.

* The tenderer is to procure the issuance of any performance or other required guarantee to replace the bond guarantee after the contract is established.

If the tender is not awarded, the expiry date is the award date or several days after the award date. On the other hand, if the tender is awarded, the expiry date is between 3 to 6 months till the signing of the awarded contract or the issuance of a performance guarantee or other required guarantee.

As a rule, the amount of a tender guarantee is at a specific percentage, 1% −5% of the project value. The purpose of the said guarantee is to safeguard the beneficiary (the party inviting tenders) against the principal's (the tenderer's) breach of such undertakings so as to prevent the submission of frivolous tenders.

Tender Guarantee or

FORM FOR BID SECURITY

Issuing Date _____

To:_____

Bid Security for Bid No. _____

for supply of _____

This Guarantee is hereby issued to serve as a Bid Security of _____ (name of Bidder)(hereinafter called the "Bidder") for Invitation for Bid (Bid No. _____) for supply of _____ (description of Goods) to _____(Name of the Buyer).

_____(Name of issuing bank)hereby unconditionally and irrevocably guarantees and binds itself, its successors and assigns to pay you immediately without recourse, the sum of _____ upon receipt of your written notification stating any of the following:

(a)The Bidder has withdrawn his bid after the time and date of the bid opening and before the expiration of its validity period;or

(b)The Bidder has failed to enter into Contract with you within thirty(30)calendar days after the notification of Contract award;or

(c)The Bidder has failed to establish acceptable Performance Security within thirty(30)calendar days after receipt the Notification of Award.

It is fully understood that this guarantee takes effect from the date of the bid opening and shall remain valid for a period of _____ calendar days thereafter,and during the period of any extension thereof that may be agreed upon between you and the Bidder with ontice to us,unless sooner terminated and or released by you.

Issue Bank _____

Signed by _____

(Printed name and designation of official

authorized to sign on behalf of issuing bank)

Official seal _____

2. Performance Guarantee or Performance Bond

A performance guarantee is an undertaking given by the guarantor at the request of a supplier of goods or services or a contractor as the principal in favor of the buyer or an employer as the beneficiary, whereby the guarantor undertakes to make payment to the beneficiary within the time limits for a stated sum of money in the event of non-performance of the principal.

The three immediate parties are:

(1) The Principal

The principal can be the exporter who supplies the goods and services under a sales contract or he can be a contractor whom a project contract has been awarded and he is the tenderer under the tender guarantee.

(2) The Beneficiary

The beneficiary can be the importer who buys a goods or services under a sales contract or he can be the party who awards a project contract and he is the party inviting tenders under the tender guarantee.

(3) The Guarantor

The guarantor will effect payment in the event of the principal's failure to fulfil the contract.

The purpose of a performance guarantee is to ensure the fulfillment of the contract on the part of the principal. Therefore, a performance guarantee is valid till the delivery of goods or services or the complete performance of the contract. The amount payable under this guarantee is often at 10% of the contract amount and sometimes can be more than that percentage.

Performance Guarantee or

Form of Performance Bond for Supply of _____

To: _____(Beneficiary)

Dear Sirs,

This Bond is hereby issued as the perfomance bond of _____ (Applicant)(hereinafter called the supplier)for supply of _____(the name of the goods)under the contract No. _____ to _____(the name of the beneficiary).

The _____(the name of the guarantor)hereby irrevocably guarantees itself, its successors and assigns to pay you up to the amount of _____(the amount of the guaranteed value)representing_____ percent of the contract price and accordingly covenants and agrees as follows:

a. On the supplier's failure of faithful perfomance of the contract(hereinafter called the failure of performance), we shall immediately, on your demand in a written notification stating the effect of the failure of performance by the supplier, pay you such amount or amounts as required by you not exceeding _____(the guaranteed amount)in the manner specified in the said statement.

b. The covenants herein contained constitute irrevocable and direct obligations of the guarantor, no alternation in the terms of the contract to be performed thereunder and no allowance of time by you or any other act or omission by you, which but for this provision might exonerate or discharge the bank shall in any way release the guarantor from any liabllity hereunder.

c. This performance bond shall become effective from issuing date and shall remain valld until _____(the date of expiry). Upon expiry, please return this bond to us for cancellation.

3. **Payment Guarantee ∕ Import Guarantee**

A payment guarantee or import payment guarantee is an undertaking by the guarantor at the request of the importer (the principal) to the exporter (the beneficiary), whereby the guarantor undertakes to make payment to the beneficiary within the time limits for a stated sum of money in the event of non-payment by the principal for the goods he has received on open account terms.

The three immediate parties are:

(1) The Principal

The principal is the importer who receives goods from the exporter on open account terms.

(2) The Beneficiary

The beneficiary is the exporter who supplies goods to the importer on open account terms.

(3) The Guarantor

The guarantor will effect payment to the beneficiary in the event that the principal fails to make payment to the exporter within the stipulated time period.

The purpose of a payment guarantee is to secure the payment on an open account basis. The amount payable under this guarantee should be the unpaid value of the goods delivered plus any applicable interests.

Payment Guarantee

TO:(Name of Seller)   Date _____

Re:Our Irrevocable Letter of Guarantee No.

With reference to Contract No. _____ for a total value of _____ signed between your goodselves(hereinafter referred to as"the Seller")and China National Technical Import Corp. ,Beijing,China(hereinafter referred to as"the Buyer")concerning the Buyer's purchase from the Seller of the Equipment for _____ , we at the request of the Buyer,open our Irrevocable Letter of Guarantee No. _____ in favour of the Seller to the extent of _____ covering 100% of the total value of the contract and undertake that payment will be effected by the Buyer as follows:

1.90% of the total Contract price,viz. _____ shall be paid by the Buyer after his having received from the Seller the following documents and has found them in order.

....

2.5% of the total Contract price,viz. _____ shall be paid by the Buyer after his having received from the seller one Certificate of Acceptance of the Contract Plant.

3.5% of the total Contract price,viz. _____ shall be paid by the buyer after expiry of the guarantee period of Contract Plant and his having received from the Seller one Certificate of Expiry of the guarantee period.

In connection with the above,we undertake that if the Buyer fails to pay wholly or partially we will within 3 days after receipt of the Seller's written Notice. Pay the Seller relative amount plus simple interest at the rate of 7% per annum for delayed payment,which the Buyer is liable under the Contract,provided that Buyer is unable to submit any proof that the documents presented by the Seller are not in conformity with the stipulation of the Contract,

Our liability under this letter of guarantee shall diminish proportionally with the percentage of amount paid by the Buyer. The letter of guarantee shall become effective on the date of issue and shall automatically become null and void after payment made as above stated.

For Bank of Asia

....

signature

4. **Repayment Guarantee / Advance Payment Guarantee**

A repayment guarantee or advance payment guarantee is an undertaking by the guarantor at the request of the exporter (the principal) to the importer (the beneficiary), whereby the guarantor undertakes to make payment to the beneficiary within the time limits for a stated sum of money in the event of default by the principal to repay any sum or sums advanced by the beneficiary to the principal.

The three immediate parties are:

(1) The Principal

The principal is the party who receives advance payment or down payment. He can be the exporter who is to supply the goods or services or the contractor who has been awarded the contract.

(2) The Beneficiary

The beneficiary is the party who makes advance payment to the principal. He can be the importer who buys goods or services on the term of payment in advance or the employer who has made advance payment to the contractor.

(3) The Guarantor

The guarantor will effect payment in the event of default by the principal to repay any advanced payment if the goods are not delivered or the services are not provided or if the contractual obligations are not performed.

The purpose of a repayment guarantee is to secure that the advanced payment will be repaid if the principal fails to perform the contract. The amount payable is the amount of the advanced payment and is automatically and proportionally reduced following each shipment or according to the progress in a construction project. In this way, a repayment guarantee can be used together with payment in advance to protect the importer. The period of validity of this guarantee is from the principal's actual receipt of advance payment to a specific date when the covered performance is fulfilled or when the compensation has been made by the guarantor.

Form of Advance Payment Guarantee for Supply
of _____

To: _____ (Beneficiary)

Dear Sirs,

This guarantee is hereby Issued as the advance payment guarantee of _____ (Applicant) (hereinafter called the supplier) for _____ (the name of the contract and its number) to _____ (the name of the beneficiary) (hereinafter called the buyer).

Whereas the buyer has agreed to advance to the supplier an amount of _____ (Say _____ only), whereas the buyer has required the supplier to furnish a guarantee, with an amount equal to the above said advance payment for performance of his obligations under the contract, and the _____ (the name of the Guarantor), at the request of the supplier and in consideration of the buyer's agreeing to make the above said advance to the supplier, has agreed to furnish the above required guarantee.

Now, therefore, the guarantor hereby guarantees that the supplier shall utilize the above said advance for the purpose of the contract and if he falis and commits default in fulfillment of any of his obligation for which the advance payment is made, it shall entitle the buyer to be paid not exceeding the above-mentioned amount.

Against notice in writing of any default, which the guarantor should be given by the buyer stating that the supplier has failed to fulfill its obligation to the buyer, and upon such first demand payment shall be made by the guarantor of the sum then due under this guarantee without any obligation.

The sum of this guarantee shall be automatically and proportionally reduced in step of the progress of the contract, and the guarantor's obligation under this guarantee shall not in any case exceeding the sum of _____ (Say _____ only).

This guarantee shall become effective from the date of receipt of the above said advance by the supplier and valid until _____ (the date of expiry). Upon expiry, please return this guarantee to us for cancellation.

For

5. Counter-trade Guarantee

Counter-trade occurs when export is linked with import. To define it more formally, counter-trade is an international trade transaction where export sales to a particular country or region will be carried out under the condition of undertakings to accept imports from that country or region. Counter-trade normally takes the form of compensation, processing and assembly of the manufacturing goods. In this connection, the guarantee provided for this kind of transaction is a compensation guarantee or a processing and assembly guarantee.

(1) Compensation Guarantee

A compensation guarantee is an undertaking by the guarantor at the request of the importer (the principal) of capital goods to the exporter (the beneficiary), whereby the guarantor undertakes to make payment to the beneficiary within the time limits for a stated sum of money in the event that the principal fails to supply the future output of the factory or to make payment for the capital goods plus interest, if any.

The amount payable under a compensation guarantee is normally made equal to the amount of the capital goods plus interest. The said guarantee is valid within half a month after the delivery of goods from the importing country.

（2）Processing and Assembly Guarantee

A processing and assembly guarantee is an undertaking by the guarantor at the request of the importer (the principal) of raw materials, components or machinery to the exporter (the benficiary), whereby the guarantor undertakes to make payment to the beneficiary within the time limits for a stated sum of money in the event that the principal fails to supply the finished products or make payment for the raw materials, components or machinery plus interest, if any.

The amount payable under a processing and assembly guarantee is normally made equal to the amount of the imported goods plus interest. The said guarantee is valid within half a month after the delivery date or the finished goods from the importing country.

6. **Overdraft Guarantee**

When a contractor has established a complete production unit or infrastructure project in a foreign country, it will normally open an overdraft account with a local bank to get financed. And a bank guarantee will be required before the overdraft account can be established. An overdraft guarantee is an undertaking by the guarantor at the request of the contractor (the principle) to an overseas bank(the beneficiary), whereby the guarantor undertakes to make payment to the beneficiary in the event that the principal fails to repay in due time the amount overdrawn in the account.

The amount payable is normally made equal to the stipulated overdraft facility in the overdraft account. The said guarantee is valid within half a month after the expiry date of the said account.

In addition to the above-mentioned guarantees, there are also other types of guarantees in connection with other types of economic transactions such as leasing guarantee, loan guarantee, warranty bond. In summary, whenever one party is in need of a protection, he can require the other party to issue a bank guarantee through a bank. In this way, he has the performance undertaking from a bank rather than his counterpart.

Overdraft guarantee

OUR GUARANTEE (GUARANTEE NUMBER)

In consideration of your granting advances by way of (TYPE OF BORROWING) on the account of (BORROWER) we hereby guarantee on demand being made to us in writing the due repayment of such advances in the event of (BORROWER) failing to repay such advances when required to do so by yourselves provided that the amount for which we shall be liable under his guarantee shall not exceed the sum of (AMOUNT IN FIGURES) (say,(AMOUNT IN WORDS)) inclusive of interest and Bank charges.

Unless previously renewed by us this guarantee is to be determined on (EXPIRY DATE) ("EXPIRY")subject to your right to cancel the facility prior to that date if you should think fit so to do,and to our right to determine our liability hereunder by giving notice in writing and upon receipt of such notice by you no further advances are to be made with recourse to us.

Claims under this guarantee must incorporate your declaration that the amount claimed represents outstanding advances by way of (TYPE OF BORROWING)on the account of (BORROWER) as aforesaid,inclusive of interest and Bank charges,which have not been repaid by (BORROWER) as requested by you, and must be received by us at this office in writing or by authenticated telex/cable not later than 30 days after the above-mentioned expiry date,or not more than 40 days after the date of our prior notice of determination of liability,after which time this guarantee shall become null and void, whether returned to us for cancellation or not,and our liability hereunder shall terminate.

This guarantee is personal to yourselves and is not transferable or assignable.

This guarantee shall be governed by and construed in accordance with the Laws of England.

ALTERNATIVE

and in addition interest and bank charges for a period not exceeding six months.

Section Three   Practices and Characteristics of a Guarantee

1. **Practices of a Letter of Guarantee**

In establishing a letter of guarantee, the following points should be borne clearly in mind:

(A) The undertaking clause must be definite and precise.

The undertaking clause expresses the terms and conditions for demanding payment under which the guarantor will effect payment to the beneficiary. Expressed in various terms under different guarantees, the undertaking clause should always state clearly whether the guarantees is subject to *Uniform Rules for Contract Guarantee* or to *Uniforms Rules for Demand Guarantee*.

If the guarantee is subject to *Uniform Rules for Contract Guarantee*, normally a documentary proof issued by a neutral third party (either an arbitrary award or a court judgement) or an approval to the claim from the principal in writing to attest the non-performance of the contract will be required.

If the guarantee is subject to *Uniform Rules for Demand Guarantee*, normally a written demand by the beneficiary stating that the principal is in default of the contract will be sufficient.

(B) The guaranteed amount should be made definite.

The guaranteed amount should be definite for two reasons. Firstly, it is the amount payable by the guarantor in the event of default by the principal. Secondly, it is also the base for the bank to charge a suitable fee for issuing the guarantee. The bank charge is usually a stated annual percentage of the bond's value. The percentage normally varies between 0.5% and 1.5% a year. In addition, if a local bank is involved, it will charge between 2% to 3% per annum.

(C) The period of validity should be limited.

The expiry date of a bond means that the responsibility of the guarantor will end by this date. This is important to the guarantor bank in the sense that he can cancel the bond on this date. Any obscure expression will bring additional risks to the guarantor.

(D) A counter indemnity from the principal.

In the case of indirect guarantee, the guarantor has the right to require a counter indemnity from the principal at the time when a counter guarantee is issued. The bank (the instructing party) will be authorized by this counter guarantee to debit the principal's account with the cost of any payments made under a guarantee. That is to say, if the principal fulfils its obligations and no payment is called for under the bond, he will only pay the issuing charge to the bank. If the principal fails to meet his obligations, the instructing party will debit the account to compensate for the amount made to the beneficiary in addition to the issuing charge.

(E) Exercise certain cautions under a counter guarantee.

In the case of a counter guarantee, the principal's bank will only act as the instructing party who has no control over the guarantee issued by the foreign bank. As the beneficiary will make his claim in a foreign country, the overseas bank (the guarantor) alone will have the right to decide whether the claim is justified. The instructing party has no say in this case and does not have the right to check whether the foreign beneficiary is cheating or not.

(F) A letter of guarantee can never be made revocable and transferable.

The purpose of establishing a guarantee is for the beneficiary to seek a bank's payment undertaking in the event of default by the principal. Revocability is against the original intention of a bond. For this reason, neither the guarantee nor the counter guarantee can be revocable once issued. Because forgery of documents is simple under letter of guarantee operation, especially under demand guarantee, a guarantee will not be transferable once issued in order to protect the guarantor against additional risks resulting from transfer.

（G）Examine documents under a letter of guarantee.

Although banks will never get involved in the contractual disputes between the principal and the beneficiary, banks shall make reasonable examination on the documents whether they appear on the face to be in consistence with the terms of the guarantee before payment is effected.

（H）The law of the place of issue.

Letter of guarantee should abide by the law of the place of issue. That means, the counter guarantee should abide by the law in the country of the instructing party and the guarantee should be subject to the law in the country of the guarantor. If a guarantee is required to be governed by the law of another third country rather than the issuing country, it is unfavorable to the issuing bank.

2. Characteristics of a Guarantee

The characteristics of a guarantee will be made clearer in comparison with those of a letter of credit. As two commonly used payment methods, they share some similarities though they are different in many aspects.

（A）Similarities between a letter of guarantee and a letter of credit.

A letter of guarantee and a letter of credit are similar in the following points:

＊ Both of them are based on banker's credit. This means that the issuing bank will undertake to effect payment to the beneficiary on behalf of the contracting parties.

＊ In both cases, underlying contract is legally independent from the letter of guarantee or the letter of credit. Banks under L/G and L/C will not be concerned and bound by the said contract.

＊ In both cases, banks deal with documents and banks effect payment only against correct documents whereby the principle of strict compliance should always be observed.

＊ Banks bear no responsibilities for the form, sufficiency, accuracy, genuineness, or falsification of the documents.

（B）Differences between a letter of guarantee and a letter of credit.

＊ Application

A letter of credit is applicable only to trade settlement where payment undertaking by the issuing bank is extended to the exporter on behalf of the importer.

A letter of guarantee is applicable to both trade and non-trade transactions where the payment undertaking of the issuing bank as a performance guarantee can be extended to either party at the request of the other party. For example, where the exporter is the beneficiary under a payment guarantee, the importer is the beneficiary under a repayment guarantee.

＊ Payment undertaking

The purpose of letter of credit is to effect payment against the beneficiary's fulfillment. In this sense, the issuing bank of L/C bears primary liability to the beneficiary. The documents required under a documentary credit should include those commercial documents such as bills of lading and/or insurance policy which are evidence of fulfillment.

On the other hand, the purpose of letter of guarantee is to effect payment against the principal's non-performance. In this sense, the issuing bank bears secondary liability to the beneficiary. That is to say, in the event of fulfillment, the amount under a L/G will not be called for. The documents under a L/G should attest the non-performance of the principal. The correct documents can either be a written demand by the beneficiary or other documentary proof from a neutral third party.

* Banks effecting payment

Under letter of credit, a number of banks can effect payment to the beneficiary. They are the issuing bank, the confirming bank, the paying bank, the accepting bank or the negotiating bank. Therefore, the place of the presentation of documents can be made at the counter of any of these banks according to the stipulations in the credit.

There is only one bank can effect payment to the beneficiary. In the case of a counter guarantee, it is the instructing party who will effect payment and in the case of a guarantee, the bank effecting payment shall be the guarantor. On all occasions, the presentation of documents should be made at the counter of the guarantor.

* The governing law

Letter of guarantee should be subject to *Uniform Customs and Practice for Documentary Credits Per ICC* publication No. 500 (UCP 500). However, UCP 500 is only a set of rules and it does not stipulate the governing law and jurisdiction to be followed when there are any disputes.

Letter of guarantee should be subject to either the *Uniform Rules for Contract Guarantee and Uniform Rules for Demand Guarantee*. Although both of them are also rules, they indicate clearly the law and jurisdiction to be followed where there are any disputes, which are settled in the place of business of the guarantor if it is guarantee and that of the instructing party if it is a counter guarantee.

* Revocability and transferability

Letter of credit can be revocable and transferable whereas letter of guarantee can be made neither revocable nor transferable.

3. Cancellation of a Letter of Guarantee

In the case of fulfillment by the principal, letter of guarantee can be cancelled either after the expiry date or the return of the original guarantee by the beneficiary without any claim being made by him. In the case of non-performance, however, the guarantee will be cancelled by payment being made to the beneficiary against his correct documents with or without the return of the original guarantee.

Section Four   Stand-by Letter of Credit

1. Definition

According to UCP 500, a stand-by credit is defined as a letter of credit or a similar arrangement, however named or described, which represents an obligation to the beneficiary on the party of the issuing bank to:

(a) Repay money borrowed by, or advanced to or for the account of the applicant, or

(b) Make payment on account of any indebtedness undertaken by the applicant, or

(c) Make payment on account of any default by the applicant in the performance of an obligation.

The stand-by credit originated in the United States where the issuance of a letter of guarantee is not allowed under the federal banking law. In order to satisfy the customers' demand of guarantee on his behalf, a stand-by credit is issued which carries with it the characteristics of a guarantee.

Under a stand-by credit, the payment will be called for only when the applicant fails to repay the loan or fails to fulfil its obligations. In other words, a stand-by credit will not by called for when the obligations are performed by the principal. In the event of fulfillment, it will just "stand-by" and will never be called for. In a stand-by credit, the parties do not normally expect that the presentation of documents will occur.

From a legal point of view, a stand-by credit is in effect a letter of guarantee, or we can say that the stand-by credit is an alternative to a guarantee when the latter is not permitted in some countries. The difference between a stand-by credit and a demand guarantee is not of law but of practice and business terminology. As a credit, stand-by credit is also subject to UCP 500. Therefore, many operations for a normal credit are also applicable to those of the stand-by credit. For example, a stand-by credit can be confirmed by another bank and the bank effecting payment can be the issuing bank or other banks, etc. This is different from a guarantee governed either by the *Uniform Rules for Contract Guarantee* or the *Uniform Rules for Demand Guarantee.*

2. **Major Types of Stand-by Credit**

(1) Performance Stand-by Credit

In contractual construction, the tenderer is the contractor once the tender has been awarded to him. It is the responsibility of the contractor to sign a contract with the employer/owner and to submit a performance stand-by credit in favor of the employer/owner, whereby the lssuing bank will effect payment to the beneficiary in the event that the principal has defaulted in the performance of the terms and conditions of the credit with the beneficiary.

(2) Repayment Stand-by Credit

It is usually made for the purpose when a local enterprise intends to obtain loan facilities from a foreign bank. A repayment stand-by credit is issued at the request of a local enterprise in favor of a foreign bank whereby the issuing bank will effect payment to the beneficiary in the event that the principal fails to make repayment in due time. The amount payable under this credit will represent the unpaid principal and the accrued interest as agreed upon.

3. **Similarities between a Stand-by Credit and a Documentary Credit**

(a) Both types of credits are separate documents independent from the underlying contract.

(b) Payment will be effected against correct documents and payment undertaking is effected from the issuing bank.

4. Differences between a Stand-by Credit and a Documentary Commercial Credit

(a) A documentary commercial credit is used for the purpose of trade settlement while a stand-by credit can be used as a non-trade guarantee

(b) The issuing bank's responsibilities under a documentary commercial credit end when payment is effected; the amount under a stand-by credit may not be called for when the principal's obligations are fulfilled.

(c) Documents required under a documentary credit are drafts plus those commercial documents evidencing the fulfillment on the part of the beneficiary; documents required under a stand-by credit are drafts plus a statement attesting the non-performance on the part of a principal. For this reason, stand-by credit is normally a clean credit and it is not typically used as a payment arrangement.

(d) A documentary commercial credit is subject to all the articles stipulated in UCP 500. However, some articles under UCP500 are not applicable to a stand-by credit.

5. Differences between a Stand-by Credit and a Letter of Guarantee

(1) Payment Availability

Stand-by credit is also a letter of credit. Its payment can be made available by sight payment, deferred payment, acceptance and negotiation with the issuing bank, the confirming bank, the paying bank, the accepting bank and the negotiating bank.

However, under a letter of guarantee, amount will be payable only by payment with the issuing bank. That is to say, only the guarantor or the instructing party can effect payment under a guarantee or a counter guarantee.

(2) Place of Presentation of Documents

Under a stand-by credit, documents may be presented to the bank effecting payment. This means that the beneficiary may be required to present the documents to the counter of the issuing bank, confirming bank, paying bank, accepting bank or negotiating bank as stipulated in the credit.

As there is only one bank effecting payment under a letter of guarantee, documents will be presented to the counter of the guarantor under a guarantee and that of the instructing party under a counter guarantee.

Performance Stand-by Credit

NAME OF ISSUING BANK First Union Trust Bank of Dallas PLACE AND DATE OF ISSUE Dallas, 20 July,19--	IRREVOCABLE STAND-BY CREDIT Date and place of expiry, Cairo, 30 Nov. , 19--	NUMBER 45612

Applicant Ewing Oill Company Inc. 2425 John Ross Avenue, Dallas, Texas.	Beneficiary United Arab Pipelines Co. , Farouk Palace Square, Alexandria, Egypt.

Advising Bank Bank of the Nile, Cairo.	Amount USD1,000,000.00(say US dollars one million only)

Partial shipments ☐allowed☐not allo.	Transhipment ☐allo☐not allo.	Credit available with Bank of Nile, Cairo by

Shipment/dispatch/taking in charge from/at for transportation to	☒PAYMENT☐ACCEPTANCE ☐NEGOTIATION against presentation of the documents detailed herein ☒and of beneficiary's draft at sight drawn on Bank of the Nile, Cairo

.Signed statement of United Arab Pipelines Co. that Ewing Oill Company Inc. failed to perform its contractual obligations under the agreement concluded on 30 June, 19-- between Ewing Oil Company Inc. and United Arab Pipelines Co. in which Ewing Oil Company Inc. was the successful bidder.

Special Conditions:

It is agreed upon that we may be released from our liability under this Letter of Credit prior to the expiry date, only if we receive notification from Bank of the Nile by tested telex to the effect that Bank of the Nile has been duly advised by United Arab Pipelines that the above agreement has been completely performed by the Ewing Oill Company Inc. Bank of the Nile to advise the beneficiary adding its confirmation. We hereby authorise Bank of the Nile to draw on us by means of tested telex for the value of all drafts drawn under this Credit, provided the telex states that all terms and conditions have been complied with.

We hereby issue this Stand-by Credit in your favour, it is subject to the International Stand-by Practices.

For First Union Trust Bank of Dallas
Signature

Chapter Eleven   Documents (Ⅰ)
−Draft, Commercial Invoice, Packing List and Insurance Policy

Section One   General Introduction to Documents

1. Types of Documents Used in International Settlement

Based on our previous discussion we know that documents used in international settlement can be classified into two broad groups: financial instruments and commercial documents. Financial instruments(documents) refer to credit instruments used to collect/make payments. Of the three commonly used credit instruments, bills of exchange are the most popular one compared with cheques and promissory notes. Commercial documents are documentary evidence of performance on the part of the exporter. In the following chapters and sections, we will talk about some popular types of the commercial documents.

Commercial documents can be further divided into basic documents and auxiliary documents. Basic commercial documents are those that should be supplied by the exporter according to the requirement of incoterms like CIF, CIP or FOB. They are the commercial invoice, insurance policy and transport documents. Auxiliary documents refer to those ones which should be submitted according to the laws and regulations of the importing country or the special requirements of the importer concerning the conditions of the goods. They are mainly the certificate of origin, packing list and weight list, inspection certificate, customs invoice and consular invoice.

2. The Importance of Documents

The importance of documents in modern international settlement can be seen in the following points:

(A) Modern international settlement centers around documents.

Modern international settlement has evolved from cash settlements to non-cash settlements where credit instruments have taken the place of cash as mediums of exchange. In the settlement process, the relevant parties, that is, the traders and the banks are dealing with documents rather than the physical goods.

(B) Commercial documents are the evidence of performance of the sales contract.

A sales contract will normally describe and stipulate the conditions of the goods, its shipment and insurance requirements and payment terms. All these items will be reflected in the corresponding commercial documents. For example, commercial invoice, packing list and inspection certificate will describe the price, packing, quantity and quality of the goods. The transport documents will show evidence that the goods are not only delivered, but also delivered in the timely fashion required. Similarly, the insurance policy will indicate whether the goods are correctly covered and the payment methods will express clearly the way to collect/demand payment.

(C) Documents represent title to the goods.

With the development in international settlement, some commercial documents have e-volved to become title documents signifying the ownership of the holder to the physical goods. Therefore, it is safe to make the conclusion that title documents equal to the physical goods. For this reason, banks will effect payment against correct documents; the exporter will be deemed to make delivery once he surrenders the documents and the importer is considered to be in possession of the goods with the title documents in hand.

(D) Documents will indicate the involvement of other parties in addition to the traders.

One major characteristic of modern international trade and international settlement is that every transaction can not be completed by traders alone. The involvement of other parties such as banks, transport companies, insurance companies and other government agencies will be re-flected through the required documents.

Section Two   Draft under Remittance, Collection and Letter of Credit

As a commonly used credit instrument in international settlement, draft is used to collect/ make payment. In addition, finance can be arranged by means of a draft and a discharged bill may also serve as a receipt of payment. In this section, we will discuss the different character-istics of drafts under various payment methods.

1. Draft under Remittance

In remittance, the direction of the movement of the draft will be the same as that of the flow of the funds. Of the three types of remittance, draft is only required in D/D and the draft used is a banker's demand draft. It is an unconditional order in writing addressed by the remit-ting bank to its overseas head office/branch or correspondent, the paying bank, signed by the remitting bank giving it, requiring the paying bank to whom it is addressed to pay on demand a sum certain in money to or to the order of the exporter. The three immediate parties to the draft are:

(1) The Drawer

The drawer is the remitting bank located in the importer's country.

(2) The Drawee

The drawee is the paying bank located in the exporter's country.

(3) The Payee

The payee is the exporter.

It should be noted that although a banker's draft is used in D/D, remittance remains a payment method based on trader's credit rather than on banker's credit. A review of the proce-dure under D/D will show clearly that the remitting bank will not draw a draft until he receives proceeds directly from the importer or until he debits the account of the importer with the amount to be paid out. In other words, the issuing of a banker's draft depends on the payment of the importer in the first place.

Bank Draft

REF. NO.	THE ROYAL BANK, LIMITED	
	Hong Kong	
no. R 12345		Date: June 8, 1997
Pay to the order of:	Mr. CHAN H. K. R. **	

The Sum Of: CANADIAN DOLLAR TEN MILLION ONLY*** | CAD10,000,000**

TO:
The Royal Bank of Canada
International Centre   The Royal Bank,
22 XY ST. Toronto, Canada   Mongkok Br. HK

2. Draft under Collection

Draft under collection can be defined as an unconditional order in writing addressed by the exporter to the importer, signed by the exporter giving it, requiring the importer to whom it is addressed to pay on demand or at a fixed determinable future time a sum certain in money to or to the order of the exporter himself. The three immediate parties are:

(1) The Drawer

The drawer is the exporter.

(2) The Drawee

The drawee is the importer.

(3) The Payee

The payee can be the exporter / the remitting bank / the collecting bank.

When dealing with draft under collection, it should first remember that collection is a reverse remittance where the direction of the movement of the draft is opposite to that of the flow of funds. This is the reason why the draft is issued by the creditor (the exporter) on the debtor (the importer). Another point to be noted is that collection is a payment method based on trader's credit. For this reason, the drawee of this kind of draft will always be made on the importer. Normally, in the case of a documentary collection, the draft will also specify the type of collection to clearly indicate whether the documents are released against sight payment (D/P sight), deferred payment (D/P after sight) or acceptance (D/A).

Documents are to be delivered only against payment of this bill
representing % of the value of our Invoice No.

号码
汇票金额
Exchange for USD19,800.00   上 海   Shanghai, DEC.25   19 86
No. TA.501042

见票 日后(本 汇 票 之 副 本 未 付)付 交
at D/P 60 days from date of shipment this **FIRST** of Exchange (Second of Exchange
being unpaid) Pay to the order of Bank of China

金 额
the sum of **U.S.DOLLARS NINETEEN THOUSAND EIGHT HUNDRED ONLY**

此 致
To M/S Ahmed Akabar General Trading,   中国纺织品进出口公司上海市家用纺织品分公司
Post Box No.1489,   CHINA NATIONAL TEXTILES IMPORT & EXPORT CORPORATION
Dubai (U.A.E.)   SHANGHAI HOME TEXTILES BRANCH

(SIGNATURE)

3. **Draft under Letter of Credit**

Draft under letter of credit can be defined as an unconditional order in writing addressed by the exporter to the bank, singed by the exporter giving it, requiring the bank to whom it is addressed to pay on demand or at a fixed future time a sum certain in money to or to the order of the exporter himself or the exporter's bank. The three immediate parties are:

(1) The Drawer

The drawer is the exporter.

(2) The Drawee

The drawee is a bank.

(3) The Payee

The payee is the exporter himself or his bank.

Similar to collection, letter of credit is also a reverse remittance. Therefore, the drawer of the draft under L/C will be the exporter instead of the importer. Unlike collection, letter of credit is a payment method based on banker's credit in the sense that the payment undertaking is giving by the bank on behalf of the importer. For this reason, the draft drawn under letter of credit should be drawn on a bank and can never be on an importer.

Sight payment credit may or may not require a sight draft. In countries such as France, Spain and Sweden etc. , a simple receipt or a commercial invoice may take the place of a draft. A negotiable credit requires a sight draft whereas a time draft is required under acceptance credit and draft is not applicable under deferred payment credit.

Draft drawn under letter of credit should be made in strict compliance with the terms and conditions of the credit. The following points deserve special attention:

(1) Drawn Clause

Under documentary credit, draft must contain a "drawn clause" indicating that the draft is established under a documentary credit. The drawn clause should be made in strict compliance with the stipulations in the credit and will usually indicate the name of the issuing bank, the issuing date and the credit No.

(2) The Amount

The draft amount is normally for the full 100% invoice value and should not be made exceeding the amount of the credit or the amount permissible under the credit. In the event that the invoice value exceeds the credit amount, the beneficiary should present a supplementary draft of the excess amount for collection. In certain special cases when commission charges are reflected on the credit, the draft amount will be made less than the invoice value with the balance being the commissions distracted from the invoice value.

The amount of the draft can also be made payable with interest at a certain percent per annum. The interest should be paid by the applicant.

Draft amount in words is exactly equal to its amount in figures and both amounts should indicate the currency as stipulated in the credit.

(3) Place of Issue

The place of issue should be made in consistence with the place of the issuer.

(4) Date of the Draft

The date of draft is the issuing date of the draft and is normally the negotiating date. It should be made no later than the latest date for presentation of documents stipulated in the credit but within the expiry date of the credit.

(5) Tenor of the Draft

The tenor of the draft indicates the time of payment and should be made in accordance with the terms of the credit on the following points:

＊ At sight

Payment should be effected immediately upon presentation or at sight.

＊ At xx days after sight

Presentation is needed for acceptance as to the calculation of the due date. Payment will be effected at maturity. The word "after" is usually omitted in the credit and the accepting date is the date when the documents are found in compliance with the terms and conditions of the credit.

＊ At xx days after date

Presentation is normally needed for acceptance in order to secure the drawee's liability on the draft.

＊ At xx days after the date of shipment

In practice, the date of the draft is based on the date of shipment and the tenor of the date is normally made "30 days after the date of shipment".

＊ At xx days after the B/L date

In practice, the B/L date is normally indicated on the tenor. For example, " at 30 days after B/L date dated 16/03/200X".

＊ At a fixed future date

Presentation for acceptance is normally required to secure the drawee's liability on the draft.

(6) Payee

Generally speaking, the payee of the draft is either the beneficiary or the exporter's bank (the negotiating bank).

When the payee is the beneficiary himself, the beneficiary will endorse the draft and present the drafts and documents to the negotiating bank for negotiation. In this case, endorsement should be made according to the stipulations of the credit. The endorsement in full will usually take the following form:

Pay to the order of

Overseas United Bank, Singapore

The ABC International Pte. Ltd. Singapore

Signature

After negotiation, the bank will become the holder in due course. If the negotiating bank chooses not to negotiate the drafts and documents, no endorsement is required and the bank will not be the holder in due course.

The advantage of making the negotiating bank the payee is that no endorsement is required. However, if the negotiating bank simply examines the documents without negotiating (giving value), the beneficiary should better make himself the payee.

(7) The Drawee

Under documentary credit, the drawee should be made on a bank as required in the credit. The drawee can never be made on the applicant. Any draft drawn on the applicant will be considered as an additional document.

Under sight payment credit or acceptance credit, the drawee bank is the nominated paying or accepting bank. Under negotiating credit, the draft should be drawn on another bank rather than the negotiating bank. Normally, negotiating credit will stipulate the draft "drawn on us", which means that the drawee bank is the issuing bank.

(8) The Drawer

As letter of credit is a reverse remittance, the drawer should be the exporter/beneficiary.

(9) Full Set

Drafts usually are made in duplicate to make a full set. In order to guard against lost in transit, the two parts will be sent separately with the first part indicating " Pay this first bill of exchange (Second bill of exchange being unpaid) " and the second part indicating "Pay this second bill of exchange (First bill of exchange being unpaid) ".

(10) Other Terms

The endorsement should not be made in restrictive order and there should be no indication of "without recourse" either on the face or the back of the draft unless it is under special authorization to do so.

E546221

Drawn under **Privatbanken, A/S. Copenhagen** 不可撤销信用证 *Irrevocable L/C No.* **704481**

Dated 日期 **20th Dec.,1985** 支息 *Payable with interest @* ％ 按 息 付款

No. 号码 **T.0456** 汇票金额 *Exchange for* **DM.129,649.95** 上海 *Shanghai,* ...... '19

见票 *at* ...... 日后（本汇票之副本未付）付交 *sight of this* FIRST *of Exchange (Second of Exchange being unpaid) Pay to the order of* **Bank of China**

金额 *the sum of* DEUTSCHE MARKS ONE HUNDRED TWENTY NINE THOUSAND SIX HUNDRED AND FORTY NINE AND 95/100 ONLY

此致 *To* **M/S. Privatbanken, A/S. Copenhagen.**

中国纺织品进出口公司上海市分公司
China National Textiles Import and Export Corporation
SHANGHAI BRANCH

Maybank

NO.

Exchange for_____   Date_____

At _____ sight pay

this **FIRST** of Exchange (Second being unpaid) to the order of Malayan Banking Berhad.

Value received and charge the same to account of _____

To _____

Malayan Banking Berhad
Form IE 30 (1/2)

Maybank

NO._____

Exchange for_____   Date _____

At _____ sight pay

this **SECOND** of Exchange (First being unpaid) to the order of Malayan Banking Berhad.

_____

_____

Value received and charge the same to account of _____

_____

_____

To _____

_____

Malayan Banking Berhad
Form IE 30 (2/2)

Section Three   Commercial Invoice and Packing List

1. Commercial Invoice

A commercial invoice is the accounting document prepared by the seller to claim payment from the buyer for the value of goods and/or service being supplied. It gives the details of the goods, the payment method, the delivery terms and a detailed breakdowns of the monetary amount due.

A commercial invoice serves as a basic document against which other documents such as drafts, transport documents, insurance documents and packing list are established. Commercial invoice can either take the form shown below or be made on the seller's letterhead with the wordings "commercial invoice" clearly indicated. It contains the following major items:

(1) Name and Address of the Seller

If the invoice is made on the seller's letterhead, this item can be omitted. The name and address in either form should be the same as those called for in the credit.

(2) Name and Address of the Buyer

The invoice must be made out to the L/C applicant with the name and address being in accordance with those appeared in the credit.

(3) The Issuing Date

The commercial invoice can be made no later than the last date for presentation and within the expiry date of the credit, or it can be made earlier than the issuing date of the credit. In practice, the issuing date of the commercial invoice can be the earliest one compared with other documents.

(4) Description of Goods

Complete description of goods will normally include the quantity, packing and specification that should be made in compliance with those in the credit. Detailed description about the goods will be found in commercial invoice whereas the information will only appear in general terms in the credit and other documents.

(5) Price and Price Terms

Price should be broken down into unit price and the seller should work out the total amount which represents the invoice value payable by the importer. Invoice value, unit price and quantity should agree with the credit stipulations. Banks are not responsible for checking the mathematical calculation.

The invoice value normally is the draft amount and is within the credit amount. In the event that the invoice value exceeds the credit amount, the draft amount will be made equal to the credit amount and thus be smaller than the invoice value. The difference between the invoice value and the draft amount will be collected through collection.

The words "about", "approximately" or similar wordings in connection with the amount, quantity or unit price stated in the credit are to be understood as allowing a difference not exceeding 10% more or 10% less than the corresponding items they refer.

Price terms refer to the incoterms such as FOB, CIF and CIP, etc. The price term should be clearly indicated as different terms will affect the actual price of a transaction.

(6) Port of Loading and Port of Discharge

(7) Shipping Mark

Shipping mark is made for the purpose of easy handling and recognition by the carrier and the consignee. It normally contains a mark, the name of the port of discharge, package No and the country of origin and it should be subject to the stipulations on the credit, if any. There may not be a shipping mark for a certain shipment, and the column "marks and numbers" will be entered with "N. M. (No marks)" or simply be left blank. However, when a shipping mark is used, the same shipping mark will also appear in other documents such as packing list or bills of lading in order to tie them up.

(8) Payment Method

Payment method such as D/P, D/A or documentary credit should be indicated in the invoice. In the case of settlement by documentary credit, the name of the issuing bank, the L/C No. and the issuing date of the credit should be indicated in the commercial invoice.

(9) Name of the Vessel, Cost of Freight and Insurance

The name of the vessel should be entered in the blank after s. s. / M. V. _____ . If the goods are consigned to air transportation, the name of the airliner and the flight number may be included.

The commercial invoice may also bear the breakdowns of the costs of freight and insurance. However, it is not always necessary for the seller to supply this information.

(10) Signature of the Exporter

Unless otherwise stipulated in the credit, invoice needs not to be signed.

Specimen of an invoice

INVOICE FACTURE FACTURA RECHNUNG FACTUUR

SELLER Name, Address, VAT No		Sheet No.
The American Exporter Co. Inc. 17 Main Street Tampa, Florida	**Invoice No. & Date (Tax Point)** 19 May 27, 1994	**Seller's Reference** 657
	Buyer's References	**Other References**

Consignee	Buyer (If not Consignee)
The French Importer Co. 89 rue du Commerce Paris, France	

	Country of Origin of Goods U.S.A.	Country of Destination France
	Terms of Delivery and Payment	
	CIP INCOTERMS 1990	

Vessel/Aircraft etc. Fawn	Port of Loading Tampa
Port of Discharge Le Havre	

Marks and Numbers and Container No.	Number and Kind of Packages Description of Goods	TT Code No.	TT Gross Wt (Kg)	Total Cube (m³)
1/24 U.S.A.	Machinery and spare parts as per pro-forma invoice number 657 dated December 17, 1993 CIP Incoterms 1990		3900	

Item/ pkges	Gross/Net/Cube	Description	Quantity	Unit Price	Selling Price
24		Machinery and spare parts as per pro-forma invoice number 657 dated December 17, 1993 CIP Incoterms 1990			US$100,000
				Invoice Total	US$100,000

The American Exporter Co. Inc.
17 Main Street
Tampa, Florida

Name of signatory

Place and Date of Issue

Signature

SPECIMEN Commercial Invoice

FUDA TRADING CO,. LTD. (PTE)
Commercial Building 19A Singapore
Tel:(65)22100 Telefax:221045
COMMERCIAL INVOICE

No. 1824

Date:10th August 19 ____

Invoice of Spare Parts of HTP—Type Ⅰ,Ⅱ,Ⅲ×30 sets

For account of Messrs. Powell International Trading Co. ,Ltd,Malaysia

Shipped by Fuda Trading Co. ,Ltd. (Pte)Singapore

Shipped per Medaly

Sailing on or about 15th August 19 ____
from Singapore to Malaysia

L/C No. MS1812

Contract No. 90129

MARKS & NOS.	DESCRIPTION OF GOODS	QUANTITY	UNIT PRICE	AMOUNT
MADEIN SINGAPORE 30 SETS)	1. SPARE PARTS OF HTP —TYP Ⅰ 2. SPARE PARTS OF HTP —TYP Ⅱ 3. SPARE PARTS OF HTP —TYP Ⅲ	10SETS 10SETS 10SEYS	F. O. B. SINGAPORE US $ 2000 US $ 3000 US $ 5000	20,000.— 30,000.— 50,000.— US $ 100,000.—

Say One Hundred Thousand U. S. Dollars Only.

Drawn Under:L/C No. MS 181 issued by Commercial Bank Malaysia Dated 10th June 19 ____

Insurance:Insurance to be effected by Buyer

Fuda Trading Co. ,Ltd. (Pte)
Singapore

Authorized Signature _____
MANAGER

E. & O. E

宏 發 國 際 有 限 公 司
HONGFA INTERNATIONAL (PTE) LTD

1 Colombo Court #08-03   Singapore 0617   Fax: 3395034
Tel: 3383676, 3383677, 3368320 Telex: RS26004 HAGSCO

INVOICE NO: 1014   *Date,* _____

Invoice of: _____

Shipped by the undersigned from Singapore _____ to _____

Per: _____ on/abt: _____ for.

Messrs: _____

Drawn under _____ L/C No. _____

Dated: _____ Import Appl. No. _____

DESCRIPTION	Quantity	Unit Price	Amount

for **HONGFA INTERNATIONAL (PTE) LTD**

E. & O.E.

It is understood that the above mentioned goods/work have been examined by the customers
at time of delivery/completion in good order and condition.

2. Packing List / Weight List

Packing list / Weight list details the packing of goods item by item such as assortment, weight and measurement and serves as a supplementary document to the commercial invoice. It is made more convenient for the custom and buyer to check the goods upon arrival at the foreign port.

Items such as description of goods and shipping marks on the packing list / weight list should be made in consistent with those on the commercial invoice, but those items pertaining to the unit price and amount should not be included in the list. The date of the packing / weight list can be made the same or a little later than but not earlier than that of the commercial invoice.

宏 發 國 際 有 限 公 司
HONGFA INTERNATIONAL (PTE) LTD

1 Colombo Court #08-03 Singapore 0617 Fax: 3392363
Tel: 3398211 (3 Lines) Telex: RS26004 HAGSCO

PACKING LIST

Date, _____

Name of Buyer: _____

Merchandise: _____

Shipped from Singapore _____ To_____

Per: _____ ;on/abt: _____

Drawn under: _____

L/C No: _____

Import Appl. No: _____ dated_____

Pkg. No.	No. of Pkg.	PARTICULARS

E. & O. E.

Section Four   Insurance Documents

1. Insurance for the Goods

The insurance of goods in this section refers to the marine insurance. The responsibility to insure the physical goods during transit can fall either upon the exporter or the importer as a result of their negotiation and should be cleared indicated in the sales contract right at the beginning of the transaction. In the case of CIF and CIP, it may be agreed that the exporter will insure the goods for the whole sea journey. And in the case of FOB, FCA and CFR, the responsibility may fall on the part of the importer.

As sea voyage is a risky journey, the cargo should be insured against possible loss under any shipping terms. As shipping terms are description of the responsibilities from the point of view of the exporter's, any obligation which dose not appear in a particular term must/may be the responsibility of the importer.

2. Definition

An insurance document is a contract of indemnity between the insurer and the insured stipulating the premium, the amount insured, risks to be covered, procedures to establish a claim and other terms and conditions applicable, thereby indemnifying or making compensation to the latter by the former in the event that a covered loss occurs. Concurrent with bills of lading, insurance documents have developed to become title documents.

The two parties under an insurance document are:

(1) The Insurer

The insurer refers to the insurance company who will make compensations against an insurance document.

(2) The Insured

The insured is the party who will claim compensation from the insurer against an insurance document in the event of a loss. He can be either the exporter or the importer.

3. Types of Loss

According to the causes, losses can be divided into maritime losses and losses of external causes.

(1) Maritime Losses

All natural disasters and accidents are referred to as maritime losses. Such disasters may happen when heavy weather, lightning, storm, earthquake and flood cause the vessel and /or the cargo to be stranded, sunk or burned down. According to the degree of damage, the maritime losses can be further divided into total loss and partial loss.

(A) Total loss

The degree of damage is the most severe in a total loss where all the goods are lost or become worthless. It can take the following forms:

* Actual total loss

When the cargo has been completely destroyed or lost, the loss is referred to as actual total loss.

　　* Constructive total loss

A constructive total loss occurs when the damage may not reach the actual total loss but the repairing of the cargo will cost more than its original value.

　　* Total loss of a proportional part

It refers to the total loss of a separate part of goods. That is to say, for this part of the goods, it is a total loss though it may not be the total loss of the entire shipment.

　　(B) Partial loss

Partial loss is also termed as "average" which indicates that some of the goods are lost or damaged but still have some value or the necessary expenses to replace the goods will not exceed their original value. According to the causes of average, partial loss can have the following subdivisions:

　　* General average (G. A.)

It refers to a loss that one part of goods is intentionally sacrificed or an expenditure is voluntarily made by the captain in time of danger for the common benefit of all parties concerned. General average will be inclusively sustained by all the parties involved.

　　* Particular average (P. A.)

It refers to a loss that accidentally has occurred to part of the cargo and is not caused by the deliberate act of a party for the common benefit. Particular average will be sustained exclusively by the party upon whom the loss falls.

　　(2) Losses from External Causes

Losses from external causes refer to losses other than the maritime losses. They can be further divided into two types:

　　(A) General risks.

General risks are caused by mishandling in the process of transit. Although a detailed knowledge of the 11 subdivisions is not required in this course, a general understanding is a must in connection with their names and natures.

　　(a) TPND.

TPND are the initials for the risk of theft, pilferage and non-delivery. It refers to the risk that the cargo may be stolen in transit or may be lost or damaged due to improper unloading or some other types of mishandling.

　　(b) Risk of leakage.

　　(c) Risk of clash and breakage.

　　(d) Risk of hook damage.

　　(e) Risk of fresh water and/or rain damage (FWRD).

　　(f) Risk of shortage.

　　(g) Risk of intermixture and contamination.

　　(h) Risk of taint of odor.

　　(i) Risk of sweat and heating.

　　(j) Risk of rust.

　　(k) Risk of breakage of packing.

　　(B) Special risks.

Special risks refer to the damage or losses caused by political, military, administrative practices and procedures or any changes made in this regard. There are 9 types of special risks:

    (a) Failure to deliver.

    (b) Import duty.

    (c) On deck.

    (d) Rejection.

    (e) Aflatoxin.

    (f) Fire risk extension clause (FREC).

    (g) War risk.

    (h) Risk of import duty.

    (i) Risk of strike riots and civil commotion (SRCC).

4. Types of Coverage / Risk

It should first be kept in mind that the word "risk" is sometimes used to refer to a loss while some other times used to refer to the coverage. The correct understanding of the word comes from the context in which it is used.

Various types of coverage are made to cover different risks or losses, though it should be understood that the risks may be overlapping with one another.

(1) Basic Marine Insurance Coverage

Three types of coverage will make the basic marine insurance coverage in the sense that they can be insured on their own and will be selected first before other additional types of coverage being chosen.

(A) Free from particular average (FPA).

FPA means that the insurer is free from being claimed for any particular average losses. The name of FPA can be misleading because it will only provide coverage for the total loss and general average. Compared with other types of risk, FPA provides the least coverage.

(B) With average (WA) or With particular average (WPA)

WA covers all the maritime losses. It can not be understood to cover the particular average only. However, it can be understood to provide coverage for the FPA plus particular average.

When a WA dose not cover small-amount losses, it normally states the percentage over which the loss will be covered. The minimum percentage of a loss to be covered is called a franchise. The percentage can be 3% or 5% of the insured amount. However, it is a tendency that a policy will not take the franchise into consideration. IOP means irrespective of percentage indicating that the insurer provides complete coverage of the risk, no matter how small the loss is in monetary terms.

(C) All Risks.

All risks cover the maritime losses and the general risks. All risks can not be understood as to cover all the risks occurred in the sea voyage.

(2) Additional Risks

Additional risks are made for the purpose to cover the 11 types of general risks and 9 types of special risks though each risk can be selected separately. Additional risks are so called because they can not be insured on their own and can only be selected when one or more of the basic marine insurance coverages have been chosen. With the knowledge of the different coverage of the risks, the risks should be selected according to the following combinations:

* When FPA or WA is chosen, the option is still open for selection from general risks and special risks.

* When all risks are chosen, the option is only open for selection from special risks since general risks are included in all risks.

The following chart will illustrate the coverage of the risks:

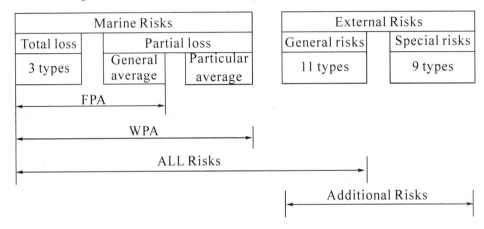

5. Insurance Clauses

It should bear in mind that in international insurance market, different marine associations (insurance companies) have their own insurance clauses concerning the risks. A detailed knowledge of these standard clauses are not required in this course, but we should have a general understanding of those aspects of the clauses which are in connection with risks.

(1) London Institute Cargo Clause (ICC)

ICC is constituted by the Institute of London Underwriters in 1963 and revised in 1982. ICC has found its wide application in the world insurance market as well as in China. The institute has divided the coverage into two groups: the basic Marine Risks and War/Strike Risks.

For Marine Risks:

(A) Institute Cargo Clause A.

This clause covers all risks except War/Strike Risks.

(B) Institute Cargo Clause B.

This clause covers WA.

(C) Institute Cargo Clause C.

This clause covers FPA.

For War/Strike Risks:

(A) Institute War Clause.

(B) Institute Strike, Riots and Civil Commotion Clauses.

(C) Institute Theft, Pilferage and Non－delivery Clauses.

(2) Ocean Marine Cargo Clause of the People's Insurance Company of China (CIC)

CIC is constituted in 1972 and revised in 1976 and 1981. It can be divided into two broad groups: Ocean Marine Cargo Insurance including FPA, WA and All Risks and Ocean Marine Cargo Insurance for Additional Risks.

6. **Contents of the Insurance Document**

The standard form of the insurance will be pre-printed by the insurer and be filled in by the insured at the time when the latter decides to insure his goods with the former. The major items are as follows:

(1) The Name and Signature of the Insurer

The insurer is the insurance company, the insurance underwriter or their agent. As an insurance document is normally preprinted on the insurer's letterhead, it is always pre-signed by the insurer.

(2) The Name and Signature of the Insured

If the shipping term is FOB or CFR, the insured will be made out to the importer.

If the shipping term is CIF or CIP, the insured should be made out to the exporter.

Under letter of credit, if the credit bears the stipulations such as "insurance document issued to the order of xx bank / to our order", the insured party should be made to the order of xx bank or to the order of the credit issuing bank. On some occasions, the credit may also require the insurance document to be made to the beneficiary of the credit.

The signature of the insured is required to validate the certificare.

(3) Endorsement

Although the endorsement is made on the back of an insurance document, it is also an important item. The insured should make proper endorsement as required by the credit or as the case may be at the time presentment is made by the exporter.

When the insured is the importer, no endorsement is required since the actual insured is the importer himself. In the case when the exporter is the insured, he will be required to endorse the document at the time when the presentment is made. Under letter of credit, the L/C stipulations will normally require the endorsee to be the issuing bank or another nominated bank. The endorsee bank will in turn endorse the document to the importer upon his payment to retire documents. Under collection, the exporter may endorse the document directly to the importer who will get the isurauce document and other relevant documents upon his payment (D/P) or his acceptance (D/A) to his bank (collecting bank). In the case that the L/C issuing bank is sbown to be the insured, the bank will endorse the document to the importer against his payment.

(4) Description of Goods

No detailed description is required on an insurance document and a general one will serve the purpose. However, other items such as the shipping mark, quantity and packing will be made consistent with the invoice and other documents.

(5) The Amount Insured

The amount insured is the amount to be claimed by the insured. As the importer will become the actual party insured through the process of endorsement and delivery, he is usually the party who will file the claim when the covered loss occurs. On the other hand, it also serves as the basis for the calculation of the premium.

The amount will be expressed both in figures and in words. Normally the sum insured will be expressed in the same currency as that in the invoice and is at 110% of the invoice value. The 10% is to cover part of the profits which the importer would make as well as any associated costs.

(6) The Rate and the Premium

Different rates will be decided by the insurer according to the type of goods, the type of risk, the type of vessel and the distance between the port of loading and the port of discharge. In practice, it usually will appear as "as arranged" and need not to be filled in by the insured.

The premium is the commission charged by the insurer on the insured, either the importer or the exporter. The formula will take into account both the amount insured and the rate:

Premium = The insured amount × rate.

As the rate is not stated in the document, the premium will also appear as "as arranged"

.

(7) Conditions /Coverage

It should be remembered that the basic marine coverages could be made on their own while the additional risks will be made only after the basic risks have been selected.

It should also be noted that the complete information of a coverage consists of the type of the risk, its insurance clause and the effective date of the insurance clause.

(8) Shipping Particulars

The name of vessel should be entered into the blank after "per conveyance S. S. _____" and the B/L date or the wordings "as per B/L" should be entered into the blank after "sailing on or about _____". After "from" the port of loading is entered and after "to" the port of discharge is entered. All the items concerning the shipping particulars should be made in consistent with the bills of lading.

(9) Issuing Date

The issuing date signifies the date on which the coverage takes effect. This dated can be earlier than or the same as the B/L date but no later than the B/L date. The later issuing date of the insurance document indicates that the goods have been uninsured for some time and it is often found unacceptable on the part of the bank.

(10) Claim Payable at

It should be clearly indicated in the insurance document as to the place where the claim is payable as well as the details of the agent to whom the claim is to be directed.

The claim is normally made payable at the place of discharge, that is, the country of the importer. The claim payable should be made in compliance with the stipulations in the credit when applicable.

(11) Full Set

Normally, insurance document in one original and one copy makes a full set. However, insurance document in two originals may also be required as a full set.

中 国 人 民 保 险 公 司
天 津 分 公 司
The People's Insurance Company of China

TIANJIN   BRANCH
总 公 司 设 于 北 京   一 九 四 九 年 创 立
HEAD OFFICE: BEIJING   ESTABLISHED IN 1949

地址: 中国天津和平区曲阜道保险大楼
Insurance Building, Qu Fu Road
Heping District, Tianjin, China.

CABLE: 42001 TIANJIN
TEL: 315366, 315367
TLX: 23262 PICC CN
FAX: (86) (22) 301297

发票号次 TBS/203023098
INVOICE NO.

保 险 单
INSURANCE POLICY

保险单号次 TT03/ 1201071193302512
POLICY NO.

中 国 人 民 保 险 公 司 （ 以 下 简 称 本 公 司 ）
THIS POLICY OF INSURANCE WITNESSES THAT THE PEOPLE'S INSURANCE COMPANY OF CHINA (HEREINAFTER CALLED "THE COMPANY")

根   据   TIANJIN TEXTILES I/E CORP.
AT THE REQUEST OF

（ 以 下 简 称 被 保 险 人 ） 的 要 求 ， 由 被 保 险 人 向 本 公 司 缴 付 约
(HEREINAFTER CALLED "THE INSURED") AND IN CONSIDERATION OF THE AGREED PREMIUM PAID TO THE COMPANY BY THE
定 的 保 险 费 ， 按 照 本 保 险 单 承 保 险 别 和 背 面 所 载 条 款 与 下 列
INSURED, UNDERTAKES TO INSURE THE UNDERMENTIONED GOODS IN TRANSPORTATION SUBJECT TO THE CONDITIONS OF THIS POLICY
特 款 承 保 下 述 货 物 运 输 保 险 ， 特 立 本 保 险 单
AS PER THE CLAUSES PRINTED OVERLEAF AND OTHER SPECIAL CLAUSES ATTACHED HEREON.

标 记 MARKS & NOS.	包装及数量 QUANTITY	保险货物项目 DESCRIPTION OF GOODS	保险金额 AMOUNT INSURED
As per Invoice No. TBS/203023098	4 CTNS	ART NO.42518 65%P.35%V.GABARDINE	USD1,769.00

总 保 险 金 额 U.S. Dollars One Thousand Seven Hundred and Sixty Nine Only.
TOTAL AMOUNT INSURED:

保 费 AS ARRANGED   费率 AS ARRANGED   装 载 运 输 工 具 TIAN YAN V. 721
PREMIUM   RATE   PER CONVEYANCE S.S.

开 赋 日 期 as per B/L   自 Hsinkang   至 Hongkong
SLG ON .OR ABT.   FROM   TO

承 保 险 别
CONDITIONS
Covering All Risks as per Institute Cargo Clauses (1.1.1963) and Risk of War as per Institute War
Clauses (11.3.80). (Warehouse to Warehouse Clause is included)

顺 保 货 物 ， 如 遇 出 险 ， 本 公 司 凭 本 保 险 单 及 其 他 有 关 证 件 给 付 赔 款
CLAIMS IF ANY,   PAYABLE   ON   SURRENDER   OF   THIS   POLICY   TOGETHER WITH OTHER RELEVANT DOCUMENTS
顺 保 货 物 ， 如 发 生 本 保 险 单 项 下 负 责 赔 偿 的 损 失 或 事 故
IN THE EVENT OF ACCIDENT WHEREBY LOSS OR DAMAGE MAY RESULT IN A CLAIM UNDER THIS POLICY IMMEDIATE NOTICE
应 立 即 通 知 本 公 司 下 述 代 理 人 查 勘
APPLYING FOR SURVEY MUST BE GIVEN TO THE COMPANY'S AGENT AS MENTIONED HEREUNDER:

THE MING AN INSURANCE CO.(H.K.) LTD.
INTERNATIONAL BUILDING,14TH FLOOR 141,DES VOEUX ROAD,CENTRAL HONG
KONG.

中国人民保险公司天津分公司国外业务部
THE PEOPLE'S INSURANCE CO. OF CHINA
TIANJIN BRANCH FOREIGN BUSINESS DEPT.

赔 款 偿 付 地 点 Hongkong in USD
CLAIM PAYABLE AT

日 期 28TH JUN., 199-   天 津
DATE   TIANJIN

7. Types of Insurance Document

Broadly speaking, insurance document can be divided according to two criteria. That is to say, according to the way to determine the maturity, it can be divided as time policy, voyage policy and mixed policy. According to whether the insured value is specified at the time the insurance contract is established, it can be divided into unvalued policy and valued policy while the latter can be further divided into insurance policy, insurance certificate, combined certificate and open policy.

(1) According to the Way to Determine the Maturity

(A) Time policy.

When goods are insured for a fixed period of time, they are insured under a time policy. A time policy is often used in hull insurance when the coverage is made for the ship as well as its machinery and equipment. For this reason, time insurance is rarely used in trade transactions.

(B) Voyage policy.

A voyage policy means that the goods are insured for transportation from one port to another port. Careful reading of the stipulations in a voyage policy is necessary for the insured as it is often the case that the insurer may state in a policy that the covers will not be extended until the goods are actually on board the conveyance and that the insurer is not liable for the loss of or the damage to the goods occurred in transit from the shore to the ship.

(C) Mixed Policy.

A mixed policy means that the goods are insured for a particular voyage as well as for a certain period of time.

(2) According to Whether the Insured Value is Specified

(A) Unvalued Policy.

An unvalued policy does not specify the insured value and the value is to be determined by a certain percentage based on the market value on the cargo's arrival at its destination. It is less popular than a valued policy.

(B) Valued policy.

A valued policy means that the insured value for the goods is clearly stated at the time when the policy is established. The great majority of insurance policies will be valued ones. A valued policy may take the following forms:

(a) Insurance policy.

An insurance policy is a written contract between the insurance company (the insurer) and the trader (the insured), containing all the terms and conditions of the agreement with full details of the risks covered. The provisions concerning the rights and responsibilities of the two parties will normally be made on the reverse of the policy. An insurance policy is a legal evidence of the agreement to insure and is often established at the time when the sales contract is made, or on a later date.

(b) Insurance certificate.

An insurance certificate is a document similar to an insurance policy with the same details except that the provisions of the policy are abbreviated. However, the provisions under an insurance policy are also applicable to an insurance certificate. An insurance certificate takes the same effect as an insurance policy from the legal point of view. But, in some countries, the insured must have a policy before he can take a legal action against the insurer. That is to say, a certificate alone is insufficient to sue the insurer.

(c) Combined certificate.

Combined certificate is an insurance certificate combined with an commercial invoice. That is to say, an item indicating that the goods are under an insurance coverage is made on the face of the commercial invoice. Combined certificate is also referred to as a risk note.

(d) Open policy.

When an exporter sells goods on a regular basis, he will normally arrange an open policy of insurance to cover all his exports during a specific time period which provides insurance coverage at all times according to agreed terms and conditions. The insurance policy/certificate is pre-printed and pre-signed by the insurer and to be held by the exporter. Each time a shipment is made, the insured (the exporter) will declare the details of the goods and pay a premium to the insurer. A certificate of insurance is then issued/signed by the exporter who will in turn send one copy to the insurance company for his file and records.

The benefit of the open cover system is that it avoids the need to negotiate insurance terms each time a shipment is made and the necessity of issuing a separate policy for each individual shipment. If an exporter sells goods on a one-off basis, it is not necessary for him to arrange an open policy. In this case, the exporter will negotiate terms with the insurer and an insurance policy will be issued.

Chapter Twelve　Documents (Ⅱ)
− Transport Documents

Transport documents mainly refer to marine bills of lading, seaway bills, airway bills, combined transport documents, inland transport way bills and parcel receipts.

Section one　Marine Bills of Lading

1.　Definition

A bill of lading is a transport document which is issued and signed by the shipping company or his agent (the carrier) and given to the shipper acknowledging that goods have been received for shipment to a particular destination and stating the terms on which the goods are to be carried. When the goods are transported by ship, marine bill of lading is one of the most important shipping documents.

2.　Functions of a Bill of Lading

(1) A Receipt of Goods

A bill of lading serves as a receipt for goods shipped, acknowledging that the goods have been received in said quality, quantity and in apparent good order for the purpose of shipment on board a vessel. It is the responsibility of the carrier to deliver the goods accordingly to the consignee named in the bill(s) of lading.

(2) A Contract of Carriage

A bill of lading is a contract of carriage made between the carrier and the shipper. The detailed provisions will be made on the reverse of the document which stipulate the rights and responsibilities of the two parties. On one hand, it is the responsibility of the carrier to transport the goods by sea and make the delivery to the consignee. On the other hand, the obligation for the shipper is to consign the goods in apparent good order and in agreement with packing requirements of the shipment.

(3) A Title Document

A bill of lading is a title document in the sense that the legal owner of the bill of lading is the legal owner of the goods. The carrier will only release the goods against the production of the original bill of lading. Original bills of lading are usually issued in sets of two, three or four (the number of originals should be indicated on the bill of lading). As any one original B/L will enable the possessor to obtain the goods, possession of a full set is required before ownership of the goods is secured. When a bill of lading is transferred, the ownership over the goods has also been transferred. As a result, constructive delivery has come into being on the basis that bills of lading have become title documents.

(4) A Negotiable Document

As a title document, a bill of lading can also be a negotiable document. However, it is not a negotiable instrument in the true sense but a quasi-negotiable instrument, important for the payment arrangements. Any transferee who takes possession of an endorsed bill of lading for value obtains a good title to it.

3. **Parties of a Bill of Lading**

The carrier and the shipper are the two parties on the bill of lading and they are the basic parties to such a document. In addition to these two, other parties will include the consignee, the notify party and the transferee/holder.

(1) Carrier

The carrier is a shipping company who can either be the owner of the ship or the hirer of the vessel. In the case when the contract is made through an agent of the shipping company, the carrier should be the shipping company instead of the agent. It is the shipping company who enters into the contract of carriage with the shipper.

(2) Shipper

The shipper is also called the consignor who dispatches the goods to the carrier. He is usually the exporter.

(3) Consignee

The consignee is the party who obtains ownership over the goods and who has the right to take delivery of the goods at the stated destination. The consignee can be made out to different orders:

(A) Demonstrative order.

A demonstrative order can be made "to order", "to the order of shipper", "to the order of the issuing bank" and "to the order of the importer". The word "order" indicates that the bill of lading of this type can be transferred by endorsement and delivery.

(a) "To order" and "to the order of shipper".

"To order" indicates that the ownership of goods belongs to the exporter/shipper. So in effect, it is the same as "to the order of shipper". Letter of credit may require B/L to be made out this way and this kind of B/L may also be used under collection. Under either payment method, the exporter is required to make blank endorsement to his bank who will endorse the B/L one more time and release it to the importer when he honors the draft presented to him.

(b) "To the order of the issuing bank".

Under a letter of credit, the credit may require B/L to be made "to the order of the issuing bank" in order to show the ownership of the issuing bank over the goods. The issuing bank will endorse and release B/L to the importer against his payment.

(c) "To the order of the importer".

When a bill of lading is made out this way, no endorsement of the importer is required when he takes delivery of the goods. This kind of B/L is used under situations similiar to restrictive order B/L discussed below.

(B) Restrictive order.

When a bill of lading is made out to a named consignee, it is a restrictive order and the named consignee is the importer. In this case, the importer can obtain the goods by presenting the original bill of lading upon his identification is proved. Under a restrictive order bill of lading, the exporter is at the risk of non-payment once the goods are delivered. This type of bill of lading is used under open account, payment in advance or other non-commercial transactions with the purpose to enable the importer to obtain goods as soon as possible.

(C) Bearer order.

Bearer order bill of lading is made out "to bearer". It can be transferred by delivery without endorsement and it is difficult to be replaced once lost. It is seldom used in practice.

(4) The Notify Party

As the importer is seldom shown to be the consignee, information of the notify party will be required. The notify party is the person whom the shipping company will notify on arrival of the goods, usually he is the importer or his agent. When a bill of lading is made out "to order", "to the order of the shipper" or "to the order of the issuing bank", the name and address of the importer or those of his agent will be indicated as the notify party. When a B/L is made out "to the order of the importer" or "to the named consignee (importer)", the notify party will be left blank.

(5) The Endorsee/Holder

The holder is the person who will become the owner of the goods under a given B/L by endorsement or by delivery. The holder is the transferee or the endorsee who will not appear on the face of the B/L and who is the result of the negotiation. The transferee/endorsee/holder may be the importer, a bank or any other third party. When the importer wants to further transfer the B/L.

Endorsement is required and applicable when a bill of lading is a demonstrative order B/L. The endorsement can take the form of blank endorsement and special endorsement. When the endorsee is a bank, the exporter is usually required to make blank endorsement. In the case when the endorsee is the importer, a special endorsement is to be made. In practice, a bill of lading is usually required to be made out "to order and blank endorsement" under L/C.

4. Contents of a Bill of Lading

A bill of lading normally contains the following items:

① The name of the shipping company (the carrier).

② The name of the shipper, who is usually the exporter or the exporter's agent.

③ The name of the consignee.

There are different ways that a bill of lading can be made out to. Please refer to item 3 for a detailed analysis. Normally a B/L is made out to order and endorsed by the exporter. It is unusual for the importer to be shown as the consignee.

④ The notify party.

When a B/L is made out to order without the importer shown as the consignee, information of the importer or his agent should be shown in the notify party, otherwise the notify party should be left blank.

⑤ The name of the carrying vessel and the voyage No.

⑥ The two ports.

One port is called the port of receipt, the port of loading or the port of shipment and the other port is referred to as the port of destination, the port of discharge or the port of delivery. When a B/L is made for port to port shipment, the name of the two ports only will serve the purpose. On other occasions, however, a B/L may be made for combined transport shipment where door to door service is provided. In this case, a place of receipt, usually the premises of the exporter and a final place of delivery, usually the premises of the importer, are mentioned in addition to the two ports.

⑦ Marks and numbers.

The marks and numbers should be made consistent with those on the other documents such as the invoice or the packing list. The same marks and numbers will appear on the boxes, cartons or cases where the goods are contained so as to indicate that they are covered by the same bill of lading.

⑧ Description of goods.

A general or a brief description of the goods will do. If the transaction is under L/C, the credit number, the name of the issuing bank and the credit issuing dated should be indicated here.

⑨ Total packages.

This shows how many boxes/cartons/cases into which goods are packed.

⑩ Freight charges.

Freight charges can be made as prepaid or collect. Freight prepaid indicates that the freight costs have already been paid by the exporter, which is usually the case under the incoterms like C&F and CIF. Freight collect means that the payment of the sea-freight is due to the importer and it is to be collected on arrival at the destination, which is usually the case under FOB.

⑪ Number of original B/L.

This indicates how many original bills of lading will make a full set. In practice, full set may contain 2, 3 or 4 originals. An original bill of lading is one which is signed by the ship's master, or by an agent of the shipping company. If it is an original, the very word "original" should be clearly indicated thereon so as to distinguish itself from a copy. Shipping companies often issue unsigned copies of bill of lading for record purposes, these unsigned copies are not documents of title.

⑫ The signature of the carrier.

For a bill of lading to be original, it should be signed on behalf of the shipping company. Shipping companies often issue unsigned copies of the bill of lading for record purpose. These unsigned copies are not title documents and can not be taken as original bills of lading.

⑬ The B/L issuing date and B/L number

This is the date when the shipping company receives the goods for shipment and/or when the goods are loaded on board the ship.

If the transaction is under L/C, the B/L date should be made consistent with the stipulations of the credit and is usually be made between the invoice date and the latest date of shipment.

BILL OF LADING FOR COMBINED TRANSPORT SHIPMENT OR PORT TO PORT SHIPMENT

Shipper Speirs and Wadley Ltd. ② Adderley Road Hackney London E8 1XY England	OVERSEAS ① CONTAINERS LIMITED B/L No. 45969648 Booking Ref 1234567 Shipper's Ref Job 5678 **OCL**

Consignee To Order ③	SPECIMEN

Notify Party. Address Woldal Ltd. ④ New Road Kowloon Hong Kong	Place of Receipt (Applicable only when this document is used as a Combined Transport Bill of Lading) Speirs and Wadley Ltd. Adderley Road Hackney London E8 1XY England
Intended Vessel and Voy No Cardigan Bay ⑤ 0415 Intended Port of Loading London	Place of Delivery (Applicable only when this document is used as a Combined Transport Bill of Lading) Woldal Ltd. New Road Kowloon Hong Kong
Intended Port of Discharge Hong Kong ⑥	

Marks and Nos. Container Nos. ⑦	Number and kind of Packages, description of Goods		Gross Weight (kg)	Measurement (cbm)
WL 124 HONG KONG 1/5	5 Wooden Cases containing 400 ELECTRIC POWER DRILLS Model LM 425 2 Speed (900RPM/2400RPM) 425 Watt high-torque motor 2 chucks – 12.5mm and 8mm supplied with each drill	⑧	950	2.376

ABOVE PARTICULARS AS DECLARED BY SHIPPER

✱ Total No of Containers/Packages Packages or pieces ⑨ 5 Movement LCL. Depot/LCL. Depot Freight and Charges (indicate whether prepaid or collect) Origin zone transport charge Prepaid Origin Terminal Handling/LCL Service Charge Prepaid Ocean Freight Prepaid ⑩ Destination Terminal Handling/LCL Service Charge Prepaid Destination zone transport charge Prepaid	Received by the Carrier from the Shipper in apparent good order and condition (unless otherwise noted herein) the total number or quantity of Containers or other packages or units, indicated✱, stated by the Shipper to comprise the Goods specified above, for Carriage subject to all the terms hereof (INCLUDING THE TERMS ON THE REVERSE HEREOF AND THE TERMS OF THE CARRIER'S APPLICABLE TARIFF) from the Place of Receipt or the Port of Loading, whichever is applicable, to the Port of Discharge or the Place of Delivery, whichever is applicable, in accepting this Bill of Lading the Merchant expressly accepts and agrees to all its terms, conditions and exceptions, whether printed, stamped or written, or otherwise incorporated, notwithstanding the non-signing of this Bill of Lading by the Merchant. When this document calls for Combined Transport it is a negotiable Combined Transport Document the terms of which are based upon the Uniform Rules for a Combined Transport Document (ICC Publication No 298)
ICS CT B/L Apsil 78	Number of Original Bills of Lading ⑪ Two (02)	Place and Date of Issue London ⑬ 01 08 19.. IN WITNESS of the contract herein contained the number of originals stated opposite has been used, one of which being accomplished the other(s) to be void For the Carrier A.J. S/ilhury ⑫

COBRA B/L 2 9/831

Specimen Bill of Lading

UNIGLORY
UNIGLORY MARINE CORPORATION

BILL OF LADING
NOT NEGOTIABLE UNLESS CONSIGNED TO ORDER

Shipper/Exporter S INTERNATIONAL PTE LTD 40 WOODLANDS INDUSTRIAL PARK E INGAPORE 2775 Shipper code	(5) Document No. OBTN688258KSG **FIRST ORIGINAL** (6) Export References
Consignee (complete name and address) / (unless provided otherwise, a consignment 'To Order' means To Order of Shipper.)) THE ORDER OF IRST COMMERCIAL BANK	(7) Forwarding Agent-References
Notify Party (complete name and address) JSCO INDUSTRIAL CORP .O. BOX 84-252 AIPEI TAIWAN ROC Notify code	(8) Point and Country of Origin (for the Merchant's reference only) (9) Also Notify Party (complete name and address)

Pre-carriage by	(13) Place of Receipt/Date SINGAPORE /CY	In Witness Whereof, the undersigned, on behalf of Uniglory Marine Corporation, the Master and the Owner of the Vessel, has signed the number of Bill(s) of Lading stated below, all of this tenor and date, one of which being accomplished, the others to stand void.
Ocean Vessel/Voy. No. JI OBTAIN 0517AN-029	(15) Port of Loading SINGAPORE	(10) Onward Inland Routing/Export Instructions (for the Merchant's reference only)
of Discharge AOH IUNG	(17) Place of Delivery KAOHSIUNG /CY	

Particulars furnished by the Merchant

Container No. And Seal No. Marks & Nos.	(19) Quantity And Kind of Packages	(20) Description of Goods	(21) Measurement (M') Gross Weight (KGS)
ONTAINER NO./SEAL NO. GTU8228498/40'/53780 FUSCO OLOUR/NO AOHSIUNG ADE IN SINGAPORE	/000930/PKG/(FF) S.T.C. : 960 PACKAGES 1X40'	BUILDING MATERIALS MORTAC SEALER, CEMENTITIOUS STUCCO AND STUCCO SPRAY GUN SHIPPED ON BOARD " OCEAN FREIGHT COLLECT " SHIPPER'S LOAD & COUNT	23004.000 50.0000

			(23) Declared Value $_____ If Merchant enters actual value of Goods and pays the applicable ad valorem tariff rate, Carrier's package limitation shall not apply
OTAL NUMBER OF ONTAINERS OR PACKAGES N WORDS)	ONE(1) CONTAINER ONLY		

4) FREIGHT & CHARGES	Revenue Tons	Rate	Per	Prepaid	Collect
	FREIGHT AS ARRANGED				

B/L NO. GMU 70660081998	(27) Number of Original B(s)/L THREE (3) (28) Place of B(s)/L Issue/Date SINGAPORE NOV.28,1996	(29) Prepaid at (31) Exchange Rate	(30) Collect at DESTINATION (32) Exchange Rate
Service Type/Mode CL/FCL O/O	(33) Laden on Board the Vessel NOV.28,1996	**R T W SHIPPING (S) PTE. LTD.** By AS AGENTS FOR THE CARRIER UNIGLORY MARINE CORPORATION	

(TERMS OF BILL OF LADING ARE CONTINUED ... ACK HEREOF AND
RM NO. DOC-001-00 ENLARGED VERSION OF BACK CLAUSE IS AVAI... UPON REQUEST)

5. Types of Bill of Lading

There are many different types of bill of lading according to different criteria:

(1) According to Whether or not the Goods are "on Board"

(A) On board B/L or shipped B/L.

An on board B/L bears the wordings "Shipped in apparent good order and condition ... " which confirm that the exporter has delivered the goods on board the vessel at the port of shipment. Date of issuance of a shipped B/L will be deemed to be the date of shipment. An on board B/L is a satisfactory type to the shipper for an early settlement.

(B) A received for shipment B/L.

A received B/L bears the wordings "Received in apparent good order and condition ... " which merely express that the goods have been handed over to the carrier and are in his custody. The absence of the word "shipped" will make the bill of lading unacceptable by the bank for settlement unless provisions have been made in the credit otherwise. For this reason, A received for shipment B/L needs to be converted to an on board B/L by adding an on board notation with the name of the vessel on which the goods have been loaded as well as a clearly indicated on board date. For a received for shipment B/L, the date of the on board date, rather than the date of issuance, is the date of shipment.

(2) According to Whether or not the Goods are Damaged at the Time of Boarding

(A) Clean or unclaused B/L.

When the statement " Shipped/Received in apparent good order and condition... " is not modified by the carrier, such a bill of lading is regarded a "clean" or "unclaused" one. When a carrier finds no defective conditions concerning the goods or the packing, he will issue a clean bill of lading. A clean and on board bill of lading is most favored by banks for settlement.

(B) Unclean or claused B/L.

If the carrier dose not agree with the statement "Shipped/Received in apparent good order and condition ... ", he will add a clause indicating the defective conditions of the goods or the packing. Such a clause will make the bill of lading a "claused" or "unclean" one. An unclean bill of lading is not acceptable to the bank.

These clauses that frequently appear on the bill of lading are: Contents leaking, packaging spoiled by contents, packaging broken/holed/torn/damaged, packaging contaminated, goods damaged/scratched, packaging badly dented, packaging damaged and contents exposed, insufficient packing, cases short shipped, goods unprotected/unboxed/partial protected, etc.

(3) According to Whether or not the B/L is Negotiable

(A) Negotiable B/L.

(a) Order B/L.

An order B/L refers to the demonstrative order B/L. This type of bill can be made to order, to the order of shipper, to the order of the issuing bank and to the order of the importer. An order B/L can be transferred by endorsement and delivery.

(b) Bearer order B/L.

A bearer order B/L is made out to bearer. It is also referred to as open B/L. This type of B/L is negotiable by mere delivery without endorsement. In practice, it is rarely used because of its higher degree of risk.

(B) Non-negotiable B/L.

A non-negotiable B/L refers to a Straight B/L or a named consignee B/L. It is made out to a named consignee and is not negotiable. The wordings "Consigned to ... (the named consignee)" mean that no one except the named consignee can take the delivery. The named consignee is usually the importer. In this case, the exporter will suffer a loss in the event that the importer refuses to pay after he has taken the delivery because the legal owner of the goods is made to be the importer by such a B/L. As a result, this type of B/L is often used in non-commercial basis, open account or payment in advance with the purpose to enable the importer to obtain goods with the least formalities.

(4) According to the Modes of Transportation

(A) In a single mode where only the sea voyage is involved.

(a) Direct B/L.

A direct B/L is issued when the goods are shipped by one vessel directly from the port of loading to the port of discharge without transhipment being made on the route.

When the transaction is under L/C and if the credit bears such indications as "transhipment not allowed", then a direct B/L will be required.

(b) Transhipment B/L.

Transhipment B/L is issued when there is no direct service between the port of loading and the port of discharge where two vessels will be involved. The goods will be transhipped from one vessel to another at the port of transhipment.

When the transaction is under L/C and if the credit bears such indications as "transhipment allowed", then a transhipment B/L will be issued by the carrier.

(B) In multi-modes with at least one part of the journey to be the sea voyage.

(a) Combined Transport Documents (CTD).

According to UCP500, CTD are newly developed shipping documents to cover at least two different modes of transport from the place of departure to the place of final destination by sea, inland waterway, air, rail or road. In a single mode of transportation under a marine/ocean bill of lading, the carrier will only provide port to port service; whereas in multi-modes transportation under CTD, the carrier can provide door to door service. As a result, since the 1980s, the name of marine/ocean B/L has been changed to bill of lading applicable to either the combined transport shipment or port to port shipment.

Parties to CTD are:

＊ Combined Transport Operator (CTO)

The CTO is the counterpart of the carrier under a marine bill of lading. He issues CTD and will be responsible for the whole journey no matter whether he actually arranges the whole journey or just a part of the transportation.

＊ Consignor

The consignor is the counterpart of the shipper under a marine bill of lading. He consigns the goods for transportation to the CTO and enters into CTD with him.

＊ Consignee

The consignee is the person entitled to take delivery of the transported goods at destination. Similar to the consignee under a marine bill of lading, the consignee of CTD can also be made out to order, to bearer or to a named consignee. When the CTD is made out to order, it is negotiable by endorsement and delivery. When it is made out to bearer, it is negotiable by mere delivery and when it is made out to a named consignee, it is not negotiable.

The differences between a CTD and an ocean bill of lading are as follows:

Ocean Bill of Lading	CTD
The issuer must be a carrier, namely a shipping company.	The issuer is a CTO who can be either the carrier or a manager of the whole journey.
The carrier provides a port to port shipment by a single mode.	The CTO provides a door to door service where at least two modes of transportation will be involved.
The responsibility of the carrier will commence from the time when the goods are received or loaded on board the ship at the port of loading and will cease when they are discharged from the ship at the port of destination.	The CTO assumed the liability from the place where the goods are taken into his charge from the exporter's premises to the place of the final destination at the importer's premises.
The carrier shall not be liable for the loss or damages to the goods before they are received or put on board the ship and after they are discharged from the vessel.	The CTO is responsible for the loss or damages to the goods whenever and wherever occurred during the course of the whole journey.

(b) Through B/L.

A through B/L resembles a CTD except that a through B/L is issued by the first carrier who will only be responsible for his part of the journey only.

(5) According to Whether or not Detailed Information of the Contract is Attached

(A) Long Form B/L.

A long form B/L is a complete form of bill of lading with full details of the contract of carriage printed on the reverse of the B/L.

(B) Short Form B/L.

A short form B/L is a regular bill of lading except that the detailed information of the contract of carriage is omitted and is subject to that contained in the carrier's long form bill of lading. Banks will normally accept this type of B/L unless stated otherwise in the credit.

(6) According to the Types of Vessel

(A) Liner B/L.

A liner B/L is issued by the carrier when the goods are shipped on a regular line vessel with scheduled route and reserved berth at destination. The most obvious advantage of a liner B/L is that the carrier can inform the shipper, before or shortly after the sea voyage, the estimated date of departure (ETD) and the estimated time of arrival (ETA) so that the importer will also be informed that the goods are dispatched and will arrive on a set date. The majority of bills of lading are liner B/L.

(B) Chartered B/L.

A chartered B/L is issued by a hirer of a ship to the exporter. The terms of the bill of lading are subject to the contract of hire between the ship-owner and the hirer. A chartered B/L
usually contains such wordings "subject to the charter party" and it is used when the shipments
are large enough to take up the entire available space of a vessel such as the shipments of oil,
chemical, grain, coal, cotton, automobiles. Compared with a liner's B/L, a chartered B/L is
cheaper for the shipper to charter a vessel than to pay the sea freight measured by ton or cubic
foot. In addition, a chartered B/L is more flexible as there is no strict schedule for the journey.

Banks normally will not accept a chartered B/L unless stated otherwise in the credit. The
type of B/L is not very popular in international trade.

(7) Other Types of B/L

(A) Stale B/L.

A bill of lading will be regarded as a stale one when it is presented to the bank later than 21
days after the B/L date. The stale bill is not acceptable to the bank under a credit.

(B) Container B/L.

A container B/L is issued when the goods are packed in either less than a container load
(LCL) or full container load (FCL). The carrier will provide services from a container yard in
the exporting country to a container yard in the importing country. With container shipping
services, containers can be hauled to the premises of the exporter's and those of the importer's
by a forwarder, thus the goods can be loaded by the exporter and unloaded by the importer.
However, not all seaports can offer container shipping services.

Again, it should be remembered that the classifications of bills of lading are based on their
various functions and there is no clear-cut among them. It is allowed that one B/L can simultaneously take several types in combination.

Section Two   Sea Waybill and Air Waybill

1. Sea Waybill

A sea waybill is a shipping document which can be issued by a shipping company as an
alternative to a bill of lading.

A sea waybill only performs two functions of a bill of lading, namely as a receipt of goods
and a contract of carriage. However, unlike a bill of lading, a sea waybill is not a document of
title and it is not negotiable. As a result, a sea waybill can only be made out to a named consignee － the importer.

When an exporter agrees to sell the goods on open account terms, payment in advance or
on a non-commercial basis, it follows that the exporter should ask the shipping company for a
sea waybill rather than a bill of lading with the purpose that the importer can obtain goods with
minimum formalities. Waybills can meet this requirement because the goods will be released by
the carrier to the named consignee (the importer) against identification even without the pro-
duce of an original waybill, in which case only a faxed copy will do.

When a seaway bill is compared with a straight B/L, the similarity lies in that both of
them are made out to a named consignee. The difference is that a straight B/L is a document of

title and an original B/L is required before the goods are released, but a sea waybill is not a title document and an original sea waybill may not be required for the release of the goods. In this sense, sea waybill is similar to an air waybill.

2. **Air Waybill**

(1) Definition

In general terms, an air transport document is used to differentiate itself from other transport documents by sea, road or rail. In more specific terms, an air transport document refers to an air waybill (AWB) or an air consignment note. An AWB is issued by an airline when goods are dispatched by airfreight. It is a contract between the carrier (the airline) and the shipper.

(2) Functions of AWB

Similar to a sea waybill, an air transport document only performs two functions, both as a receipt of goods and as a contract of carriage. For this reason, there is no such a thing as a bill of lading with regard to air transport and the only air transport document can be issued is an air waybill or an air consignment note.

Another similarity to a sea waybill is that an AWB is not a document of title and is not negotiable. Therefore, if the transaction is under L/C, the credit should not require an AWB to be made out to order and/or to be endorsed. An AWB should be made out to a named consignee who will be the importer, the exporter's agent or the L/C issuing bank.

Disadvantages for an AWB to be made out to the importer are:

(A) Upon arrival at the airport of destination, the goods are released to the consignee (the importer) against identification even without producing the original AWB.

(B) Under letter of credit when an AWB shows the importer as the consignee, the banks have no power to intervene the release of the goods.

(C) Under letter of credit, the consignee/importer will take the delivery even when he has not made payment to the L/C issuing bank. Under other payment methods, the exporter may suffer the loss of non-payment.

Advantages for an AWB to be made out to the L/C issuing bank are:

(A) The issuing bank has the control over the goods which will be released to the importer only with the permission of the issuing bank.

(B) The issuing bank will release to goods to the importer against his payment.

Under collection, an AWB can be made out to a bank only after granting the latter's consent and permission. In order to control the goods, another alternative that an exporter can do is to make the named consignee to be the exporter's agent who will enjoy similar advantages to control the goods and secure payment for the exporter in the same way as the L/C issuing bank will.

(3) Contents of AWB

(A) The name and address of the shipper.

The shipper is normally the exporter.

(B) The name and address of the consignee.

The consignee can be the importer, or, if the exporter wants the retain the ownership over the goods till the importer makes payment, the consignee can be made out to the issuing bank under L/C or an agent of the exporter under collection who will press and collect payments from the importer. When payment is effected, the bank or the exporter's agent will issue a delivery order and instruct the airline to place the goods at the disposal of the importer. The delivery order is a letter of authority, signed by the bank or the exporter's agent, authorizing the airport to release goods to the named consignee. Readers may need to refer back to item (2) for a detailed analysis.

(C) The name of the carrier.

The carrier is the airline and the issuer of an AWB. The word non-negotiable will indicate clearly that an AWB is not a title document.

(D) Carrier's agent.

In order to facilitate businesses in different cities and/or countries, the carrier can also have its agent in various places. The information concerning the agent's name, its code and account No should be entered into the applicable boxes.

(E) The names of the airports.

The name of the airport of departure and the name of the airport of the destination together with the flight No should be furnished accordingly.

(F) The declared value for customs purposes.

A detailed knowledge of the customs procedure is not required for this course. It is helpful to know that "NVD" means no value declared.

(G) Handling information.

This corresponds to the notify party on a bill of lading. It should be entered with the name and address of the importer when he is not shown as the consignee. Otherwise, this box should be left blank.

(H) Marks.

The marks perform the same function as the shipping marks on a bill of lading. The same marks will appear on all the boxes/cartons/cases and on all the other relevant documents to tie them up.

(I) Details of the air freight charges.

(J) Brief description of the goods.

As detailed description of goods will appear in the commercial invoice and the packing list, a general description here will be enough to serve the purpose. If the transaction is under L/C, then the brief description should be made in conformity with that on the credit.

(K) Freight charges prepaid or collect.

This shows whether the air-freight is prepaid by the exporter or whether it is payable at the destination.

(L) Signature of the exporter or his agent.

The signature is made to confirm the certification shown above.

Shipper's Name and Address		Shipper's Account Number	Not Negotiable **Air Waybill** Issued by
			Copies 1, 2 and 3 of this Air Waybill are originals and have the same validity.
Consignee's Name and Address			It is agreed that the goods described herein are accepted in apparent good order and condition (except as noted) for carriage SUBJECT TO THE CONDITIONS OF CONTRACT ON THE REVERSE HEREOF. ALL GOODS MAY BE CARRIED BY ANY OTHER MEANS INCLUDING ROAD OR ANY OTHER CARRIER UNLESS SPECIFIC CONTRARY INSTRUCTIONS ARE GIVEN HEREON BY THE SHIPPER. THE SHIPPER'S ATTENTION IS DRAWN TO THE NOTICE CONCERNING CARRIER'S LIMITATION OF LIABILITY. Shipper may increase such limitation of liability by declaring a higher value for carriage and paying a supplemental charge if required.
Issuing Carrier's Agent Name and City			Accounting Information
Agent's IATA Code		Account No.	

Airport of Departure (Addr. of First Carrier) and Requested Routing

To	By First Carrier	Routing and Destination	to	by	to	by	Currency	WT/VAL PPD COLL	Other PPD COLL	Declared Value for Carriage	Declared Value for Customs

Airport of Destination			Amount of Insurance	INSURANCE — If carrier offers insurance, and such insurance is requested in accordance with the conditions thereof, indicate amount to be insured in figures in box marked "Amount of Insurance".

Handling Information

No. of Pieces RCP	Gross Weight	kg lb	Rate Class Commodity Item No.	Chargeable Weight	Rate / Charge	Total	Nature and Quantity of Goods (incl. Dimensions or Volume)

Prepaid	Weight Charge	Collect	Other Charges
	Valuation Charge		
	Tax		
	Total Other Charges Due Agent		Shipper certifies that the particulars on the face hereof are correct and that insofar as any part of the consignment contains dangerous goods, such part is properly described by name and is in proper condition for carriage by air according to the applicable Dangerous Goods Regulations.
	Total Other Charges Due Carrier		
			Signature of Shipper or his Agent
Total Prepaid	Total Collect		
			Executed on (date) at (place) Signature of Issuing Carrier or its Agent

ORIGINAL 3 (FOR SHIPPER)

(M) The issuing date.

This is the date on which the goods are received by the airline and in his custody. Normally, this is also the flight date.

(N) The signature of the carrier or his agent.

An AWB can be signed by the carrier or by his agent on his behalf.

(O) The full set.

Normally air waybills will be issued in three originals to make a full set. The 1st original is for the carrier, the 2nd one is for the consignee and the 3rd one is for the shipper.

Section Three　Other Transport Documents

Bills of lading and air waybills are the two most important transport documents because in international trade, goods are commonly dispatched by sea or air. In addition to these two, other transport documents will include road waybill, rail waybill and courier receipt.

All these minor types of transport documents share the same characteristics by performing only two functions of a bill of lading. That is, they act as receipts of goods by the carrier and contracts of carriage. However, similar to a sea waybill and an air waybill, they are not negotiable and are not documents of title. The word non-negotiable will appear on these documents to indicate that they can never be treated as title documents and can only be delivered to a named consignee. The rules concerning the ways to make out the named consignee under a sea waybill and an AWB are also applicable to these documents by which the exporter may or may not wish to retain his ownership over the goods.

1. Road Waybill or CMR Consignment Note

When the goods are sent by truck, a road waybill or a CMR consignment note will be issued. It is subject to the *Convention on Contract for the International Carriage for Goods by Road* (CMR) established in 1965.

A road waybill will contain the following major items:

(a) Date and place of issue.

(b) Name and address of the shipper, consignee and carrier.

(c) Place and date of receiving the goods and the place of delivery.

(d) General description of goods with their quantity expressed in weight or measurement.

(e) Marks and numbers.

(f) Carriage charges.

(g) Instructions for customs and other formalities.

(h) Signature of the carrier or its agent.

2. Railway Bill or Cargo Receipt

When the goods are sent by railway, a railway bill or cargo receipt will be issued. It is subject to the *International Convention for the Transport of Goods by Rail* (CIM) established in some form in 1893 with additional protocol made in 1970 after various revision to meet the needs of the international trade of the modern time.

A railway bill will contain the following major items:

(a) Date and place of issue.

(b) Name and address of the shipper, consignee and carrier.

(c) Place of the original railway station and the place designated for delivery.

(d) General description of goods with their packing method, quantity in weight or in measurement.

(e) Carriage charges.

(f) Instructions for customs and other formalities.

(g) Signature of the carrier or its agent.

3. Courier Receipt or Post Receipt

When the goods are sent through the post office, by a courier or an expedited delivery service, a courier receipt or a post receipt will be issued. The worldwide famous expedite services are EMS, DHL, UPS and Federal Express. This mode of transportation will be chosen when the goods are of great value, or of a small quantity such as samples and when the speed of delivery is of the greatest concern. Courier service, especially the expedited delivery services provide desk-to-desk service.

Specimen of a courier service document

Chapter Thirteen　Documents (Ⅲ)
- Other Commercial Documents and Documents Examination

Section One　Other Commercial Documents

In addition to the basic documents of commercial invoices, insurance documents and the transport document, other commercial documents may also be found in international business to meet the requirements of the importer or the importing countries. They are varied in forms. In this section, seven additional documents will be introduced.

1. Certificate of Origin

(1) Definition

A certificate of origin is a document certifying that the goods come from a particular country. Relevant details of the certificate will be supplied by the exporter and it is preferably authenticated and issued by an independent body, such as an Inspection Bureau or a Chamber of Commerce. In China, the certificate may be issued by either the Inspection Bureau or the China Council for the Promotion of International Trade. However, in some other cases, it is also found applicable that a certificate of origin is issued by the exporter himself.

Some countries may insist that a certificate of origin should be produced before goods will be allowed into the country. The reasons may be that a certificate of origin can be served as the basis for exercising discriminatory tariffs, implementing quotas and import control, ensuring that the quality of the imports meets the standards of the country of origin and conforms to the sanitation requirements of the importing country.

(2) Forms of Certificate of Origin

(A) Issued by the exporter.

When a certificate of origin is issued by the exporter, it is usually made on the exporter's company letterhead.

(B) Issued by an independent third party.

As is often the case, letter of credit will usually stipulate an independent third party as the issuer of the certificate of origin. In this case, the certificate should be made on the issuer's company letterhead and should be made into a separate document which is not to be combined with any other document.

(C) Made on a combined form.

When the credit dose not stipulate an issuing party, a certificate of origin can be made on a combined form. A combined form is a combination of a certificate of origin with a commercial invoice where a statement such as: " We hereby certify that the goods are (Chinese) origin" is inserted.

(D) General System of Preference Form.

General System of Preference (GSP) is another widely used form of certificate of origin. It is a treatment of customs duty preference imposed by the developed countries on the goods from the developing countries, with the purpose of increasing in the developing countries the revenue of export and speeding up their industrialization and their economic growth. It signifies:

* General

This favorable treatment is granted to every developing country.

* Non-discriminatory

The preference is conducted on a non-discriminatory basis.

* Non-reciprocal

The preference is granted by the developed country to the developing country without any requirements of a counter preference from the developing countries. Any exporter in a developing country will obtain this favorable treatment after he has made out the certificate on a GSP form.

A GSP certificate of origin takes a standard form worldwide and should be issued by an authorized entity in the exporting country. In China, the entity should be the Import and Export Commodity Inspection Bureau of People's Republic of China while in the other developing countries, the entity is usually the various Chambers of Commerce located in that country. The standard forms of GSP include:

General System Preference Certificate of origin Form A;

Certificate of Origin for Textile Products;

Certificate in Regard to Textile Handicrafts and Traditional Textile Products of the Cottage Industry; etc.

(3) Contents of the Certificate of Origin

Although differences may be found in these various forms, a certificate of origin should generally contain the following items:

(A) The name and the address of both the exporter and the importer. A GSP form will also require the complete name of the country of origin to be supplied.

(B) Brief description of goods with its shipping marks, weight or other quantity. In the case of a GSP form, origin criterion letter should be properly filled in. Different letters will indicate whether or not the goods are purely domestic products. For example, the letter "P" means a 100% local production, while "W" indicates that the products contain foreign ingredients or components and "F" indicates that the foreign contents are below 14%.

(C) Details of the shipment to which the certificate relates.

(D) Certifying statement to indicate clearly that the merchandize is grown / processed / manufactured in a certain country. In the case of a GSP form, a separate declaration by the exporter independent from that of the issuer is also required.

(E) The issuing date may be later than that of the commercial invoice, but it must be made no later than the latest date for presentation of documents stipulated in the credit.

(F) The signature of the issuer. In the case of a GSP form, both the signature of the exporter and that of the issuer are required.

SPECIMEN1 Certificate of Origin

CERTIFICATE OF ORIGIN

DATE _____

1. NAME OF EXPORTER _____

ADDRESS _____

2. NAME OF IMPORTER OR CONSIGNEE _____

_____

ADDRESS _____

3. THE IS TO CERTIFY THAT THE MERCHANDISE DESCRIBED IS GROWN/ PROCESSED/MANUFACTURED IN _____

(COUNTRY,PLACE)

MARK & NUMBER	DESCRIPTION OF GOODS	QUANTITY	REMARKS

THE ABOVE DESCRIBED MERCHANDISE HAS BEEN LOAD _____

(NAME OF CARRIER)

LEAVING _____ ON/ABOUT _____ DESTINED FOR
(NAME OF PORT)   (DATE)

_____ PORT.

4. THIS CERTIFICATE SHALL BE INVALID IN CASE OF ANY UNAUTHORIZED ALTERATION.

ISSUED BY _____

SPECIMEN Generalized System of Preferences Certificate of Origin

Original	
1. Goods consigned from (Exporters business name , address , country)	Reference No. **GENERALIZED SYSTEM OF PREFERENCES CERTIFICATE OF ORIGIN** (Combined declaration and certificate) **FORM A** Issued in .... (country) See Notes overleaf
2. Goods consigned to (Consignee's name , address , country)	
3. Means of transport and route (as far as known)	4. For official use

5. Item number	6. Marks and numbers of packages	7. Number and kind of packages; description of goods	8. Origin criterion (see Notes overleaf)	9. Gross weight or other quantity	10. Number and date of invoices

| 11. Certification
It is hereby certified , on the basis of control carried out , that the declaration by the exporter is correct.

....
Place and date , signature and stamp of certifying authority | 12. Declaration by the exporter
The undersigned hereby declares that the above detail and statements are correct ; that all the goods were produced in

....
(country)
and that they comply with the origin requirements specified for those goods in the Generalised System of Preferences for goods exported to

....
(importing country)
....
place and date , signature of authorized signatory |

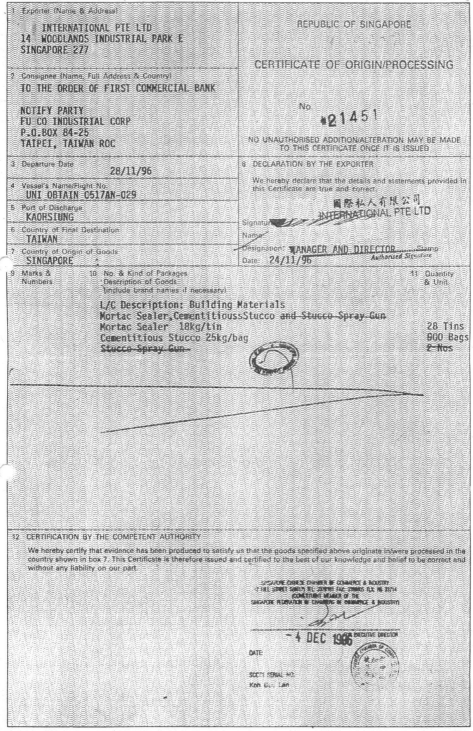

Exporter (Name & Address)

INTERNATIONAL PTE LTD
14 WOODLANDS INDUSTRIAL PARK E
SINGAPORE 277

REPUBLIC OF SINGAPORE

CERTIFICATE OF ORIGIN/PROCESSING

2 Consignee (Name, Full Address & Country)
TO THE ORDER OF FIRST COMMERCIAL BANK

NOTIFY PARTY
FU CO INDUSTRIAL CORP
P.O.BOX 84-25
TAIPEI, TAIWAN ROC

No
#21451

NO UNAUTHORISED ADDITION/ALTERATION MAY BE MADE
TO THIS CERTIFICATE ONCE IT IS ISSUED

3 Departure Date
28/11/96

8 DECLARATION BY THE EXPORTER

We hereby declare that the details and statements provided in
this Certificate are true and correct

國際私人有限公司
INTERNATIONAL PTE LTD

4 Vessel's Name/Flight No.
UNI OBTAIN C517AN-029

5 Port of Discharge
KAOHSIUNG

6 Country of Final Destination
TAIWAN

7 Country of Origin of Goods
SINGAPORE

Signature
Name
Designation: MANAGER AND DIRECTOR   Stamp
Authorised Signature
Date: 24/11/96

9 Marks &
Numbers

10 No. & Kind of Packages
Description of Goods
(include brand names if necessary)

11 Quantity
& Unit

L/C Description: Building Materials
Mortac Sealer,CementitioussStucco and Stucco Spray Gun
Mortac Sealer 18kg/tin
Cementitious Stucco 25kg/bag
Stucco Spray Gun

28 Tins
900 Bags
2 Nos

12 CERTIFICATION BY THE COMPETENT AUTHORITY

We hereby certify that evidence has been produced to satisfy us that the goods specified above originate in/were processed in the
country shown in box 7. This Certificate is therefore issued and certified to the best of our knowledge and belief to be correct and
without any liability on our part.

SINGAPORE CHINESE CHAMBER OF COMMERCE & INDUSTRY
2 HILL STREET S(0617) TEL: 2270067 FAX: 2590605 TLX NO 33714
CONSTITUENT MEMBER OF THE
SINGAPORE FEDERATION OF CHAMBERS OF COMMERCE & INDUSTRY)

- 4 DEC 1996   EXECUTIVE DIRECTOR

DATE

SCCCI SERIAL NO.
Koh Buck Lan

Printed by Authority

TDB 3

2. Inspection Certificate

(1) Definition

An inspection certificate is a document to inspect the export so as to ensure the quality, quantity, packing and other conditions of the goods. An inspection certificate may be issued either under the regulations of the authorities of the exporting country or be issued at the request of the importer and/or the authorities of the importing country. For the exporting country, an inspection certificate may enable the authorities to check the exporter's contractual performance so that its creditworthiness and competitive position in the world market can be sustained and enhanced. For the importer, his own interests will be protected and for the importing country, inferior or even dangerous goods will be kept away from entering its territory.

The issuer of an inspection certificate may be a government inspection bureau, the importer's agent who inspects the goods in the exporting country or the exporter himself. In China, the certificate is normally issued by the Export and Import Commodity Inspection Bureau of the People's Republic of China.

(2) Types of Inspection Certificate

Different types of inspection certificate are made to inspect different aspects of the exports as required. The major types are as follows:

Inspection certificate of quality

Inspection certificate of quantity

Inspection certificate of weight

Inspection certificate of health

Inspection certificate of veterinary

Inspection certificate of non-aflatoxin

Inspection certificate of plant quarantine

Inspection certificate of disinfection

Inspection certificate of sanitation

Inspection certificate of fumigation

Inspection certificate of conditioned weight

(3) Contents of a certificate of inspection

A certificate of inspection should be made on the issuer's company letterhead.

(A) Consignor.

"Consignor" should be made out to be the "shipper" of the B/L. As the exporter/beneficiary is generally the shipper, so the consignor will normally show the exporter's name.

(B) Consignee.

The consignee is generally made out "to whom it may concern" or "to order" without showing the importer's name as the consignee. One reason is that the inspection certificate is legally valid for any holder. The other reason is to make the certificate consistent with the B/L especially when the B/L is made out to order.

(C) Name of the commodity with its marks and numbers.

(D) Results of the inspection.

This space is used to state the result of an inspection which can be classified into weight, quality, quantity etc. accordingly. The purpose is to ensure that the inspection certificate conforms to the stipulations of the credit and it contains no detrimental statement as to the goods unless authorized by the credit.

(E) The date.

On one hand, the issuing date or the inspection date of the certificate should not be made later than the B/L date. On the other hand, it should not be made too early as the certificate may be expired before documents are presented.

(F) The signature of the issuer.

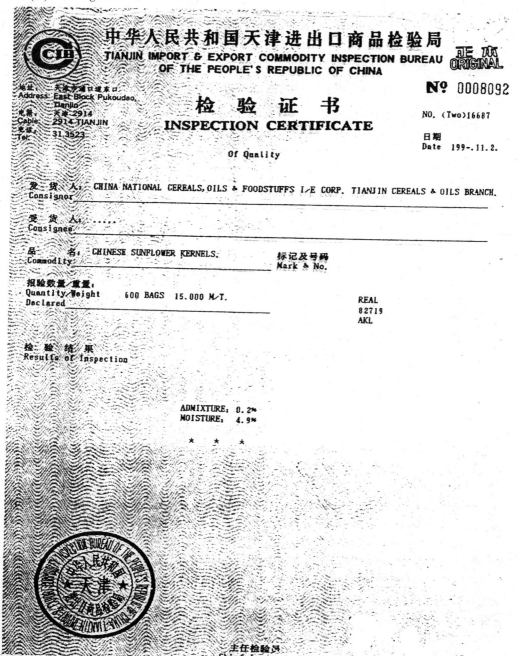

3. **Consular Invoice**

A consular invoice is a special type of invoice issued by the embassy or consulate of the importing country located in the exporting country. A consular invoice may be required by some countries as a basic shipping document to present. A consular invoice can both increase the revenue for the consulate, and perform the functions of a certificate of origin to serve as a basis for levying discriminatory duties on different countries and to prevent dumping of the foreign goods. It can also take the place of an import permit. A high tariff or even an embargo will be imposed on a shipment without a consular invoice.

As to the exporter, it is both time-consuming and costly to apply for a consular invoice, especially when there is no consulate located in the city of the exporter's premises. For this reason, the exporter, e. g. in China may ask to have the consular invoice to be issued by the China Councils for the promotion of International Trade or the Export and Import Commodity Inspection Bureau of the People's Republic of China instead, as they have branches in all the big cities nationwide.

4. **Customs Invoice**

A customs invoice is a special invoice made and specified by the customs of the importing country and to be issued by the exporter's filling in a given form specified by the customs of the importing country. It usually take three different forms:

* Customs invoice
* Combined certificate of value and origin
* Certified Invoice in accordance with xx customs regulations.

Similar to a consular invoice, a customs invoice can perform the following functions:

(A) To certify the origin of goods against which differential tariffs will be levied by the customs of the importing country.

(B) To ensure that the value of the import is not lower than its domestic value so that dumping will be prevented.

To serve these purposes, though varied in forms according to the different customs regulations of the importing countries, a customs invoice will feature the origin of the goods with detailed information on the price formation. For example, if the price term is FOB, then the net export price should be worked out by the FOB price less the packing charges and inland transportation charges or other applicable charges incurred during the process of the exportation. Under CIF, the net export price would further less out the freight and insurance premium. It should be noted that the domestic price must be lower than the net export price.

The difference between a customs invoice and a consular invoice is not in effects but in procedures. A customs invoice can be printed in the exporting country conforming to the original form of the importing country while a consular invoice will be made and printed by the embassy or the consulate of the importing country. This means that it is not necessary for the exporter to pay a fee to obtain a customs invoice while he is asked for a fee in the case of a consular invoice.

5. **Pro-forma Invoice**

Before a sales contract is established between the exporter and the importer, a pro-forma invoice may be supplied or required to take the place of a commercial invoice. It normally takes the same form with the same items as those in a commercial invoice except the word "proforma" will be indicated.

Functions of pro-forma invoice are as follows:

(A) A pro-forma invoice can be supplied by the exporter as a quotation to the importer. The price and sales terms will be negotiated between the two parties and once the terms are accepted by the importer, there will be a firm contract to be made in accordance with the contents in the pro-forma invoice, against which commercial invoice will also be made accordingly. In practice, the exporter will be required to certify on the commercial invoice such wordings: " the goods are in accordance with the pro-forma invoice xx. "

(B) As L/C is normally established before a commercial invoice is established, a pro-forma invoice is required by the importer when he applies for an import license and/or foreign exchange permit. Also, letter of credit is generally established with reference to a pro-forma invoice rather than a commercial invoice. In practice, the credit will bear a statement such as " as per pro-forma invoice No xx".

(C) Under advance payment where payment is required before the shipment, the exporter will normally forward a pro-forma invoice instead of a commercial invoice for the advancement.

(D) Under consignment where goods are in the hands of a middleman, a pro-forma invoice will serve as a reference to him in his offer to a potential buyer. Under this situation, a commercial invoice will not be issued as it will be established only after a buyer is available.

(E) In international bidding, a pro-forma invoice is required by the party inviting tender from the tenderer. The party inviting tender will make comparisons against pro-form invoices submitted from different tenderers before he makes a decision and establishes a sales contract with the most competitive candidate.

6. Beneficiary's Statement

It is a statement made out on the exporter/beneficiary's company letterhead to certify that he has performed certain tasks according to the stipulations in the credit. For example, the tasks may generally include the mailing of a part of shipping documents to the importer or cabling the issuing bank that the shipment has been made, etc. Always the beneficiary's statement will be accompanied by a post registered receipt or a courier receipt from EMS, DHL, Federal Express, UPS, etc. , as evidence.

INTERNATIONAL

Beneficiary's Certificate

L/C No.:6NF2/00508/1163　dd 08/11/1996　Under
FIRST COMMERCIAL BANK

This is to certify that one set of shipping documents, including 1/3 clean on board Bill of Lading had been sent to the applicant.

International Pte Ltd
國際私人有限公司
INTERNATIONAL PTE LTD

Authorised Signature

Date:02/12/96

国际私人有限公司
INTERNATIONAL PTE LTD
14 WOODLANDS INDUSTRIAL PARK　SINGAPORE 277　• TEL:　　　• FAX:

7. Shipping Company's Certificate

This is a certificate issued by the carrier to evidence the voyage, the ship's nationality, its age and its scheduled line.

Section Two   Documents Examination

As international settlement is carried out around documents in the sense that both the delivery and payment are made against documents. Documents should be examined properly so that traders' responsibilities and obligations can be fully met. Documents examination should be carried out by banks, which signifies the role of banks in international settlement. The following is the guideline in documents examination under a documentary credit.

1. General Principle in Documents Examination

(1) The Principle of Independence

As we have already known, the principle of independence signifies that the credit is a separate document independent from the sales contract or the credit application form on which it is based. This means only the wordings in the credit have the binding on banks.

(2) The Principle of Strict Compliance

This principle is made by the International Chamber of Commerce to govern the documents examination throughout the world. It means that documents must comply with terms and conditions of the credit on the one hand and they must be consistent with each other on the other hand. Any failure of these two requirements will result in "discrepancies" of documents, causing problems to obtain payments.

(A) When documents are found to be in strict compliance, the responsibilities of the issuing bank are to take up the documents and make reimbursements to the nominated bank after payment has been effected by payment, acceptance or negotiation to the beneficiary.

(B) When documents are found not to be in their face to be in consistence with the principle of strict compliance, banks may reject them and give notice by telecommunication stating all the discrepancies within 7 banking days after the receipt of the documents.

(3) Banks Deal Exclusively with Documents

In international settlement, banks will deal with documents rather than with the physical goods. Banks will never be involved in contractual disputes between the traders about the actual conditions of the goods while they should ensure that the documents presented meet the principle of strict compliance.

However, non-stipulated documents will not be examined by banks. When banks receive such documents, they shall return them to the presenter or pass them on without responsibility.

(4) Escaping Clauses

(A) Banks are required to examine documents with reasonable care but assume no responsibilities for the authenticity, form or validity of the documents. Banks are not the carrier, the insurer or the trader so they can not be expected to be an expert in every aspect of international trade. "Reasonable care" means that banks should make use of their background and professional knowledge to make sure that the documents presented are in face consistent with the credit and with each other. In addition, banks are not responsible for the presentment of false or forged documents.

(B) Banks are not liable for the act of a third party involved in the operation. The third party may be another bank when the original bank, acting as the issuing bank, instructs the latter, as his correspondent bank, to advise, confirm, and/or negotiate the credit but whose act is beyond the control of the original issuing bank.

(5) Reasonable Time

According to UCP500 article 13, the issuing bank, the confirming bank or the nominated bank shall each be allowed a reasonable time to handle the documents. The time period is usually made within and not to exceed seven days from the receipt of the documents.

2. Documents Examination

The following will serve as a summary or generalization of the points to be considered in the bank's examination of each individual document. As a detailed analysis of each document has been discussed in their relevant sections or chapters, readers may refer back to them so as to understand the reasons behind these points.

(1) Draft Examination

When examining a draft, the following points should be noted:

(A) Ensure that a drawn clause is included to indicate that the draft is established on the bank specified in the credit. This means that the drawee should always be a bank and can never be the importer, may it be the issuing bank, the confirming bank or other nominated bank as the accepting bank, or the paying bank. The draft should not be drawn on the applicant.

(B) Ensure that the credit number, the name of the issuing bank and the issuing date will be included in the drawn clause.

(C) Ensure that the draft is issued within 14 or 21 days after the B/L date but within the validity date of the credit. Ensure that the draft is presented before or on the latest date of presentation which will fall on the earlier date of the above mentioned two dates.

(D) Ensure that the tenor is as required by the Credit. Ensure that the time draft is made payable on an determinable future date.

(E) Ensure that the draft amount does not exceed the balance available in the credit. The amount of the draft expressed in figures and words should be made identical. Ensure that the value of the draft and that of the invoice corresponds.

(F) Ensure that the draft is properly endorsed and there are no restrictive endorsements.

(G) Ensure that the signature and the name of the drawer correspond with the name of the beneficiary.

(2) Examining a Commercial Invoice

(A) Ensure that the invoice is not a "pro-forma" invoice.

(B) Ensure that the invoice is issued by the beneficiary of the credit to the applicant of the credit. Ensure that it is not made out to the name of a third party other than the applicant, unless otherwise stipulated in the credit.

(C) Ensure that the description of goods is in agreement with that shown in the credit. As only a general description of goods is made in the credit, the additional and detailed information of the description of goods in the invoice should not be considered inconsistent with the requirements of the credit.

(D) Ensure that the details of the goods, the price terms and the breakdowns of prices as mentioned in the credit are included in the invoice.

(E) Ensure that any other information supplied in the invoice, such as marks, numbers, transportation information is in agreement with that of the other documents.

(F) Ensure that the value of the invoice corresponds with that of the draft and it does not exceed the available balance of the credit. Ensure that the currency of the invoice is the same as that of the credit.

(G) Ensure that there is no such notation in the invoice to indicate that the goods are "used", "secondhand", "rebuilt" or "reconditioned" when not authorized by the credit.

(H) Ensure that the invoice value covers the complete shipment if partial shipments are not allowed in the credit.

(I) Ensure that the invoice is signed when required by the credit.

(J) Ensure that the correct number of original(s) and copy(s) are presented.

(3) Examining a Marine Bill of Lading

(A) Ensure that the B/L is a "clean" and "on board" one. Banks will not accept a B/L which contains a clause to render it "foul" or "unclean". Ensure that an "on board" notation is dated and made on a "received for shipment" B/L.

(B) Ensure that the B/L bears the name of the shipper or his agent.

(C) Ensure that the B/L is made out to the consignee as required in the credit. If the importer's name is not shown as the consignee, it will be shown as the notify party as required in the credit.

(D) Ensure that the B/L is correctly endorsed as required in the credit.

(E) Ensure that the general description of goods are identical with that shown in the credit and that the shipping marks and numbers as well as other specifications, if any, are in agreement with those appeared on the other documents.

(F) Ensure that the "freight prepaid" or "freight collect" is indicated correctly on the B/L as required by the terms of the Credit.

(G) Ensure that the full set of originals issued is presented. In practice, however, full set may not be required by the credit.

(H) Ensure that the B/L is not a charter party transport document or a forwarder's transport document unless authorized in the credit.

(I) Ensure that the B/L is presented no later than 14 or 21 days after shipment but within the validity of the credit.

(J) Ensure that all other conditions stipulated in the appropriate transport articles of UCP500 are complied with.

(4) Examining an Insurance Document

(A) Ensure that the insurance document is the right type of policy, certificate or declaration required by the credit.

(B) Ensure that it is issued and signed by an insurance company, an underwriter or their agent.

(C) Ensure that if it is issued to the order of the beneficiary of the credit, the insurance document is correctly endorsed so that the title can be transferred to the applicant of the credit.

(D) Ensure that the document does not bear a date later than the B/L date or the date of shipment.

(E) Ensure that the insured amount is as required in the credit and is expressed in the same currency as that of the credit, unless otherwise stated in the credit. Banks will not accept an under-insured document.

(F) Ensure that the general description of goods corresponds with that in the credit and other details such as the shipping marks and numbers are consistent with other documents.

(G) Ensure that it covers the goods from the designated port of loading or place of taking in charge to the port of destination or the place of delivery.

(H) Ensure that the claim under the insurance document is made payable at the destination.

(I) Ensure that the risk(s) is correctly chosen and covered as required in the credit.

(J) Ensure that the full set is issued and presented.

(5) Examining of the Certificate of Origin

(A) Ensure that the country of origin specified meets the requirement of the credit.

(B) Ensure that if a certificate of origin is required under the credit, it is a separate document and not combined with any other document(s).

(C) Ensure that the certificate of origin is issued, signed and legalized as required by the credit.

(D) Ensure that the right form of certificate of origin is issued and presented.

(E) Ensure that the description of goods is consistent with that of the other documents.

(F) Ensure that correct number of original(s) and copy(s) are issued and presented.

(6) Examining the Inspection of Certificate

(A) Ensure that the inspection certificate is issued and signed by the party required in the credit.

(B) Ensure that the certificate is the right type complying with the inspection requirements of the credit.

(C) Ensure that the certificate is issued on a date earlier than the shipment date on the B/ L.

(D) Ensure that the document contains no detrimental clause as to the goods, specifications, quality, packaging, etc. , unless authorized by the credit.

(7) Examining the Packing/Weight List

(A) Ensure that it is a separate document and not combined with any other document(s) .

(B) Ensure that it contains a detailed list as to show its packing, weight or measurement in accordance with the requirements of the credit.

(C) Ensure that the data on it is consistent with that of the other documents.

(D) Ensure that it is signed if it is required in the credit.

(8) Examining of Other Miscellaneous Documents

According to Article 21, UCP500, when miscellaneous documents other than commercial invoice, transport documents and insurance documents are called for, the credit should stipulate by whom such documents are to be issued, their wordings and their data content. If the credit dose not so stipulate, banks will accept such documents as presented, provided that their data content is not inconsistent with any other stipulated documents presented.

(9) Examining the Covering Letter

When the exporter presents the documents to the bank for payment, acceptance or negotiation, he will usually fill in a standard form pre-printed by and addressed to the bank covering

L/C stipulated documents with their number of original(s) and copy(s) as well as other instructions clearly indicated therein. This standard form will serve as a covering letter and will be placed on the top of the other documents which will be orderly arranged according to the sequence of their appearance in the covering letter. When a bank examines a covering letter, it should:

(A) Ensured that the letter is addressed to this bank.

(B) Ensure that it has a current date.

(C) Ensure it is correctly related to the credit number reference.

(D) Ensure that the documents enumerated are attached in correct number of original(s) and copy(s) with the same amount and currency.

(E) Ensure that the bank remitting the documents is acting as a paying, accepting, negotiating bank.

(F) Ensure that the payment instructions are clear and understandable. It should clearly indicate whether any discrepancy(s) has been noted and whether payment, acceptance, or negotiation has been effected against an indemnity or under reserve.

To Malayan Banking Berhad

Date

Dear Sirs

We enclose draft/s and documents as listed, please follow the instruction marked ☒

☐ PURCHASE/DISCOUNT/NEGOTIATE subject to final payment

☐ PURCHASE/DISCOUNT/NEGOTIATE subject to final payment (without advance) and to credit our account only upon receipt of funds
from the reimbursement/paying bank.

OR

☐ Present to issuing bank for payment.

Our Ref. No.	Drawees & Address						Term		Bill Amount	

Documents Attached	Draft	B/L	Comm. Inv.	Ins. Cert.	Cert. Orgn.	Pkg List	Wt. Note	Bene. Cert.	Shpg Co. Cert.	AWB	D/O	
Number of Copies												

Enclosed also: 1 copy of Invoice and 1 photocopy of the original transport document for your files.

Covering

Draw under L/C No. _____ issued by _____

_____ _____ dated _____

Please follow instructions marked ☒

__Instructions__

☐   Advise acceptance and maturity date by cable/telex.   ☐

☐   In case of dishonour advise us by cable/telex giving reasons.

Please utilise against Forward Contract No.

Date   For

Please credit our Current Account No.   with you.

It is expressly agreed and we hereby undertake to repay or hold you harmless and fully indemnify you on demand the amount which you have paid us or will pay to us together with all costs and charges which you may have incurred, if payment is not made to you by the drawee of the draft and or the issuing bank of the letter of credit which has been discounted/purchased/negotiated or presented for payment by you for any reasons whatsoever including but not limited to any discrepancies in the documents.

We further agree that your bank assumes no responsibility for the authenticity or genuineness of documents delivered to your bank, nor for the quantity, quality, condition, genuineness, identity, title or delivery of the goods to which the documents relate.

For Bank's Use		
Bank Ref. No.	Date E. P.	Initial

Yours faithfully,

Authorised Signatories & Company's Stamp

Malayan Banking Berhad
IE 67 (1/2)

Section Three   Bank's Common Practices in the Event of Documents Discrepancies

1. The Practice of the Nominated Bank

In the event that the documents presented are inconsistent with the terms and conditions of the credit and/or with each other, the nominated bank will adopt the following practices:

(A) Return all the documents or just the discrepant documents to the beneficiary/exporter to have them corrected or amended for resubmission within the validity of the credit and before the latest date for presentation of documents.

(B) Upon requested by the exporter, cable or write to the issuing bank/confirming bank, if any, for authority to pay, accept, or negotiate against such discrepant documents. For example:

"Documents presented under your L/C No. _____ Bill's amount _____ Our reference No. _____, all terms are complied with except _____ . Pleas cable us whether we may negotiate the documents. "

(C) Call for an indemnity from the beneficiary or from his bank to pay, accept or negotiate with the understanding that any payment, acceptance or negotiation made will be refunded by the party issuing the indemnity, together with the interest and all charges if the issuing bank refuses to make reimbursement against these discrepant documents. In this case, the nominated bank should indicate clearly in the covering letter that " due to discrepancy(ies) we have paid/ negotiated documents against Letter of Indemnity. "

(D) Based on practical experience and with the agreement of the beneficiary, pay, accept or negotiate "under reserve", i. e. the bank retains the right of recourse against the beneficiary if the issuing bank refuses to make reimbursement against the discrepant documents. In this case, the nominated bank will indicate clearly in the covering letter that "due to discrepancy (ies), we have effected payment under reserve. "

(E) Return all the documents to the beneficiary/exporter for his direct action to forward them to the issuing bank.

2. The Practice of the Issuing Bank

When the documents presented by the beneficiary or sent by the nominated bank abroad are found to be on their face to be consistent with the terms of the credit and with each other after checking, the issuing bank is bound.

(A) To effect payment to the beneficiary or make reimbursement to the nominated bank who has paid, accepted or negotiated under the credit.

(B) To take up the documents.

When the documents are found to be inconsistent, the issuing bank may seek advice from the applicant and if the applicant accepts the discrepancy(ies), the issuing bank will deliver documents against applicant's payment of the invoiced amount and effect payment to the beneficiary or to the nominated bank. If the applicant dose not accept the discrepancy(ies), the issuing bank may exercise the right of refusal and no payment will be effected. The issuing bank will not be entitled to exercise the right of refusal until it has acted in accordance with the following requirements stipulated in Article 13 and 14 of UCP500:

(a) Payment is refused on the basis of documents discrepancies but not of goods discrepancies. This is because that document examination is made on documents but not on the physical goods.

(b) Issuing bank gives the notice of refusal at the time of no later than the close of the seventh banking day following the day of receipt of the documents. The issuing bank may make the decision to dishonor on its own or it is the result that the issuing bank fails to approach the applicant for the latter's approval of the discrepancies.

(c) Issuing bank gives the notice of refusal by SWIFT, Cable or Telex but not by airmail. It should be clearly stated in the message that the dishonor comes from the issuing bank and not from the applicant. For example, any message containing "Buyers refuse . . . " or " Our customer rejects . . . " or similar wordings is wrong because letter of credit is a payment method based on banker's credit.

(d) The notice of refusal must state all discrepancies. Issuing bank is not allowed to raise discrepancies in several notices. According to Article 196 of UCP500, the issuing bank will not be entitled to raise subsequently any further discrepancies if the first discrepancy mentioned in the notice of refusal turned out to be inadequate grounds for rejection of documents.

(e) Notice of refusal must also state that issuing bank is holding the documents at the disposal of, or is returning them, to the presenter (the exporter or the nominated bank). The issuing bank is not permitted to give notice of refusal on the one hand and deliver the documents to the applicant on the other hand.

If the nominated bank draws the attention of the issuing bank to any discrepancies in the documents and advises the issuing bank that it has paid, accepted or negotiated the documents under reserve or against an indemnity with regard to such discrepancies, the issuing bank shall not be relieved from their payment obligations under the credit. Therefore, the issuing bank must examine documents to find out the discrepancies and approaches the applicant for approval of the discrepancies. If the applicant does not accept the discrepancies, the issuing bank must give notice of refusal by telecommunication stating all discrepancies and documents being held at the disposal of the presenter.

If the documents are sent on approval or on collection, it is subject to *Uniform Rules for Documentary Collection ICC* No. 322. The issuing bank is in no way to effect payment if the applicant refuses to pay because the payment method has changed from L/C to collection. That is to say, the payment will rely on the importer's credit rather than the issuing bank's payment undertaking as stipulated by UCP500.

In reality, however, it is possible that an issuing bank without a reputable credit standing may collude with a dishonest applicant to refuse payment on alleged discrepancies. In this case, the beneficiary and the negotiating bank, the paying bank or the accepting bank must be cautious and work closely with each other to make effort to receive payment as soon as possible. If the discrepancies raised by the issuing bank are not reasonable, the nominated bank shall cable or write to the issuing bank immediately to press for prompt payment with incurred interest for delayed payment, if any. If an actual discrepancy does exist, the beneficiary must present the correct documents immediately within the time limit and contact the applicant directly, asking him to accept the discrepant documents and effect payment.

Bibliography

1. John Black. Oxford Dictionary of Economics [M]. New York：Oxford University Press, 1997.

2. Poh Chu Chai. Law of Negotiable Instruments[M]. 3e. Singapore：Longman, 1994.

3. Cecilia Ting. Hong Kong Banking System and Practice[M]. 4e. Hong Kong：The Hong Kong Institute of Bankers, 1998.

4. Clive M. Schmitthoft. Export Trade, The law and Practice of International Trade[M]. London：Stevens and Sons,1990.

5. 王玉奇,罗丙志. 新编国际结算[M]. 广州:华南理工大学出版社,1999.

6. 广东外语外贸大学国际经贸学院教材编写组. 国际贸易实务[M]. 广州:广东高等教育出版社,1999.

7. 苏宗祥. 国际结算. 增补本[M]. 第二版. 北京:中国金融出版社,1998.

8. 沈锦昶,等. 国际支付与结算. 修订本[M]. 上海:上海外语教育出版社,1996.

9. 姚新超. 国际贸易运输[M]. 北京:对外经济贸易大学出版社,1997.

10. 刘崇仪. 国际贸易[M]. 成都:西南财经大学出版社,1988.

11. 应诚敏,刁德霖. 国际结算[M]. 上海:立信会计出版社,1999.

12. 张耀麟. 银行进出口贸易融资[M]. 北京:中国金融出版社,2000.

13. 蔡慧娟. 国际结算[M]. 成都:西南财经大学出版社,1997.

图书在版编目(CIP)数据

国际结算教程/傅泳主编. —2 版. —成都:西南财经大学出版社,2012.8
ISBN 978 - 7 - 5504 - 0795 - 4

Ⅰ. ①国… Ⅱ. ①傅… Ⅲ. ①国际结算—教材 Ⅳ. ①F830.73

中国版本图书馆 CIP 数据核字(2012)第 194346 号

国际结算教程(第二版)

主编:傅 泳

责任编辑:汪涌波
封面设计:穆志坚
责任印制:封俊川

出版发行	西南财经大学出版社(四川省成都市光华村街55号)
网 址	http://www.bookcj.com
电子邮件	bookcj@foxmail.com
邮政编码	610074
电 话	028 - 87353785 87352368
照 排	四川胜翔数码印务设计有限公司
印 刷	郫县犀浦印刷厂
成品尺寸	185mm×260mm
印 张	15.5
字 数	405 千字
版 次	2012 年 8 月第 2 版
印 次	2012 年 8 月第 1 次印刷
印 数	1— 3000 册
书 号	ISBN 978 - 7 - 5504 - 0795 - 4
定 价	29.80 元